Clinical Social Work Practice

Clinical Social Work Practice

An Integrated Approach

SECOND EDITION

Marlene G. Cooper

Fordham University

Joan Granucci Lesser

Smith College

Boston • New York • San Francisco
Mexico City • Montreal • Toronto • London • Madrid • Munich • Paris
Hong Kong • Singapore • Tokyo • Cape Town • Sydney

Series Editor: *Patricia Quinlin*
Series Editorial Assistant: *Annemarie Kennedy*
Marketing Manager: *Kris Ellis-Levy*
Senior Production Editor: *Annette Pagliaro*
Editorial Production: *Walsh & Associates, Inc.*
Composition Buyer: *Linda Cox*
Manufacturing Buyer: *JoAnne Sweeney*
Cover Administrator: *Kristina Mose-Libon*
Electronic Composition: *Publishers' Design and Production Services, Inc.*

For related titles and support materials, visit our online catalog at www.ablongman.com.

Between the time Website information is gathered and then published, it is not unusual for some sites to have closed. Also, the transcription of URLs can result in unintended typographical errors. The publisher would appreciate notification where these errors occur so that they may be corrected in subsequent editions.

Library of Congress Cataloging-in-Publication Data

Cooper, Marlene G., 1942–
    Clinical social work practice: an integrated approach / Marlene G. Cooper, Joan Granucci Lesser.—2nd ed.
      p.   cm.
    Includes bibliographical references and index.
    ISBN 0-205-40811-7
    1. Psychiatric social work.   I. Lesser, Joan Granucci, 1952–   II. Title.

HV689.C65 2005
361.3'2—dc22   2004050596

Printed in the United States of America
10 9 8 7 6 5 4 3 2   09 08 07 06 05 04

To our patients and students

Contents

Preface

This book grows out of our experiences as practitioners and as clinical faculty at our respective schools of graduate social work. Both of us have taught clinical practice to students over the years and have struggled with ways to build on the foundation level curriculum so that the advanced year could become a meaningful expansion of both knowledge and skill. The mandate of the social work profession is ever growing, as is the two-year MSW curriculum. We have the challenge of teaching—and the students have the challenge of learning—multiple theoretical practice models. What has been increasingly obvious to us in our teaching of clinical practice is that this focus on breadth, while appropriately inclusive of the wide range of thinking in the field, contributes to problems with depth. It is indeed a challenge to help students understand the constructs of a theory and also help them to use that theory to guide assessment, establish goals, and plan interventions. This process is multidimensional and involves integration on many levels. Students must integrate respect for client self-determination with professional expertise; social work values and ethics with the constraints of a managed health/mental health care environment; a strengths perspective with attention to client's symptoms; and the use of self with theory and practice.

We chose the term *clinical social work practice* over the more generic term *social work*. We recognize the tension within the profession regarding whether our mission is social change or individual and family change. We agree that the overall commitment of the profession is to facilitate social change so that individuals have fewer problems resulting from conditions of poverty and oppression. We also strongly believe that we have a professional and ethical responsibility to work therapeutically with those individuals and families whose lives have been profoundly affected by these larger social issues.

There has been conflict, over the years, as to the language used to describe the clinical social worker and the client. In the Freudian model, the client was referred to as a patient, and the therapist, as a doctor. Some social workers today are referred to as therapists; others are practitioners, clinicians, consultants, trainers, teachers, providers, and even conductors. In some settings, clients are called members; in others, consumers. The language that describes the participants in the therapeutic relationship is often a reflection of the theoretical perspective being used. Different theories use different language, and there is room for all of these terms.

We are aware that social work education today is quite broad. However, we are firmly committed to teaching clinical knowledge and skill, for it is these components that enable our students to evolve into true professionals. Our book, therefore, has taken on that charge. We have included an array of theories that are psychodynamic, cognitive, behavioral, and postmodern. Despite their differences, the theories we have included in this book all view the therapeutic process as being created by the therapist and client in an atmosphere of mutuality and collaboration.

We have tried to make our theoretical chapters "student friendly" by illustrating technique with dialogue from actual work with clients. Our clients reflect the larger social issues of our times: They are survivors of child abuse and neglect, domestic violence, discrimination, racism, and mental illness. Our case discussions show both clients' and social workers' struggles with change and the therapeutic process. We include process recordings that reflect our work with individuals, families, and groups of different cultural, racial, ethnic, and religious backgrounds. We have attempted to present our clinical work authentically, describing our successes as well as our mistakes.

The book is divided into fourteen chapters. In the first chapter, we present our model for integrating theory and practice, using the core practice class as a laboratory for knowledge building, skill development, evidence-based practice, and the acquisition of a professional self. Process recording from an interview with a Latina woman struggling in her role as wife and daughter describes the integration in detail. In Chapter 2 we discuss some key issues in clinical practice. We begin with the contemporary perspective of brief treatment. Ethical and boundary concerns, suicide, and the complexities of clinical practice in a technological, managed care environment are also discussed. We conclude this chapter with some comments on the importance of therapist's self care.

In Chapter 3, we move into the clinical interview and the processes that evolve during the beginning, middle, and end stages of treatment. Discussion and case material focuses on several meetings with a teenage boy diagnosed with a conduct disorder. In Chapter 4, the psychosocial study, we discuss the preparation of the psychosocial summary on an advanced level. We present a clinical example of an out-of-control 7-year-old African American boy who was placed by his mother in a residential treatment facility. This material serves as a model for teaching the conceptualization of a theoretical formulation and a diagnostic impression based on the DSM-IV and the mental status exam.

Chapter 5 is devoted to a discussion of cross-cultural practice. It is our belief that sensitive, skilled clinicians can meet the challenge of working effectively with clients of different cultural backgrounds. We include two cases—a Vietnamese adolescent with substance abuse problems and an African American woman attempting to establish a bicultural identity. These cases illustrate treatment that is culturally sensitive and culturally competent.

Chapters 6 through 12 present clinical illustrations through the lenses of specific theoretical models. Each of these chapters includes a detailed discussion of a theory, assessment, and treatment. Dialogue is used to illustrate how theory guides practice. We have selected theories that offer insight into clinical social work practice with individuals, families, and groups of clients whose lives have been profoundly affected by social, cultural, political, sexist, racist, and emotional forces.

In Chapter 6 we present object relations, a psychodynamic theory, and its relevance to contemporary social work practice with vulnerable client populations. Clinical intervention with a female survivor of severe childhood abuse illustrates this concept. Chapter 7 presents the theory of self psychology and its application to brief treatment. The theory is illustrated in interviews with an elderly woman seeking counseling to understand why her son has undergone a sex change and how she can relate to him now that he has become her daughter. This case further shows the complexity of doing clinical social work practice against the backdrop of social stigma. Also in this chapter is a discussion of the application of self psychology to brief group therapy with heterosexual women who have experienced domestic violence. In Chapter 8, self-in-relation theory—a feminist perspective—is introduced. Group treatment with women who are learning to assert themselves in their work and family relationships demonstrates this model.

In Chapters 9 and 10 we discuss cognitive and behavioral social work practice. We illustrate cognitive theory with the treatment of a client suffering from anxiety and depression because of distortions in her thinking. Behavioral theory is explicated in Chapter 10 in the case discussion of the brief treatment of woman who suffers from obsessive-compulsive disorder.

Chapters 11 and 12 illustrate two postmodern theories—narrative and solution-focused therapies. Both chapters also demonstrate family treatment. Treatment of a Puerto Rican family grappling with intergenerational differences as they attempt to acculturate to U.S. society illustrates the narrative model. The application of a solution-focused approach to family treatment with a child who is lying is presented in Chapter 12.

Chapter 13 addresses clinical practice with children and adolescents. It includes developmental assessment, childhood psychopathology, play therapy, learning disturbances, and the clinical interview with the child or adolescent and the parent(s). Our case material describes play therapy with a 10-year-old Latina girl suffering from selective mutism, behavioral therapy with the parent of a 4-year-old child with temper tantrums, and behavioral treatment of a 12-year-old African American boy diagnosed with ADHD and ODD.

Chapter 14 addresses research and evaluation in social work practice. Single-subject design methodology provides a model for accountable practice and is graphically illustrated. The subject of this research is the client suffering from obsessive-compulsive disorder. Qualitative inquiry is also detailed and illustrated by interviews with focus group participants from Kingston, Jamaica, West Indies, who participated in a cross-cultural international study of violence against Jamaican children.

We hope that this book will provide students and mental health professionals with the knowledge and skills that are required to practice on an advanced clinical level and that they will learn as much by reading it as we have by writing it.

Acknowledgments

We acknowledge with gratitude all of those whose contributions have made this book a reality. Included is our thanks and praise of Steven Bogatz, for his technical support and research assistance; Lee Badger, Katherine Walsh Burke, and Phebe Sessions for their critical review of material; and Ann Bernales, Catherine Boyer, Constance Crain, Laurie Engstrand, Heide Eriksen, Farnsworth Lobenstein, Janice Malin, Jennifer Cass Markens, Alina Patton, Ariel Perry, Carol Rayl, Karen Seltzer, and Helen Solomon for case material. We would also like to thank Yunena Morales, President of the Jamaica Association of Social Workers, and the Executive Board for their generous research collaboration; Fanteema Barnes and William Stetson for library assistance; and Kenneth Cunningham, Robin Keim, Verna Leduox, Joseph MacKay, Bridgett Sergue, Carrie Boucher, and Sue Gunsalus for their administrative support.

A very special thanks to Dr. Mary Ann Quaranta, Provost, Marymount College at Fordham University; Dean Peter Vaughan, Fordham University Graduate School of Social Service; Dean Francine Vecchiolla of Springfield College and Dean Carolyn Jacobs of Smith College School for Social Work for their support and guidance; and to the Brown Foundation, Inc., the Smith College School for Social Work Clinical Research Institute, Fordham University Graduate School of Social Service Research and Development Fund, and the Fordham University Office of Research and Sponsored Programs for their financial support.

Joan gives special thanks to her husband, Martin, for his heartfelt emotional support, her children Eric, Rebecca, and Julia, for providing joy and inspiration, to her mother for her standards of excellence, and to her father, who would have been so proud.

Marlene gives special thanks to her parents, for their pride and confidence, and to her son, Alex, who was able to wait patiently for his mother while she labored at the computer, and whose presence makes all things possible.

In addition, we would like to thank the following reviewers of the first edition text whose comments contributed to the book's development: Marilyn A. Biggerstaff, Virginia Commonwealth University; Elizabeth Dungee-Anderson, Virginia Commonwealth University; Alice Leiberman, University of Kansas; Mary Katherine Rodwell, Virginia Commonwealth University, Maureen Braun Scalera, Rutgers University; and Jan Wrenn, St. Andrews University. Reviewers of the second edition were Carol P. Kaplan, Fordham University; Robert H. Keefe, Syracuse University; and Carole A. Winston, University of North Carolina at Charlotte.

1

An Integrated Approach to Clinical Practice

Theoretical Base for Clinical Social Work Practice

Clinical social work must be guided by theory as well as principles. Harry Guntrip (1969), a noted object relational theorist, considered all theories of human nature to be influenced by the cultural era, the prevailing intellectual climate, and the dominant ideas of their time. Turner (1996, p. 12), writing in contemporary times, echoes Guntrip's earlier observations about theories: "Each is recognized and prized to differing degrees, at different times, in different parts of the profession, and at different stages in the lives of colleagues."

Clearly, social work educators today face many challenges. Students need to learn how to practice from a theoretical base; examine these theories as applied to social work practice with diverse clients in their field work settings; develop a professional, ethical, and creative use of self in clinical practice (Barbour, 1984; Gomory, 2001; Munro, 2002; Thyer, 2001); and find the best evidence for selecting their interventions and the means to evaluate the effectiveness of their work.

In this chapter we offer an integrative model for clinical social work practice. The Integrative Model has five components: (l) practice class as laboratory, (2) the integrative journal, (3) clinical supervision, (4) faculty field advisement, and (5) evidence-based practice. This model is not linear—it is reflexive. There is a back-and-forth sharing among its parts. For example, sections of the integrative practice journal that contain process records are shared with the clinical supervisor and faculty advisor, and evidence-based practice occurs in both class and field. For purposes of clarity, we discuss the components in discrete sections below. However, the reader should bear in mind that the overarching component of this model is the practice class as laboratory.

1

The Integrative Model

Practice Class as Laboratory: Learning to Integrate

The practice class is the forum for integrating the various components of the model. When designed as a laboratory, the students are given both the conceptual framework for practice, and the opportunity to try out various aspects of their learning in class and field.

The Integrative Journal

The basic linking tool for class and field is the *integrative journal.* Journaling is a highly effective learning tool: It helps students deconstruct and demystify theory. Writing about their understanding of different theories, testing the application of theory to clinical material, planning interventions and evaluative measures, and seeking best practice evidence give students the opportunity to reflect on their use of self, their personal style, their emerging self-awareness as practitioners, their understanding of difficult concepts, and their ability to listen to what clients have to say on multiple levels.

Godwin (1996) points out that journaling helps you to look at things from different perspectives and brings you closer to the actual experience. Writing naturally leads to learning because it is a constructive, reflexive process. The therapeutic process is about communication, and writing helps to improve communication skills. The journal is a window into the unique way in which each student is absorbing the material. For the instructor, the journal is a tool that helps her to attend to each student's learning style and needs. The instructor's written comments throughout the student's journal entries offer support, guidance, clarification, and constructive criticism. Student feedback to the instructor allows for modification and adjustment of course content. Journaling operationalizes the collaborative learning process that takes place in the classroom.

Initially, journaling can be difficult and arouse anxiety in students. They question what should be written, how often should they write, and how many pages should they write. General guidelines help to give structure, and a sample journal assignment appears at the end of this chapter. Journaling should be done in preparation for each class, and students should bring their journals with them to class and share them either in small groups or with the larger class to promote discussion. Journals can include comments on required readings, excerpts from student work with clients, and material from supervisory conferences or classroom discussions. Students are encouraged to write about what they are learning and practicing. Once again, this is an individual process. As the instructor learns more about what type of progress the student is making, she can give help and redirection. As the students progress in their journaling, they become more spontaneous in their writing and less concerned with the number of pages.

The instructor is very active during classroom exercises where journals are shared, meeting with each individual group to listen, clarify, and participate in the process of explicating themes from the students' case material and drawing on specific theoretical concepts from the literature that would be helpful in determining treatment goals and/or guiding treatment interventions. The students then practice these interventions by doing role-plays in the small group settings. Following the small group exercise, the students convene as a whole, and each of the groups has an opportunity to discuss its process and role-play with the entire class as an audience. At this juncture, the classroom instructor invites other students to expand the role-play by considering additional clinical themes and/or introducing other theoretical models that may also be relevant. The students often need assistance from the instructor to "stay in role" and to test their developing skill in applying the theory to practice (i.e., what they will actually say to clients). This is perhaps the most challenging aspect of the classroom exercise for the students because they may feel exposed and, understandably, may need help and redirection when they first begin. The instructor again sets the tone by ensuring that the students become collaborators in helping each other learn both the science and the art of therapeutic communication.

Process Recording.   Process recording, a time-honored tradition in clinical social work practice, has gone in and out of favor over the years and, in our technological age, has been considered outdated. Nonetheless, in sitting alone, painstakingly trying to remember what transpired in the counseling session, the student learns about himself as well as his client. There may also be some benefit in the selective memory process that occurs when one is retrospectively recording what happened in an earlier session. We concur with Neuman and Friedman (1997, p. 237), who write that ". . . the student's recollection provides insight into her total experience of the interaction. . . . process recordings offer insight into the student's thinking process and conscious and unconscious behavior during the interview."

Students are asked to include sections of process recording in their journals. The recordings selected should reflect the students' attempts to talk with clients within the framework of different theoretical models. Students can use their journals initially to reflect on their understanding of the theory. They can then use their process recording to see what their interaction with clients has been, and then try to apply theoretical concepts to their work with clients.

We are aware that students resist writing process recording, and that busy supervisors often allow summary recording to be substituted for verbatim dialog. However, it is the actual dialog that takes place between the student and the client that must be studied in order to ascertain how the student is applying the theoretical constructs (Graybeal & Ruff, 1995). We believe that process recording is critical to learning and should continue to be taught to social work students at both the BSW and MSW levels. Abramson and Fortune (1990, p. 376) point out that "what is important is what field supervisors do with process recordings, rather than simply how often students are required to submit them." Field instructors are often not clear about the use of the process recordings. Models of process recordings are not standardized, and field supervisors and students grapple with what is to be included. Our model for process recording encourages the use of a different three-column approach. Note that the third column asks students to comment on the application of theory. This requires students to think on a higher conceptual level than the more commonly used approach that addresses only dialog, student's thoughts, and feelings. It is important that supervisors be trained with the model of process recording used in the practice class and that they learn how to most effectively use this model in supervision with clients.

Dialog	Student's Self-Reflection	Student's Application of Theory

Three-column model for process recording.

Example of Student Process Recording.   The student, a male graduate intern, attempts to use self-psychology in his work with a 38-year-old Dominican woman who is experiencing depression. This theory he selects—self-psychology—is described in detail in this book. The student struggles with the concept of *mirroring* (Kohut, 1971, 1977). This concept relates to a mother's ability to recognize and reflect back to the developing child an appreciation of his capabilities and talents. The mother acts as a self-object—a person who is experienced intrapsychically as providing an enduring sense of availability, which fosters the developing self. When the child does not have this experience, the internalization of psychic structures cannot occur and shame and humiliation result. This section of process recording demonstrates the student's use of the three-column approach as he attempts to understand the theory of self-psychology in his work with his client.

The student writes: "Mrs. Diaz came to the session with her 3-year-old daughter. I asked a case aide if she could watch her while we talked. The aide initiated an argument with me in front of Mrs. Diaz. The process picks up after the case aide leaves me in the interview room with Mrs. Diaz and her daughter."

Dialog	Student's Self-Reflection	Student's Application of Theory
Intern: Don't worry, Mrs. Diaz. The two of us will clear things up later. It is her job to supervise children while parents are in session. Can I comment on something that I have noticed? Mrs. Diaz: Yeah, sure.	She's always feeling responsible for other people. Now she feels responsible for me (would Kohut see this as Mrs. Diaz being the *selfobject* for others?)	I am trying to be the *selfobject* for Mrs. Diaz.

Dialog	Student's Self-Reflection	Student's Application of Theory
Intern: You had nothing to do with the situation with the aide, and yet you felt really guilty about what had happened.		Offering *reassurance* and *interpretation* but I think I need to be more *empathic*—maybe say "you really feel responsible for many things . . ."
Mrs. Diaz: I don't know . . . I just feel responsible somehow. I feel responsible for my husband's depression, my sister's unhappiness, and my mother's too.	She takes on a lot.	Listening and exploring
Intern: Wow, you are responsible for a lot of people . . . your daughter, your husband, mother, sisters, etc.	Mrs. Diaz nods with a forced smile. I must have hit on something here. In the past, Ms. Diaz told me that she was reared to be the caregiver for the younger children in the family, and that this role was typical in Latin-Caribbean cultures. Her situation was compounded by the sense of abandonment she felt when her mother left for New York without her. She was deprived of the chance of having a mutually empathic relationship with her mother and may have begun to feel unworthy. This client is not able to achieve warm and fulfilling relationships with others because of the lack of foundation set by the mother.	I am trying to use *mirroring,* but I don't think I really understand how to do this.
Intern: When you were trying to separate from Mr. Diaz, who supported you during that time?		I think I move away from theory here. I have to try harder to stay with Mrs. Diaz's experience.

Dialog	Student's Self-Reflection	Student's Application of Theory
Mrs. Diaz: No one at that time . . . even my mother came and put a guilt trip on me so I would stay with him.	She's so alone. Her own mother wouldn't take her side.	
Intern: That must have been really hard on you.		I attempt another self-psychology intervention here, providing *empathy*—a *mirroring* response—I think. Am I using mirroring correctly now?
Mrs. Diaz: Yes, it was . . . no one ever supports me, not even my friends.		
Intern: What are your friendships like?	I wonder why I was questioning this here.	*Exploration*—but maybe I should have continued *mirroring*.
Mrs. Diaz: Well, my friends are like my sisters. They all have these problems with their husbands and their children, they all need help, too.	She seems sad.	
Intern: It sounds as if you are overburdened being a mother to everyone. I can understand how you feel, actually I can feel the heaviness when you walk into the office.		I am using *empathy* here.
Mrs. Diaz: I am a mother to everyone.	I made a good comment here. She seems to be *reflecting* on what I said.	
Intern: No one deserves to feel that way, especially when you have so many positives going for you.	I'm feeling sad for her. I want to raise her self-esteem.	I am trying to continue offering *support*—being *empathic*—offering myself as a *selfobject*.
Mrs. Diaz. I don't feel like I have any positives.		
Intern: You said that your mother is always yelling for you to clean your apartment even more than you do . . . right? Your apartment looks beautiful.	Her apartment is always immaculate. She doesn't see her own worth.	I am helping to *build her self-esteem* by *providing support*.

Dialog	Student's Self-Reflection	Student's Application of Theory
Mrs. Diaz: Yes, she wants me to be the perfect Dominican housewife, while my husband stares at the wall doing nothing.	She seems angry. He sounds like a real loser.	Perhaps I should ask something about Dominican culture? Is this the norm for all marriages? Or, is this another example of how her mother can't put her first?
Intern: So you are expected to do everything for your family while your husband sits and rests all day.	How can she stay with him?	
Mrs. Diaz: Yes, I am not going to have it.	Good. She's sounding stronger.	*Empowering.*
Intern: I think we are getting somewhere today.		I use the "we"—a self-psychological concept called *twinship*. I will try to show her that I am allied in the work with her.
Mrs. Diaz: (crying) No one is there for me.	I wish I could take away her sadness.	
Intern: I can see how this must have been very upsetting to you. You love your mother, yet she wasn't always there when you needed her.		*Validating* and *mirroring.*
Mrs. Diaz: No, she wasn't at all. She left my sisters and me with our cousin while she went to New York to follow her dreams.		
Intern: So as a mother, would you say she was excellent, very good, good, or poor?		*Scaling.*
Mrs. Diaz: I love my mother, she is not a bad person . . . she just . . . well she was not very good . . . she always sent money and we had food and clothing, but she wasn't there when I needed her.		

Dialog	Student's Self-Reflection	Student's Application of Theory
Intern: That must make you angry.	Mrs. Diaz has been socially conditioned to show empathy for others in her roles as caregiver, mother, and wife. She often feels guilty when she does something for herself. She's beginning to show anger at others—her husband and mother—who do not show empathy toward her. I view her anger as a strength, because it shows that she has not been taken over by the oppressive forces or social conditioning.	My goal is to provide her with an *empathic relationship*. That is different from what she has experienced. I am again using *mirroring*.
Intern (continuing): This must be a really difficult situation for you. Instead of concentrating solely on getting daycare and job training over the next couple of weeks, could we talk about how your relationship with your parents has impacted all of your other relationships?	I want to continue exploring the past and how it relates to her present situation. I am trying to be empathic, but this is becoming challenging. I'm afraid of overstepping my boundaries by talking about "we" and "us."	*Empathy*—I use the concept of *twinship* here when I talk about the "we." This is the *partnering self object*—I show her that we're in this together.

If the student shares this process recording in class, he will benefit from the feedback. Most certainly, the practice instructor and the field supervisor should read the journal entry and make comments on the process record, and it should travel with the student to his next supervisory conference, providing linkage between the classroom and the field.

Clinical Supervision: The Learning Alliance

Supervision is a contractual learning process that begins with an agreement between the supervisor and the supervisee (student) on what is to be learned and how the learning will take place. The supervisor must be selective and goal oriented, focusing on the process recording, the student's comments and use of theory, and, above all, the client. Too much focus on the student's feelings makes the client an involuntary co-participant in the supervisee's therapy (Burns & Holloway, 1990; Moldawsky, 1980). While examination of countertransference issues should, when appropriate, be part of the supervisory process, giving primacy to student self-reflection over the development of skill, particularly at this early stage of clinical education and experience, often leaves students practicing from instinct or intuition, rather than a sound knowledge base. It is also important for the supervisor to be mindful that students should reflect on feelings that may have influenced certain choices within the context of the client's needs. This distinguishes supervision from therapy and keeps the professional boundaries intact (Congress, 2001).

Several authors have written about supervisors' tendencies to train students and workers in the model of therapy that they themselves either have been trained in or use more frequently in their practice (Holloway & Brager, 1989; Putney, Worthington, & McCulloughy, 1992). While this is understandable and can certainly be of value to the student, supervisors also need to be attentive—as appropriate to the agency and client population—to incorporating models of practice that the student may be learning and/or interested in discussing. Supervision, too often, is removed from the learning going on in the classroom. Supervisors do not communicate with practice instructors (or vice versa) unless those teachers are advisors to their students (Fortune, McCarthy, & Abramson, 2001; Knight, 2001). In the integrative model, the supervisor reads the student's process recording with a focus on the development of knowledge and skill. The supervisor should be clear about the importance and use of this teaching tool and that the student has presented this dialog to her practice class. This allows input from two sources and enables the student to have time to think critically about his intervention.

The Clinical Agenda.   The clinical agenda is a working document that provides the beginning clinician with a tool to improve practice skills and develop professional awareness. The agenda brings focus to the supervisory conference as both the supervisor and the student prepare for the meeting by writing an agenda of clinical issues that they each would like to discuss. The supervisee is responsible for preparing agenda items that reflect her view of clinical practice with clients, considering emerging themes that suggest areas of struggle or concern. This agenda should be given to the supervisor in advance of the conference. The supervisor's agenda, written after a careful review of the supervisee's process recording, should include observations and comments about the student's process record that will help the student translate the theory into dialog. The student should have this before he meets with his supervisor.

The classroom dialog and exercises provide a direct link to supervision because students' participation in the practice laboratory (class) helps them to develop a clinical agenda based on their own unique learning needs. Through this process, the classroom instructor and the student make the field supervisor aware of what is occurring in the practice class. In turn, the supervisor contributes to students' development in the field by providing important feedback that they can integrate into process records, journals, and classroom discussion and exercises.

Following are two examples of clinical agendas. The first was written by the student intern following his interview with Mrs. Diaz. The second is the supervisor's clinical agenda, written after reviewing the same process recording.

Example of Student's Clinical Agenda.

1. I think I felt embarrassed that the case aide and I had an argument in front of Mrs. Diaz. It threw me and I forgot for the moment that I was using the self-psychology model with Mrs. Diaz. How should I have handled it within the framework of self-psychology?
2. I'm worried about how Mrs. Diaz sees me. I am a male intern with white privilege, and she is an immigrant Latino woman living in poverty. She has problems with her husband, whom she claims is abusive. Should I address the gender and cultural issues with her? Would I be able to do that within the self-psychology model? Or am I coming from my own anxieties instead of focusing on being more empathic with Mrs. Diaz?
3. Mrs. Diaz was traumatized by her mother's early migration and what she perceived as abandonment. I, too, have some early abandonment issues. I feel very close to Mrs. Diaz when she talks about this. I'm afraid of overstepping my boundary because I am very identified with her struggle. What do you think? How do you think I can I guard against this?
4. I struggled with the concept of mirroring—I would like to review the places in the process recording where I attempted to use it.

Example of Supervisor's Clinical Agenda.

1. Self-psychology is an excellent model to use because it demonstrates the use of empathy. Did you select this theory intuitively, or did you find some evidence that this was the model of choice?
2. You are highly empathic during most of the interview. Can you recognize the times during the interview when you move from the empathic response to another intervention? Do you know what you were thinking or feeling during those times? How could you continue to be empathic and what would you say?
3. What was your practice evidence for using a scaling intervention during the interview? What theoretical model were you incorporating into your work? What were you feeling at that time?
4. In the interview you speak about raising Mrs. Diaz's self-esteem. Can you think about how this would be accomplished within a self-psychological framework?
5. How would raising the gender and cultural issues help your client? What do you think about her marital expectations within the context of her culture?
6. Let's talk more about your concerns re: boundary issues.
7. How might you begin to think about evaluating your practice interventions?

Faculty Field Advisement

The role of the faculty field advisor is a critical one. It provides linkage between the field and the classroom curriculum. It is ideal, but not always possible, to have faculty advisors serve as practice instructors. It is most difficult in large schools where students have different specializations, and practice classes house too many students for one advisor to manage. However, we feel strongly that faculty advisors and supervisors should be oriented to the practice curriculum, to the three-column method of process recording described, and to the integrative model. Students should be able to remove process recordings from their journals to ensure confidentiality. The practice instructor should be the only person to have access to the entire integrative journal, as this allows the student to freely struggle with complex material without fear of repercussions from the field work faculty. Faculty advisors who are not practice teachers should attend training workshops, as should field supervisors, so that they will be familiar with the theoretical models taught in the curriculum. We suggest that they receive Continuing Education credits for their participation and that distance learning also be incorporated into the curriculum. Finally, guidelines and models for all of these materials—the integrative journal, the process record, the clinical agenda, and the supervisory conference—should be included in the field work manual and the student manual, so that students, supervisors, and advisors all are clear about the guidelines and requirements.

Evidenced-Based Practice

The Council on Social Work Education (CSWE) mandates the use of scientific inquiry throughout the social work curriculum (CSWE, 1984), and most social work students will enter a field where both public and private funding sources will insist on results-oriented outcomes to ensure high-quality service (Rock & Cooper, 2000) and where practice evaluation will be a professional necessity. Addis and Waltz (2002) point out that, although the different rationales for psychotherapy dissemination research have been well articulated, the most effective means for bringing research products to clinical practice have yet to be determined, and there is a lack of research on training in the integration of science and practice at the undergraduate, graduate, and postgraduate levels. In the integrative model, students are asked to seek the best evidence for their choice of theoretical approach in their work with clients. They are required to search the literature for support for the efficacy of using their interventions, and also to provide a plan—and sometimes a product—evaluating the effectiveness of their work. Ideally, the practice class and the research class would be linked so that students would learn practice evaluation and theory application simultaneously during a semester. We realize that this is not always the case, and so we provide, in Chapter 14 of this book, two methods for integrating research and practice. Strong research-oriented students can be taught to carry out the designs that are described, while others may simply be able to provide evidence for the theoretical models they select and offer an evaluation plan. All research designs should be linked to the field, and clinical supervisors should participate in helping students select clients whose cases are appropriate for measurement.

Summary

信奉する

Social work has evolved over the years, taking on the challenges of the times. The profession now espouses a breadth of theoretical approaches and treatment modalities, a commitment to diversity and social justice, and a trend toward empirical evaluation of practice. Graduate social work education is, for many, the first step to becoming a skilled clinician. Schools of social work have the challenge of integrating classroom learning with clinical practice. In the integrative model illustrated in this chapter, we have presented a guide that students and instructors can use to ensure that students will truly know how to bring their knowledge of theory into the interview and counseling meetings with their clients. We hope this model will be used by students in the practice class, field supervisors, and faculty advisors so that an integrative learning experience will take place.

Learning Assignments

1. Keep a practice journal and write in it weekly. Bring it to each class for discussion. Try to include some or all of the following in each journal entry:
   a. A discussion of some readings that are relevant to your work with a particular client(s) (individual, group, or family).
   b. A piece of (or full) process record(s) of a session with a client, using the three-column model described in this chapter. Use dialogue from a session that illustrates how you have integrated learning from the reading(s). Discuss how the reading(s) might influence your future work with this client.
   c. A critique and evaluation of your session with this client. Consider your assessment and/or intervention and discuss the evidence for selecting this intervention and what your next steps will be.
   d. A clinical agenda for your next supervisory meeting that raises a few questions that you would like to discuss, based on your work with this client and your classroom learning.
   e. A discussion of your practice class, learning needs, and/or areas of further interest.
   f. A discussion of the outcome of your supervisory meeting.
   g. Discuss how you intend to evaluate the effectiveness of your work.

2. Prepare a formal oral case presentation. Choose a client from your field practicum (with your supervisor's assistance and involvement, when possible) and provide descriptive psychosocial information. Present the theoretical framework you found useful in working with the client, the evidence for using that particular theory with the client, and a process recording of an interview in which you demonstrate your use of the theory. Raise two questions about your work that you would like the class to help you with.

3. Submit a formal psychosocial study that includes clearly defined treatment goals based on a theory. Explain the theory, the evidence for your choice, and provide a sample process recording of an interview that demonstrates your ability to use this theory in your work with a client. Discuss how you might evaluate the effectiveness of your intervention.

References

Abramson, J., & Fortune, A. (1990). Improving field instruction: An evaluation of a seminar for new field instructors. *Journal of Social Work Education, 26,* 273–286.

Addis, M., & Waltz, J. (2002, November). Implicit and untested assumptions about the role of psychotherapy treatment manuals in evidence-based mental health practice. *Clinical Psychology: Science and Practice, 9*(4), 367–378.

Barbour, R. (1984). Social work education: Tackling the theory-practice dilemma. *British Journal of Social Work, 14,* 557–567.

Burns, C. I., & Holloway, E. L. (1990). Therapy in supervision: An unresolved issue. *Clinical Supervisor, 7*(4), 47–60.

Congress, E. (2001). Dual relationships in social work education: Report on a national survey. *Journal of Social Work Education, 37*(2), 255–267.

Council on Social Work Education (CSWE). (1984). *Handbook of accreditation standards and procedures.* Washington, DC: Author.

Fortune, A., McCarthy, M., & Abramson, J. (2001). Student learning processes in field education: Relationship of learning activities to quality of field instruction, satisfaction, and performance among MSW students. *Journal of Education in Social Work, 37*(1), 111–127.

Godwin, G. (1996). How to keep a journal. *Behavioral Health Treatment, 2*(7), 551–552.

Gomory, T. (2001). Critical rationalism (Gomory's blurry theory) or positivism (Thyer's theoretical myopia): Which is the prescription for social work research? *Journal of Education in Social Work, 37*(1), 67–79.

Graybeal, C., & Ruff, E. (1995). Process recording: It's more than you think. *Journal of Social Work Education, 31,* 169–181.

Guntrip, H. (1969). *Schizoid phenomena, object relations and the self.* New York: International Universities Press.

Holloway, S., & Brager, G. (l989). *Supervising in the human services: The politics of practice.* New York: The Free Press.

Kohut, H. (1971). *The analysis of the self.* New York: International Universities Press.

Kohut, H. (1977). *The restoration of the self.* New York: International Universities Press.

Knight, C. (2001). The process of field instruction: BSW and MSW students' views. *Journal of Social Work Education, 37*(2), 357–381.

Moldawsky, S. (1980). Psychoanalytic psychotherapy supervision. In A. K. Hess (Ed.), *Psychotherapy supervision. Theory, research and practice* (pp. 126–135). New York: John Wiley & Sons.

Munro, E. (2002). The role of theory in social work research: A further contribution to the debate. *Journal of Social Work Education, 38*(2), 461–471.

Neuman, K. M., & Friedman, B. D. (1997). Process recording: Fine-tuning an old instrument. *Journal of Social Work Education, 33*(2), 237–243.

Putney, M. W., Worthington, E. L., & McCulloughy, M. E. (1992). Effects of supervisor and supervisee theoretical orientation and supervisor–supervisee matching on interns' perceptions of supervision. *Journal of Counseling Psychology, 39,* 258–265.

Rock, B., & Cooper, M. (2000). Social Work in Primary Care: A Demonstration Student Unit Utilizing Practice Research. *Social Work in Health Care, 31*(1).

Thyer, B. (2001). What is the role of theory in research on social work practice? *Journal of Social Work Education, 37*(1), 9–26.

Turner, F. J. (Ed.). (1996). *Social work treatment: Interlocking theoretical approaches* (4th ed.). New York: The Free Press.

2

Key Issues in Clinical Practice

In this chapter we will discuss those key issues that require special consideration. We include content on brief treatment, ethics and boundaries, suicide, managed care, and therapist's self-care.

Brief Treatment

Research Perspective

Currently, brief treatment perspectives are influencing social work practice—they are considered one of the primary strategies for managing third-party costs for outpatient mental health services. However, brief treatment has become the treatment of choice for reasons other than just cost containment. Outcome studies in which clients were randomly assigned to either time-limited or time-unlimited treatment showed no difference in the effectiveness between these two treatment modalities regardless of diagnosis (Corwin, 2002). Pekarik (1996), in studies of the effectiveness of a variety of brief treatment perspectives with no-treatment control groups, found that those persons who received brief treatment functioned more effectively than control group members. Koss and Butcher (1986), in well-designed psychotherapy studies, with experienced therapists, clinically representative clients, and appropriate controls and followup, demonstrated that brief therapy was as effective as longer courses of treatment. Large numbers of clinical studies determined that even when clinicians decided on the need for long-term treatment, in actual practice, most treatment was unplanned brief treatment, with the average number of sessions being between six and eight (Koss & Burcher, 1986; Smyrnios & Kirby, 1993). Howard, Kopta, Krause, and Orlinsky (1986) found that clients make their greatest improvements in functioning in the early sessions of therapy. Garfield (1994) studied the expectations of therapy of seventy clients in an outpatient clinic and found that over a third thought that therapy sessions would last a half hour or less, 73 percent anticipated some improvement by the fifth session, and 70 percent expected treatment to last ten sessions or less.

Models of Brief Treatment $3717°$

Koss and Butcher (1986) identified fifty-three models of brief treatment in the literature. Since that study was published, new models have appeared. Epstein and Brown (2002), trying to minimize the difference among the models, break the classifications into three categories: psychodynamic, problem-solving, and mixed-eclectic. Psychodynamic brief treatment makes use of psychoanalytic principles such as uncovering, working through of repressed material, analysis of defenses, transference, countertransference, and resistance. The goals are fairly flexible, and analysis of conflict is supplemented by environmental management. (Examples of psychodynamic brief treatment appear in our theoretical chapters on object relations and self-psychology.) Problem-solving models involve a focus on target problems, selection of mutual goals, teaching of problem-solving strategies such as skill acquisition, and discussion of alternatives and obstacles. Cognitive behavioral treatment would fall into this category. (For a detailed description and case examples, see Chapters 10 and 11 on cognitive and behavior social work practice.) The third approach, mixed eclectic, is composed of a diverse selection of the psychodynamic and problem-solving components plus additions and rearrangements constructed by particular theorists (for a review of the literature on the mixed-eclectic approach, see Budman & Gurman, 1988; Cummings, 1990; Parad & Parad, 1990; Strupp & Binder, 1984).

The First Meeting

The initial contracts in brief therapy can be reviewed and renegotiated, but it is essential to establish the parameters of the treatment, including a clear definition of patient and therapist responsibilities. Detailed information about the presenting problem is rapidly obtained, and the clinician moves quickly from general, open-ended questions to more specific questions as the interview proceeds (Kadushin, 1997). Time must be used flexibly. Budman and Gurman (1988) suggest that some clients may benefit from more intensive meetings at the beginning of therapy and less frequent meetings as the therapy progresses. Budman, Hoyt, and Friedman (1992) consider the first session to be critical in brief treatment. They delineate eleven tasks that need to be accomplished in the first meeting: (1) establishing rapport; (2) orienting and instructing the patient on how to use therapy; (3) establishing an opportunity for the patient to express his or her thoughts and feelings; (4) assessing the patient's strengths, motivations, expectations, and goals; (5) evaluating possible psychiatric complaints, such as biological factors, suicide/homicide risk, and substance abuse; (6) mutually formulating a treatment focus; (7) making initial treatment interventions and assessing their effects; (8) suggesting homework tasks; (9) defining the treatment parameters; (10) scheduling future appointments; and (11) handling issues such as confidentiality, fees, insurance, or releases, as indicated. Single-session solutions (Hoyt, 1995) may be appropriate for those who come to solve a specific problem for which a solution is in their control; patients who essentially need reassurance; and patients who come for evaluation and need a referral for medical and/or other nonpsychotherapy services.

The Working Relationship

The clinician must develop an immediate positive working relationship in brief treatment. A high level of activity is demanded of the therapist, as well as a collaborative mindset, and an ability to stay focused and intensely alert throughout the course of treatment. Within the context of this positive relationship, therapist and client agree on goals and objectives and contract for the number of sessions needed to achieve these. Goals are focused, and reflect those issues that are most compelling to the client (Corwin, 2002). Problems in the therapeutic alliance are dealt with in the here and now, and signs of resistance are handled in the moment so that therapist and client can work toward a better therapeutic relationship.

In the middle phase of brief treatment, client and worker maintain the focus and make progress toward the stated treatment goals. In some brief treatment models, such as cognitive and behavioral therapies, homework assignments keep the therapy moving between sessions and help the client to progress more rapidly.

Termination is built into brief treatment, beginning with contracting the number of sessions and followed by end-of-session reviews that summarize the meeting and the progress made toward goal attainment. Feelings of loss are not ignored, but there is less exploration of these issues. It is expected that clients may return to the therapist in the future if problems recur. Because the relationship in brief treatment is less intense than in open-ended therapy and centered on client's strengths, there is less dependence on the therapist (Corwin, 2002).

Selection Criteria

Brief treatment can utilize broad or narrow selection criteria in determining whether patients are appropriate candidates. Briefly stated, brief treatment conducted with broad selection criteria excludes few prospective patients, proposing instead that everyone start with a time-limited role. Contraindications for brief treatment models that utilize narrow selection criteria include patients who do not give the impression they can develop a working alliance with the therapist, those who have not had at least one significant relationship in their lives, and patients who do not seem motivated to change. Additional contraindications for brief treatment may include patients with serious depression who are unable to form a rapid therapeutic alliance, patients with acute psychosis, patients with severe narcissistic disturbances, or those with a history of severe trauma. Schizoid patients and patients unable to identify a central focus are also not considered appropriate (Bloom, 1997; Clarkin & Frances, 1982).

Ethics and Boundaries

Sexual Relationships with Clients

The National Association of Social Workers (NASW) Code of Ethics (1996) states that "social workers should under no circumstances engage in sexual activities or sexual contact with current clients, whether such contact is consensual or forced." The code further admonishes against sexual contact with clients' relatives or other individuals with whom clients maintain close personal relationships when there is a risk of exploitation or potential harm to the client. Engaging "in sexual activities or sexual contact with former clients because of the potential for harm to the client" is also prohibited.

In spite of these warnings, sexual contact between social workers and clients does occur. A study of 300 closed adjudication cases for the years 1982 to 1992 on record at the NASW national offices found that sexual activity with a client accounted for 29.2 percent of the 72 substantiated complaints against social workers, almost double the next most common complaint of having dual or multiple relationships with clients or former clients in which there is risk of exploitation of or potential harm to the client (National Association of Social Workers, 1995; cited in Berkman, Turner, Cooper, Polnerow, & Schwartz, 2000). Reamer (1995) found that between 1969 and 1990 sexual impropriety was the second most common malpractice claim (18.5%) filed against social workers.

We believe that there is never a circumstance that would justify sexual relations between worker and client. And we further caution social workers not to engage in sexual relations with former clients or friends or relatives of a client. We say this without equivocation. It is *never* in the client's interests and can only serve to harm. The therapeutic relationship involves client vulnerability and practitioner influence (Kagle & Giebelhausen, 1994). The repercussions for the client are just too severe and the damage too extensive to ever warrant an exception to the rule: Never engage in sexual relationships with clients. Entering into a sexual relationship with a client post-termination can still be exploitative. The client has shared her intimacies with you, and by so doing, has been made vulnerable to you. The therapeutic relationship is, by its very nature, a relationship that is unequal, and sexual relationships between practitioner and client always carry the potential for harm.

Other Dual Relationships

Unfortunately, far less information is available on nonsexual dual relationships, but such relationships can be exploitative, pose risks to clients, and also lead to sexual intimacy between practitioners and clients (Pope & Bouhoutsos, 1986, cited in Berkman et al. 2000). But what about former clients or friends or relatives of clients? Again, as stated by the NASW Code of Ethics, the rule is "no." Clients, former clients, and friends or relatives of clients should not become part of your personal life. There is always the potential for betrayal of past confidences or the stirring up of rivalries. It places a burden on your client, who may receive knowl-edge of you that she doesn't need to know. It may prevent her from seeking your help again in the future. It may cause her to doubt the help that you provided in the past. Keep your personal and professional life separate, when you can.

We recognize that there are times and places (particularly small towns) where clients' and social workers' lives do overlap. They may belong to the same religious organizations, be parents of children in the same schools, and appear at the same community functions. I have known students who live and work in the African American community and who attend the same churches as their clients. In the lesbian community, a complete separation between personal and profes-sional contact may be impossible because there are aspects of the therapists' and clients' lives that will intersect, even when the therapist exerts great effort to avoid dual roles (Eldridge, Mencher, & Slater, 1993).

Some practitioners have adopted feminist and other empowerment models that seek to redress the power imbalance between clinician and client (Kagle & Giebelhausen, 1994). Feminist writers suggest that we recognize and validate the existence of overlapping relationships, because they may be unavoidable, and ask the therapist to accept responsibility for monitoring such relationships to prevent potential abuse of or harm to the client. They suggest that we make ethics a rela-tional process: consulting, questioning, discussing, disagreeing, and clarifying—these relational processes help to heighten our awareness and capacity to create a living ethics for relational psychotherapy.

The Suicidal Client

Perhaps one of the most heart-wrenching and troubling issues in clinical practice is the threat of a client's suicide. The importance of the relationship between the interviewer and the client cannot be overestimated when working with the suici-dal client. Trust is paramount when making an assessment, and the interviewer must be as tenacious as a detective in her inquiries. Remember, patients who are experiencing suicidal ideation (thoughts) may be reluctant to talk about it for a va-riety of reasons. They may feel ashamed or frightened that they will be hospital-ized against their will. They may also want to die and not want to share that with anyone who they think will try to stop them. Whenever possible, the interviewer should check with corroborative sources to determine whether they have noticed any behaviors that might be of concern. Talking to others who have a relationship with the patient also provides the opportunity to determine what the specific stressors and/or supports are in the patient's life.

Those who write about suicide from a self-in-relation perspective (see, for example, Kaplan & Klein, 1990) emphasize the importance of the clinical rela-tionship in work with potentially suicidal female clients. Their understanding can be extended to work with all suicidal clients, regardless of gender. They have identified three main relational functions for the therapist: (1) to monitor suicide and make contractual agreements; (2) to create a supportive, life-affirming, patient–therapist connection; and (3) to foster the client's connection to a sustaining support system. The suicidal client despairs of her capacity to maintain connection and finds safety within a process that awakens within her the possibility of finding connections. Citing Miller (1986), Kaplan and Klein (1990) point out that the sense of being deeply understood within the therapeutic relationship legitimates and validates the feelings that the suicidal client is trying to communicate and propels her toward further awareness of her relational potential and further confirmation of her right to life. The sense of being understood is life affirming. The therapist needs to engage the suicidal client with empathy, care, and concern, and to lend her own optimism that, even in the darkest of times, there are viable alternatives to taking one's life.

Guidelines for Assessing Suicide

There are some very clear general guidelines that therapists can use in assessing for suicide. Shea (1998) notes that the interviewer must be concerned with (1) the frequency of the patient's suicidal ideation, (2) the duration of ideation (how long does it last?), (3) the concreteness of the suicidal plan, and (4) the extent of action taken with regard to the plan. Having a specific plan and a lethal means available are clear indicators of imminent suicide (Bednar, Bednar, Lambert, & Waite, (1991, p. 115). A person who makes a suicide attempt at a time and a place where there is a good possibility of being discovered by someone does not represent the same risk as an attempt made where/when the possibility of discovery by another person is low (this is known as the risk/rescue ratio).

The Chronological Assessment of Suicide (C.A.S.E.) is a useful tool with a patient who has made a suicidal attempt or when suicidal ideation is intense (Shea, 1998). In step one of the C.A.S.E., the interviewer explores presenting suicidal events. She asks questions such as "How did the patient try to kill herself?" "How serious was the action taken with this method?" "To what degree did the patient intend to die?" "How does the patient feel about the fact that she did not successfully kill herself?" "Did alcohol or drugs play a part in the attempt?" In step two, the interviewer asks about recent suicidal events by gathering information on any suicidal thoughts and actions the patient may have had during the previous six to eight weeks, questioning what plans have been considered, how far the patient took actions on those plans, and how much of the patient's time was spent on these plans. Step three involves exploration of past suicidal events that inform the practitioner about the patient's safety, for example, "What was the most serious suicide attempt?" "When was the most recent attempt?" In step four the interviewer obtains information about the immediate suicidal events, any suicidal ideation the patient may be having during the interview, and the patient's prediction of future thoughts of suicide. The clinician might ask, "What would you do later tonight or tomorrow if you began to have suicidal thoughts again?" or "Right now, are you having any thoughts about killing yourself?"

Providing Safety

A referral for a psychiatric evaluation is always required when a patient is suicidal. A psychiatrist's knowledge and expertise in this area supports our own, and many psychotropic medications that only psychiatrists can prescribe help stem the depressive course. If, in conjunction with the psychiatrist, it is determined that the patient presents a suicidal risk, immediate hospitalization or another form of protection is required. Whenever possible, try to encourage the patient to agree to a voluntary hospitalization if your assessment of their risk for suicide warrants inpatient care. Remember that if the patient is suicidal, you must breach confidentiality and take the necessary steps, which might include contacting family members, a crisis center, or the police in order to ensure the well-being of the patient. This is a difficult time for the interviewer because the patient may be angry, feel betrayed, and at times, may verbally or physically lash out. Interviewers may understandably feel conflicted about pursuing a course of action that is against the patient's wishes. A discussion of whether suicide can ever be justified as being within the bounds of client self-determination is beyond the scope of this chapter. You need to remember that failure to properly assess for and or take the proper steps to prevent a suicide can be construed as professional negligence. It is also important that you clearly document your assessment of suicide risk and the steps you took to try to prevent a suicide from occurring.

If a decision is made not to hospitalize, family members or friends, if available, must be involved in monitoring the patient, calling for emergency help, or getting the patient to the hospital if there is an imminent threat of danger. They must be informed as to what constitutes suicidality in a patient and that it is important that they not leave the patient alone, even for a few minutes. It is important for the interviewer to establish a safety plan with the patient and to involve appropriate family members or friends, whenever possible. Safety contracts can provide important insights for the interview into the patient's thinking about suicide. A patient may, for example, be reluctant to sign a safety contract (Shea, 1998). Remember also that, while safety contracts can be important deterrents, they offer no guarantee that a patient will not commit suicide. Additionally, the patient should be instructed to call the primary therapist at any time, even late evenings, and the therapist must be available to receive such calls. Home phone numbers should not be given. We recommend that all clinicians who practice outside of agencies have their own emergency paging systems so that patients can have immediate access in crisis. Agencies should also have 24-hour coverage.

Child and Adolescent Suicide

Children and adolescents must be directly questioned about suicide because, as Kaplan, Sadock, and Grebb (1994) point out, parents are frequently unaware of such ideas in their children. They must be specifically questioned about their fantasies, as teenagers often glorify suicide, viewing those who do end their lives as heroes and heroines. Fantasies of an afterlife among departed relatives and loved ones are common among depressed adolescents, who see suicide as a way to be reunited with those they have lost. Because adolescents are impulsive, they may see suicide as an immediate solution without thinking about consequences or alternatives. And, because adolescents operate in the here and now without a long view of the future, their despair is all the more compelling. Because peer group identification and acceptance are so important during the development stage of adolescence, those who live on the margin are particularly vulnerable to suicide. Hispanic females have a 21 percent rate of suicide attempts, in part owing to the demands on these adolescents to balance traditional and acculturated roles (Zayas, Kaplan, Turner, Romano, & Gonzalez-Ramos, 2000). African American and non-Hispanic white female adolescents have rates of 10.8 percent and 10.4 percent, respectively. Adolescent males overall have lower rates of suicide attempts than their female counterparts (Zayas et al., 2000, citing a 1996 report from the Centers for Disease Control and Prevention). Gay youth have been found to attempt suicide at a rate two to three times higher than other adolescents (Kulkin, Chauvin, & Percle, 2000; Morrison & L'Heureux, 2001). Therapy is critical for these at-risk adolescents as it gives them the opportunity to discuss their feelings and fantasies in an atmosphere of confidentiality, with an empathic therapist who provides a safety net and a reality check, offering a way out of isolation and disconnection.

Managed Care

The management of client care is designed to meet two major goals: controlling costs while ensuring the quality of care (Corcoran & Vandiver, 1996). The oversight of health and mental health services is done by a third party, and need, duration, and continuation of these services and their rate for service reimbursement are predetermined by the payor. The notion is that by limiting unnecessary services financial costs will be kept down. White, Simmons, and Bixby (1993, cited in Berkman, 1996) predicted that, by 2000, 90 percent of all medical benefits administration will be handled by managed care.

Ethical Dilemmas under Managed Care

Of great concern to social workers are the ethical dilemmas created by the advent of managed care—in particular, the limits and scope of confidentiality. The therapeutic relationship between the therapist and the client now includes a third party. Although reimbursement by third-party insurers always involved reporting on diagnosis and treatment sessions, under managed care detailed documentation is often required. Clinicians are required to report on client's symptoms, diagnosis, goals and objectives, modalities, and length of time needed to obtain results. Most often, continued care is authorized only when need can be justified, such as a DSM-IV diagnosis of Major Depression or Bipolar disorder, both considered medical conditions. GAF scores often need to be in the fifties for continued outpatient treatment. Clients who require help with problems of living (legitimate DSM-IV diagnosis such as adjustment disorders) receive limited services. The authorization process under managed care is often cumbersome, requiring copious paperwork and numerous telephone calls. Managed care regulations often compromise the integrity of the therapeutic relationship. Situations can occur when clients may need to change insurance plans. Managed care companies have not consistently honored the relationship between client and therapist, suggesting that clients choose a therapist on their provider panel if they want continued reimbursement for their therapy. This is in spite of empirical research (Lambert, 1992a; Luborsky, Crits-Cristoph, Mintz, & Auerback, 1988; Najavits & Strupp, 1994; Strupp, 1995) attesting to the importance of the therapist–patient relationship on treatment outcome. Managed care companies also encourage therapists to rely on therapies that have been empirically tested, such as cognitive and behavioral, as opposed to narrative and psychodynamic models that may be less amenable to quantifiable measurement (Chambliss, 2000). This occurs in spite of knowledge that good practice requires that an intervention be chosen on the basis of psychosocial assessment, not the preference of a managed care company.

Reamer (1997) cautions that social workers who practice in managed care programs must be careful to avoid practices that constitute ethical violations. They need to be sure to protest utilization-review decisions that are contrary to their professional judgment; that clients are adequately informed about the risks associated with short-term or limited intervention; that clients are assessed thoroughly for risks of self-injurious behaviors, including suicide, and the potential to harm others; that other professionals are consulted when social workers believe they do not have the requisite expertise or resources to provide clients with the care they need in the time allotted; and that social workers with supervisory responsibilities monitor supervises carefully and conscientiously. Reamer offers some guidelines for ethical practice. First and foremost, the clinician must disclose to clients how delivery of services may be influenced by managed care policies and restrictions. Clients need to be fully informed of the pre- and current authorization process, their right to appeal a utilization decision, the potential invasion of their privacy by the review process, and other options available to meet their needs (Sabin, 1994a, 1994b). Reamer concludes that social workers concerned about their ability, under managed care, to meet the needs of vulnerable clients, must organize clients and colleagues to inform key participants in managed care of the risks that managed care generates, the severity of mental health problems left that are not addressed, and the benefits of high quality services.

Confidentiality and Technology: HIPAA

Managed care's reliance on technology for immediate transmission of information poses another threat to confidentiality. Telephone reviews, facsimile transmissions, voice-mail reports, and computerized databases used by managed care companies seriously compromise the guarantee of confidentiality (Davidson & Davidson, 1996, cited in Rock & Congress, 1999). In the early days of computers, data was stored primarily on one computer unit or a floppy disk; now computers often are networked both within and between agencies. This means there is no longer one case record, but in reality the case record sits on every worker's desk (Rock & Congress, 1999).

The Health Insurance Portability and Accountability Act (HIPAA) of 1996, Public Law 104-191, which became effective on April 24, 2001, set national standards for the protection of health information, as applied to health plans, healthcare clearinghouses, and healthcare providers who conduct transactions electronically. By the compliance date of April 14, 2003, covered entities had to implement standards to protect and guard against the misuse of identifiable health information. Failure to comply in a timely manner could result in civil or criminal penalties. The privacy rule established, for the first time, a foundation of federal protections to protect health information. Currently, all health and mental healthcare patients must sign forms signifying that they have agreed to allow their providers to transmit confidential information electronically. The rule does not replace federal, state, or other laws in effect that grant even greater privacy protections, and covered entities are free to adopt even more protective policies or practices. For a general overview of standards for privacy of individually identifiable health information, refer to the government website (www.hhs.gov/ocr/hipaa/guidelines/overview.pdf).

In spite of protective legislation, breaches of confidentiality should be expected to take place in electronic media, and confidentiality cannot be guaranteed. Social workers are therefore cautioned that information that is potentially life-threatening may be too risky to be stored electronically and should be secured in other ways.

Opportunities under Managed Care

Managed care presents benefits as well as disadvantages. Many marginalized clients who would otherwise be confined to the use of clinic settings with long waiting periods for services, overburdened practitioners, and overcrowded working conditions now have access to the private sector. They have a choice of providers (within the limits of their plans), with various specializations and levels of expertise (psychiatric, psychological, or social work). They have opportunities that were previously afforded only to the middle and upper class. This has brought equity into the healthcare arena and diversity into the sphere of private practice (Rock, 2001).

Therapist Self-Care

We conclude this chapter with the very important topic of therapist self-care. Using oneself authentically with a wide range of clients on a daily basis is emotionally demanding. It involves ongoing self-reflection and self-monitoring to ensure that the clinician responds professionally and empathically. Hiratsuku (1991, cited in Pieper, 1999) coined the term *compassion fatigue* to describe what could happen when the clinical social worker feels stuck with unrewarding clinical experiences. When this occurs, the therapist might find herself disclosing more of her personal life than is appropriate, raising topics with a client that the client has not expressed an interest in discussing, and, in general, gratifying her own needs and becoming less emotionally available. To protect oneself, a therapist must strive to achieve a sense of balance in her life. Therapist self-care protects from burnout by defining the balance between the therapist's caring for self and caring for others. The concept of self-care also reduces risk factors that are associated with ethical violations. Self-care enhances therapy by promoting and modeling growth and well-being (Porter, 1995, p. 250).

Fraunce (1990), writing from a feminist perspective, sees a connection in how the therapist behaves toward herself and her clients, as well as how clients behave toward themselves. She discusses the importance of the therapist's role-modeling effective self-care strategies, often something clients themselves struggle with in their own lives.

What tools can clinical social workers use to balance their own needs and the clients' well-being? We believe this begins in graduate education where the seeds for a professional clinical social work career are planted. Graduate schools of social work face a dilemma in contemporary times. There is an absolute need for flexible programs to make the profession available to those who may be economically challenged, to people of color who traditionally have been unable to pursue higher education, to those with family responsibilities and experience who may be returning to school, and to a host of others. However, a graduate program in social work is a challenging endeavor that requires time and commitment—intellectually and emotionally. This is difficult to handle when trying to balance other social and economic roles, contributing to role strain. Students are further burdened and stressed by the demands of their clients, often because they have not yet learned the importance of maintaining flexible but clear boundaries. In addition, students often have their own histories of trauma or loss that can easily be triggered in the social work practice setting. Balancing the rigors of graduate education with self-care is important because this is the time one begins to lay the foundation for professional practice. Schools of social work need to examine this issue carefully and find ways to make graduate education available and challenging while encouraging self care.

We encourage faculty to space exams and papers so that students can have time to reflect and reconstitute their energies, rather than having to produce for all courses at the same time. We suggest more informal gatherings (such as lunchtime seminars) where students and faculty can engage in stimulating conversations and exchange new ideas. We advise students to realistically assess their work, school, and family commitments, adjusting schedules to ensure some time to rest and refuel. In our fast-paced world, students and faculty alike need opportunities to slow down, think, process, and nourish their minds as well as their selves. As Eldridge and colleagues (1993, p. 5) point out, "Therapist self-care is an ethical imperative. If we are not fairly consistent in caring for our changing personal needs, it will be very difficult to prevent us from meeting those needs in our therapeutic relationships."

Summary

We encourage our students to continue discussing the important issues that have been highlighted in this chapter. Open speech in classes and supervision of potential ethical and boundary violations will help prevent clinicians from acting on unconscious feelings that might lead to behavior that is injurious to both the client and the therapeutic relationship. Clients at risk for suicide must be carefully assessed, and steps must be immediately taken to provide safety and care. It seems likely that managed care policies will continue to affect our practice: Knowledge of brief treatment is essential if we are to provide quality service within the constraints of time. And finally, we stress the importance of therapist self-care. Working with clients is demanding and not always gratifying. Clinicians need to find ways to nurture themselves so that they can continue to be empathic, nonjudgmental, self-aware, and able to act in the best interests of those they serve.

Learning Assignments

1. Working in pairs, role-play a situation where a client becomes seductive with the therapist. How does the therapist respond, especially when she might also be experiencing erotic feelings?

2. Continue the role-play, but exchange roles. In this next situation, a client invites the therapist to her son's graduation. How does the therapist handle this?

3. Write up an outpatient treatment report for a managed care company, requesting additional visits for your client. You must include the diagnosis on all four axes, a GAF score, the treatment modality and frequency, the expected outcome, and the amount of time required to attain your results.

4. Discuss the ways in which you, as student, can care for yourself given the heavy demands of your graduate education and the other stresses in your life.

References

Bednar, R., Bednar, S., Lambert, M., & Waite, D. R. (1991). *Psychotherapy with high risk clients*. Pacific Grove, CA: Brooks/Cole.

Berkman, B. (1996). The emerging health care world: Implications for social work practice and education. *Social Work, 41*(5), 541–551.

Berkman, C., Turner, S., Cooper, M., Polnerow, D., & Swartz, M. (2000). Sexual contact with clients: Assessment of social workers' attitudes and educational preparation. *Social Work, 45*(3), 223–235.

Bloom, B. L. (1997). *Planned short term psychotherapy: A clinical handbook*. Boston: Allyn and Bacon.

Budman, C., & Gurman, A. (1988). *Theory and practice of brief therapy*. New York: Guilford.

Budman, C., Hoyt, M., & Friedman, S. (1992). *The first session in brief therapy*. New York: Guilford.

Chambliss, C. H. (2000). *Psychotherapy and managed care*. Boston: Allyn and Bacon.

Clarkin, J. F., & Frances, A. (1982). Selection criteria for the brief psychotherapies. *American Journal of Psychotherapy, 36,* 166–180.

Corcoran, K., & Vandiver, V. (1996). *Maneuvering the maze of managed care*. New York: Free Press-Simon and Schuster.

Corwin, M. (2002). *Brief treatment in clinical social work practice*. Pacific Grove, CA: Brooks/Cole.

Cummings, N. A. (1990). Brief intermittent psychotherapy throughout the life cycle. In J. K. Zeig & S. G. Gilligan (Eds.), *Brief therapy: Myths, methods and metaphors* (pp. 169–184). New York: Brunner/Mazel.

Davidson, T., & Davidson, J. (1996). Confidentiality and managed care: Ethical and legal concerns. *Health and Social Work, 21,* 453–464.

Eldridge, N., Mencher, J., & Slater, S. (1993). *The conundrum of mutuality: A lesbian dialogue*. Wellesley, MA: Stone Center, Wellesley College.

Epstein, L., & Brown, L. B. (2002). *Brief treatment and a new look at the task-centered approach*. Boston: Allyn and Bacon.

Fraunce, P. S. (1990). The self-care and wellness of feminist therapists. In H. Lerman & N. Porter (Eds.), *Feminist ethics in psychotherapy* (pp. 185–194). New York: Springer.

Garfield, S. L. (1994). *Research on client variables in psychotherapy*. In A. E. Bergin & S. L. Garfield (Eds.), *Handbook of psychotherapy and behavior change* (4th ed., pp. 190–228). New York: John Wiley & Sons.

Howard, K. L., Kopta, S. M., Krause, S. M., & Orlinsky, D. E. (1986). The dose-effect relationship in psychotherapy. *American Psychologist, 41,* 159–164.

Hoyt, M. F. (1995). Single-session solutions. In M. F. Hoyt, *Brief therapy and managed care: Readings for contemporary practice*. San Francisco: Jossey-Bass.

Kadushin, A. (1997). *The social work interview*. New York: Columbia University Press.

Kagle, J. D., & Giebelhausen, P. N. (1994). Dual relationships and professional boundaries. *Social Work, 39*(2), 213–220.

Kaplan, A., & Klein, R. (1990). Women and suicide: The cry for connection. *Work in progress*. No. 464. Wellesley, MA: Stone Center Working Paper Series, Wellesley College.

Kaplan, H., Sadock, B., & Grebb, J. (1994). *Synopsis of psychiatry, behavioral science clinical psychiatry* (7th ed.). Baltimore: Williams & Wilkins.

Koss, M. P., & Butcher, J. N (1986). Research on brief therapy. In A. E. Bergin & S. L. Garfield (Eds.), *Handbook of psychotherapy and behavior change* (4th ed., pp. 664–700). New York: John Wiley & Sons.

Kulkin, H. S., Chauvin, E. A., & Percle, G. (2000). Suicide among gay and lesbian adolescents and young adults: A review of the literature. *Journal of Homosexuality, 40*(1), 1–29.

Lambert, M. (1992a). Implications of outcome research for psychotherapy integration. In J. C. Norcross & M. R. Goldfried (Eds.), *Handbook of psychotherapy integration*. New York: Basic Books.

Luborsky, L., Crits-Cristoph, P., Mintz, J., & Auerback, R. (1988). *Who will benefit from psychotherapy?* New York: Basic Books.

Miller, J. B. (1986). What do we mean by relationships? *Work in progress*. No. 22. Wellesley, MA: Stone Center Working Paper Series, Wellesley College.

Morrison, L. L., & L'Heureux, J. (2001, February). Suicide and gay/lesbian/bisexual youth: Implications for clinicians. *Journal of Adolescence, 24*(1), 39–49.

Najavits, L. M., & Strupp, H. H. (1994, Spring). Differences in the effectiveness of psychodynamic therapists: A process-oriented outcome study. *Psychotherapy, 31*(1), 114–123.

National Association of Social Workers (NASW). (1995). *Overview of a decade of adjudication*. Washington, DC: Author.

National Association of Social Workers (NASW). (1996). *Code of ethics*. Washington, DC: Author.

Parad, H. J., & Parad, L. G. (1990). *Crisis intervention: Book 2*. Milwaukee, WI: Family Service Association of America.

Pekarik, G. (1996). *Psychotherapy abbreviation: A practical guide*. Binghamton, NY: Haworth Press.

Pieper, M. H. (1999). The privilege of being a therapist: A fresh perspective from intrapsychic humanism on caregiving intimacy and the development of the professional self. *Families in Society, 80*(5), 479–487.

Pope, K. S., & Bouhoutsos, J. (1986). *Sexual intimacy between therapists and patients*. New York: Praeger.

Porter, N. (1995). Therapist self care: A proactive ethical approach. In E. J. Rave & C. C. Larsen (Eds.), *Ethical decision making in therapy: Feminist perspectives* (pp. 247–267). New York: Guilford.

Reamer, F. G. (1995). Malpractice claims against social workers: First facts. *Social Work, 40,* 595–601.

Reamer, F. G. (1997). Managing ethics under managed care. *Families in Society: The Journal of Contemporary Human Services,* 96–101.

Rock, B. (2001). Social work under managed care: Will we survive or can we prevail? In B. Rock & R. Perez-Koening (Eds.), *Social worker in the era of devolution: Toward a just practice.* New York: Fordham University Press.

Rock, B., & Congress, E. (1999). The new confidentiality for the 21st century in a managed care environment. *Social Work, 44*(3), 253–262.

Sabin, J. E. (1994a). Caring about patients and caring about money. *Behavioral Sciences and the Law, 12,* 317–330.

Sabin, J. E. (1994b). Ethical issues under managed care: The managed care view. In R. K. Schreter, S. S. Sharfsteind, & C. A. Schreter (Eds.), *Allies and adversaries: The impact of managed care on mental health services* (pp.187–194). Washington, DC: American Psychiatric Press.

Shea, S. C. (1998). *Psychiatric Interviewing: The art of understanding.* Philadelphia: W. B. Saunders Company.

Smyrnios, K. X., & Kirby, R. J. (1993). Long-term comparison of brief versus unlimited psychodynamic treatments with children and their parents. *Journal of Consulting and Clinical Psychology, 61*(6), 1020–1027.

Strupp, H. (1995). The psychotherapist's skills revisited. *Clinical Psychology: Science and Practice, 2,* 70–74.

Strupp, H. H., & Binder, J. L. (1984). *Psychotherapy in a new key: A guide to time-limited dynamic psychotherapy.* New York: Basic Books.

U.S. Department of Health and Human Services, Public Health Service, Alcohol, Drug Abuse and Mental Health Administration. (1989). *Report of the secretary's task force on youth suicide* (pp. 3–142). Rockville, MD: Author.

White, M., Simmons, W., & Bixby, N. (1993). Managed care and case management: An overview. *Discharge Planning Update, 13*(1), 17–19.

Zayas, L. H., Kaplan, C., Turner, S., Romano, K., & Gonzalez-Ramos, G. (2000, January). Understanding suicide attempts by adolescent Hispanic females. *Social Work, 45*(1), 53–63.

Zeig, J. K., & Gilligan, S. G. (Eds.). (1990). *Brief therapy: Myths, methods and metaphors.* New York: Brunner/Mazel.

3

The Clinical Interview
The Process of Assessment

Beginning, Middle, and End Stages of Treatment

In this chapter we discuss the clinical interview in the beginning, middle, and end phases of treatment. Brief therapy with an adolescent boy diagnosed with a conduct disorder illustrates both the client's and worker's responses to the various clinical issues that emerge at each stage.

The First Meeting

The initial clinical interviews are the process by which data collection takes place. The psychosocial summary, which is described in detail in Chapter 4, is the product of that therapeutic process. Initially, the worker needs to gather the information that forms the basis of the psychosocial assessment. She also begins to establish the working alliance.

Who should attend the first meeting? When a parent calls about help for a child, will the entire family attend? When you first see a new client, what do you observe? Sometimes it is how she sits in the waiting room. Is she reading, sleeping, pacing? Does she seem eager to respond to your greeting or anxious about entering your office? What and whom has she brought to the interview? How is she dressed? Seasoned practitioners seem to take in this information through their bones: Inexperienced workers will need to be very conscious and use all their powers of observation when meeting a client for the first time.

Introductions

When you introduce yourself to a new client, use your full name. Then ask the client how he or she would like to be addressed. You may call a client by a first name if so directed; otherwise, using a title and surname is more respectful. This may be particularly significant when meeting older clients and clients from minority cultural groups. Obviously, there may be individuals and settings where this general rule can be relaxed; for example, when meeting young children or adolescents for the first time. You may find yourself in a situation where you address the client by her full name and she calls you by your first name. In that case, you may want to consider whether you switch to a first name basis as well.

Be on time for your first meeting with a client (and all subsequent meetings). If a client is late for the meeting, it is important to ask about this in a nonthreatening manner. Talk to your client about this openly and collaboratively establish the guidelines for subsequent meetings. This should include a discussion of when to call if an appointment needs to be cancelled. Remember, this first meeting often sets the stage for what is to follow.

It is important to pay attention to the seating in your office. You should avoid sitting behind a desk when you are interviewing a client, because this may introduce a power imbalance in the relationship. Clients who come from cultures where the "doctor" is expected to be an authority may relate to you more formally than someone who is born and raised in the dominant culture. Take your cues from the client's behavior. Remember, the client is assessing you while you are assessing her. Keep pictures of your partners, children, and pets at home. Items that are too personal are not appropriate to display. If your client is struggling with finding a mate, she doesn't need to see you as part of a happy family. It may stir up envy and add to the client's burden.

Why Is the Client Here?

I think the best way to begin the initial interview is by learning why the client has come to see you. Questions such as "What brings you here today?" or "What is on your mind today?" are helpful in getting started. Frequently, clients are flooded in the beginning, often too overwhelmed to give much information. It's important to have a tissue box close to the seating arrangement—many clients cry as soon as they hear the comforting voice of a person whom they believe will be able to help them find a way out of their pain. It is helpful to provide structure initially and to educate your client about what is going to take place in the interview, including what kinds of questions you will be asking and why. Try to present yourself as an interested, empathic, helpful person, and not an investigator or interrogator. Make sure that you have acquainted yourself with the questions on the intake form ahead of time so that you can move smoothly into new subject areas as you collect information. Open-ended questions are best to use at this time in order to give the client an opportunity to tell her story. If you are unclear about something, a gentle interruption, such as, "What you are saying seems very important—I'd like to ask you a little more about that," may be used. Listen for clinical themes such as substance use, mood disturbance, anxiety behaviors, physical complaints, social and personality problems, difficulty thinking, and psychosis (Morrison, 1995). This will help you question about specific symptoms, which may be diagnostically helpful as well as determine your theoretical frame of reference. It is important to obtain information about the client's resources and coping capacities. Be mindful that the client needs some protection in the beginning—too quick a revelation of all her struggles and defeats may leave her feeling vulnerable and fearful of returning. Try to keep the interview moving. Long silences create anxiety, and you want your client to be comfortable in your presence.

Confidentiality

It is important to let the client know that you need to have some specific information that may be difficult to remember, such as demographic data or dates of certain events, and that you may have to write these things down. Explain what you are writing and get the client's permission before moving ahead. It is not helpful to have a completed intake form only to lose your client because she experienced you as insensitive or preoccupied with note-taking. It is also important to let the client know the parameters of the clinical relationship and what material will and will not be kept confidential. Clients should be informed of what types of information can be shared with third parties, and under what circumstances, and asked to sign service agreements that clearly address these issues.

Answering Personal Questions

Clients may sometimes ask you personal questions in an initial interview. Different theoretical models understand and address this important issue in varying ways. In general, it is important to understand the meaning that such questions have to the client and, whenever you are unsure of the meaning, to feel comfortable asking. This is not to be confused with feeling threatened by a client's asking a personal question and reacting with a response such as "Why do you ask?" which can feel disrespectful or embarrassing to the client.

In most cases, clients ask personal questions because they want to know what kind of life experiences the clinician has had and whether she will be able to understand what the client is talking about. This issue has particular significance in cross-cultural work, especially when the therapist may be from the dominant culture, and the client may be from a minority background. As greater numbers of minorities enter the helping professions, they may also find themselves working with clients from the dominant culture who may be questioning whether the minority therapist can understand their difficulties, especially as the client may be a member of a group that the therapist may equate with racism and oppression. Many years ago, a young African American female student told me how she was taken aback when a young white female client asked her how she felt about white people, since they were often mean to black people. In my own practice, I have been asked many times when working with African American clients how I feel about black people. These are difficult and complex issues for which no simple answer is available.

The key is to understand the significance to the client and to always put her best interests first. The clinician may be uncomfortable about sharing personal information even when it might be helpful to the client; in these instances, the clinician needs to acknowledge her understanding of what the client is looking for and honestly share feelings of discomfort. For example, one might say, "I'm sorry I'm not comfortable talking about my personal life with you. I can understand this may be disappointing you, but I hope we will be able to work together in spite of my decision," or "I'm not comfortable talking about my personal life with you, but I'd like to understand what asking that question means to you or whether you feel I can help you without answering personal questions."

It is important to differentiate between questions the client may be asking about your personal life from those he or she may be asking about how your training, credentials, or personal values that could compromise your ability to be of assistance. You have an ethical responsibility to answer questions that will enable the client to make an informed decision about whether to engage in treatment with you. For example, I have been asked by clients if I was a "Christian therapist," and, recently, a young couple who were devout Jehovah's Witnesses asked if I was a Witness as well. Upon hearing that I was not, they asked if I felt I could work with them and help them with their problems even though we may have different religious beliefs. You must also tell the client if you are a student or a clinical trainee, regardless of whether the client asks about your credentials. After stating your name, simply state, "I am a student (or an intern) training to be a social worker. I will be working at this agency until May. My work with you will be supervised by a licensed social worker. If you have any questions about this, I would be happy to discuss them." By inviting the client to talk about any concerns she may have, you convey a willingness to be of help, which the client will appreciate.

The Therapeutic Relationship

The concept of the therapeutic relationship has its origins in the psychoanalytic literature. Freud (in Strachey, 1953–1974) was the first to speak of the patient as an active collaborator in the treatment process. He introduced several theoretical concepts—transference, countertransference, the working alliance, the real relationship, and resistance—that have survived and, with revision, have continued to influence the theoretical relationship in clinical social work practice. In fact, every psychotherapeutic model that followed Freud (including psychoanalytic, cognitive, behavioral, and postmodern theories) has considered at least one or more of these constructs either within the context of the theoretical formulation or as a basis for departure (see, for example, DeLaCour, 1998; Greenberg & Mitchell, 1983; Jordan, Kaplan, Miller, Stiver, & Surrey, 1991; Monk, Winslade, Crocket, & Epston, 1997; Safran & Segal, 1996). Since these concepts form the core of our understanding of the therapeutic relationship, their original definitions and an understanding of their usage in current practice models will follow.

Transference and Countertransference

Transference, as originally introduced by Freud, is the "experiencing of feelings, drives, attitudes, fantasies and defenses toward a person in the present which are inappropriate to that person and are a repetition, a displacement of reactions, originating with significant persons of early childhood." Transference is based on a relationship in the past (Greenson, 1967, p. 33). Relational psychoanalytic theories place the concept of transference into the therapeutic dyad and consider that a client's transferential responses may be evoked by the therapist.

Countertransference is a controversial subject in contemporary times. It was originally defined as "a transference reaction of an analyst to a patient . . . when the analyst reacts to his patient as though the patient were a significant person in the analyst's early history" (Greenson, 1967, p. 348). Initially confined to the therapist's personal feelings, countertransference, like transference, has become more relational in scope. This concept is now considered to be both the result of the therapist's own unconscious processes and/or an appropriate reaction by the therapist to the patient—an important indicator of the patient's relational style. This reciprocal influence of the conscious and unconscious subjectivities of two people in the therapeutic relationship is called *intersubjectivity*. This concept expands the earlier definitions of transference and countertransference by suggesting that the therapist and the patient bring their own separate lives to the therapeutic encounter, but also understand and change each other during this process (Natterson & Friedman, 1995).

The Real Relationship and the Working Alliance

The real relationship is the "realistic and genuine relationship between analyst and patient in the here and now" (Greenson, 1967, p. 217). The concept of the real relationship is imbedded not only in psychoanalytic theories but in the cognitive, behavioral, cross-cultural, and postmodern models presented in this book. In many ways, the real relationship between the therapist and the patient is the precursor to the concept of the working alliance—the rapport that develops between the therapist and the patient that makes it possible to work purposefully in therapy. Bordin (1979, p. 252) concurred with Freud's view that the alliance between the therapist and the client is "one of the keys, if not the key, to the change process." He elaborated on the importance of the working alliance across theoretical models by pointing out that all models include working alliances. The effectiveness of therapy depends to a great extent on the strength of the working alliance. The strength of the alliance is determined by the "closeness of fit" (Bordin, 1979, p. 253) between the demands of the particular kind of alliance and the personal characteristics of client and therapist. The patient experiences insight, emotional growth, and increased problem-solving capabilities as a result of the therapist's understanding and contributions to this process. Saari (1986, p. 49) refers to this as the "therapeutic culture" created mutually by the client and therapist during their interactions with each other.

Resistance

Greenson (1967, p. 60) presents the original psychoanalytic definition of resistance as "a counterforce in the patient, operating against the progress of the analysis, the analyst, and the analytic procedures and processes." He quotes Freud (1912, p. 103), who states: "The resistance accompanies the treatment step by step. Every single association, every act of the person under treatment must reckon with the resistance and represents a compromise between the forces that are striving towards recovery and the opposing ones." The concept of resistance has also undergone revision in psychoanalytic thinking. Originally considered an obstacle to the therapeutic work, resistances came to be understood as the source of important information regarding the patient's ego functions. Wachtel (1982) equates resistance with the patient's conflicts about changing. Beginning therapists, in particular, often view resistance as something that has to be overcome. Wachtel suggests instead that we view resistance as the way in which the patient is trying to communicate to the therapist at a particular point in the therapy. Behaviors that are considered "resistant" by the therapist may serve as adaptive functions for the patient and may protect the patient from experiencing pain, anger, shame, or many other uncomfortable feelings. This is much more in line with postmodern theories that do not adhere to the concept of resistance and the cognitive and behavioral theories that view resistance as obstacles to the change process.

Using These Concepts in Practice

As you listen to the client's story, pay attention to the feelings that are stirred up in you. Often the best aid to forming a diagnosis comes from your own felt responses to the client and to the material that the client presents. A cautionary word is important here lest you confuse feelings that may be aroused in you by the client with acting on those feelings in an inappropriate manner. You have a responsibility to differentiate between countertransference feelings that may be aroused due to your own history and countertransference feelings that may be elicited by the client. No matter the source of the countertransference, you must always act in a professional manner and in the best interests of the client. Although this may seem obvious, when feelings in the therapist are stirred, it is easy to forget that this is a therapeutic relationship, not a personal one.

The Case of Dan—The Beginning

The Referral

Dan, a 16-year-old boy, was referred to me for treatment by the assistant principal at his school. She mandated that he attend therapy after he received twenty-one suspensions—all for being disrespectful to his teachers. He was described as a charismatic leader who was very angry. A board of education psychiatrist who saw the boy for an emergency consultation diagnosed him as having a "severe conduct disorder." The family agreed to treatment as an alternative to placement in a special school for children with disciplinary problems.

Reading and hearing this referral material would have placed me on guard had I not been experienced both the public school system and boys diagnosed with "conduct disorder" when I was a young worker in agency practice. Many of those children so diagnosed had turned out to be deprived of nurture and eager to seek approval from delinquent peer groups. And frequently the school system had been too quick to pin a label on a nonconforming child.

Dan Tells His Story

Dan came to the first interview accompanied by his father. Dan was dressed in the baggy shorts and loose T-shirt typical of teenage boys today. What was notable was the baseball cap pulled down over his forehead, the scowl on his face, and his clenched hands. This boy was obviously tense and angry. His father, who was sitting in the waiting room with him, reading, looked perfectly pleasant, with a nice smile on his face and an anxious but warm greeting. I showed Dan into the office and he took the far chair. I noted that he wanted to maintain distance by sitting far away from me. With my encouragement, he spoke readily but with anger about why he was here. According to him, he'd been in continual trouble in school because the teachers were all "idiots," and he backed this up with some credible examples. He spoke of how he had challenged their intellects as well as their authority. He had earned a reputation as a troublemaker, and no matter who was misbehaving in class, he felt that he was always singled out as the one to blame and given harsher and more frequent punishments than his peers. This had been a problem since elementary school. I also learned from him that he had lived with his mother after his parents divorced, between the ages of 6 and 13, that he "hated" his mother for physically and emotionally abusing him, that his father had tried for custody of him and his sister over the years but had not succeeded in court, and that, finally, his mother "disappeared" after some criminal activity and was last heard from two years ago on his birthday. He described her in profane terms and also said she was known to be "mentally ill." This was a lot of information to get from a teenager in an initial interview. Most of the teens referred to me were reluctant to talk. I commented to Dan that he was a good provider of information. He answered that he'd seen shrinks before, told his story before, and that it hadn't helped. I was interested in why and whether Dan had any hopes that this therapy might be helpful. He said that all the therapists did was listen but nothing ever changed in his life. He was just doing this so that he could get back into school.

My Response

During his retelling of why he had been mandated to come to see me, I remained empathic, supportive, and inquisitive. I let him know that I was glad he was here, whatever the reasons, by simply telling him so. I didn't yet know what was the reality, but I accepted his story as his experience of what had happened to him. I mentally noted that I, like Dan, had encountered many incompetent professionals in my life, and I was sure that teachers as well as therapists could be included in that list. I was interested to see if he had empathy for anyone, because I knew that if I couldn't find that quality, the prognosis would indeed be grim. He did say, when asked, that he had a lot of friends—a good sign—and that he cared about his dad. He seemed quite intelligent, and I was pleased to see that his cognitive abilities had not been impaired by the abuse he had suffered. I paid attention to my response to him. Although he was angry and challenging, I felt for him, thinking how hard it must be to be raised without a mother's love. His father, when learning that the referral had been made to a woman, commented, "I hope she is smart." I had filed that. Would he test me? Would his father? Would Dan be more comfortable seeing a man? The gender of the therapist can sometimes be of significance to certain clients, and he had been abused and traumatized by a woman. It was critical that I be as kind and caring as possible, so as to provide a different relational experience for this very wounded child.

I told Dan that I knew that he didn't want to come and see me. I agreed that there were incompetent mental health professionals as well as doctors, lawyers, teachers, politicians, and so forth, but that since therapy seemed inevitable, I would like to try to help him out of the trouble he was in so that he could be successful at school. In spite of his protests and responses about "not caring," I sensed that he cared very deeply about what people thought of him, that he had a wish to do well, and I told him so. I spoke to Dan about confidentiality, and that I would only reveal what he told me if I thought he was at risk of hurting himself or others. He had heard this before—from his previous therapists, and they were all idiots too. I acknowledged that it can be hard to hear things repeated since he had been in therapy before, but that I felt it was important for me to understand how Dan was feeling this time around. I asked if there were any times when he was feeling bad enough to want to hurt himself in any way. Dan responded: "No, not now, I just feel angry now . . . there were times in the past when I wished I could disappear, though." I said that it sounded like he may have been very discouraged at those times. "Did you ever think about ways that you might make yourself disappear?" Dan avoided eye contact with me at this point and said that there were times that he thought he might take some pills, but he didn't want to hurt his father. I replied by saying, "Thanks for telling me about that, Dan . . . . It isn't always easy to talk about these things." I spoke with Dan and his father for ten minutes together after Dan and I had finished talking. An adolescent boy in treatment needs to feel separate from his family as he deals with adolescent issues of autonomy and independence. However, I also thought it important to establish an alliance with Dan's father, although he seemed nervous and not really interested in being part of the therapy. I mentally noted how discouraged and hopeless parents feel when they have a child in constant difficulty. The man seemed more than willing to have me handle things and wanted to be left alone. Nonetheless, I felt it was important for Dan to hear his father's reasons for bringing him to see me and equally im-

(continued)

The Case of Dan—The Beginning   **Continued**

だと考える

portant for Dan's father to hear Dan's view of the situation. Seeing father and son together would also establish a framework for future joint sessions, if deemed appropriate. Weingarten (1997, p. 311) discusses the importance of seeing adolescents with
their parents: "A parent and adolescent can benefit from hearing each other's stories,
and that each may be a resource for change for the other."

My Conceptualization

Because I had made a conscious decision to be as nurturing as I could to this boy, I
began in a very concrete way, providing, in subsequent sessions, donuts and a drink.
He ate and drank easily, and I noted that he was appreciative and polite. He had good
manners—a sign that he could be respectful. Because I am an eclectic practitioner, I
found myself conceptualizing my assessment in psychodynamic, object relational
terms, thinking about some cognitive and behavioral interventions as well, all of
which are elaborated on in other sections of this book. The cognitive/behavioral approaches were important because we had to make quick progress—the school needed
results and Dan needed to feel a sense of mastery. I had a tentative working hypothesis: As Dan's story unfolded, I saw a boy who was now so vulnerable to criticism after
his long history of abuse that he misperceived any adult slight as a dismissal and in-
validation of his very being. When wounded, he felt wounded to the core, and was
very quick to retaliate the only way he knew how—by using his intelligence to plan
and strategize a way to get back, usually by humiliating the perceived perpetrator. I
would need to be very careful not to hurt him by invalidating his experience in any
way. I'd also have to help him to learn better coping strategies, because eventually I
or someone else would give an invalidating response, and Dan would have to learn to
better manage his anger so as to have a more trouble-free existence in the real world.

Follow-Up to the Initial Interview

After my initial interview, I sent for an earlier school psychological report. This would
provide important information and should always be part of your record when working with a child who has had previous evaluations. If there were no prior school reports, I might have talked with him and his father about having an evaluation done
by the school-based support team or an outside evaluator. This would help us to rule
out any learning or attentional issues as well as give a basic understanding of his intellectual capabilities. I was pleased to see that the impressions by the evaluator had
matched my own. The psychological report spoke of a boy with "superior intelligence,
who was intense, easily upset, moody and highly defensive. He appears to misinter-
pret the intentions of others and sees them as being hostile and threatening. He then
responds with anger and hostility that he feels is reasonable and justified. He has particular difficulty with direction/criticism/correction when given by a female teacher."
During these first visits I was also in contact with the assistant principal at Dan's
school. She had made the referral and seemed to view him negatively. It was important to make an ally of this woman, and so, with Dan's (and his father's) permission,
I shared some of my initial impressions. This school-based intervention was an important one in which I tried to clarify the relationship between Dan's emotional state
and his behavior in the classroom. She softened when she learned of the abuse and

began to want to work with him. She became a great resource for Dan and, ultimately, his advocate at the school.

Now I had an initial picture of Dan from listening to his story and reading his evaluations. Equally important was my own response. I sensed the vulnerable child under his aggressive demeanor, and I wanted to reach him and for him to trust me to do so. I shared the information in the psychological report with him. This was strategic—Dan wanted to know if he was "mentally ill" like his mother, and the report reassured him that he wasn't. I considered it important for Dan to know what the evaluator saw as his issues and not to paint a rosy picture. I shared her diagnostic formulation and told him that I saw it that way, too. I told him that I had some goals for him, and that one was to help him to learn what his triggers were, so he could manage his anger. I told him I would give him strategies for this—since he had a good strategic mind. I was going to appeal to his logic, which was his strength, by using a direct, truthful, and reality-oriented approach. This wasn't a child to talk with about feelings—not yet, at least. I'd appeal to his strong mind and motivation to do well (yes, he did want to go to college, if only to be able to choose his own teachers and subjects so he could avoid the "idiots" he was so accustomed to).

Intervention Planning

The most important piece of history that informed my assessment and treatment planning was the knowledge that Dan had been mistreated. This fact influenced my choice of an object relations framework of conceptualization to understand Dan, particularly as it related to childhood abuse. Mistreated children often have an unconscious need to replicate the original trauma. They are hyperalert to signals of possible abuse, misperceive, and think it is there when it may not be there, and can provoke it out of an unconscious desire for mastery (James, 1994). This framework helped me shape my working hypothesis—that Dan was trying to master the abuse he had experienced at his mother's hand by provoking those in authority who appeared dismissive or critical of him in the hopes that he would hurt them and so be empowered and triumph.

The Middle Stage of Treatment

Once the initial impressions have been formulated and the treatment plan selected, the worker has the task of moving the therapeutic process ahead to meet certain goals and objectives. The middle stage of treatment is where that process takes place. It is often referred to as the working-through stage. Before the advent of brief treatment modalities—and more recently, managed care—the worker had seemingly endless time to engage in this phase of the therapeutic process. Clients spent years in therapy gaining insight and greater understanding, and some made major personality changes. But whether treatment is long-term or short-term, in the middle phase of treatment there are some predictable occurrences that must be addressed.

There are many reasons why therapy can get "stuck" in the middle phase. It is important to remember that it is normal for clients to be fearful of the unknown. Change often threatens the stability of the client's situation, even when that stability is unpleasant. Couples may fight and appear to be unhappy in their marriages, but if change implies that the partnership will end, they may find ways to stay where they are. Resistance, or obstacles to progress as referred to in cognitive/behavioral models, takes many forms. Sometimes a missed session might indicate that the client is struggling with the therapeutic work. Arriving late or arriving early to a session might signal anxiety. Talking about the trivial, rather than the important events in a client's life can indicate some fears about making changes. It is important that the worker appreciate that there are very real factors that can also present obstacles in the treatment relationship. Many of our clients lead chaotic or disorganized lives. A single mother may have to take a child to a clinic appointment and wait in line for many hours, missing her therapy hour. Clients are often called unexpectedly to their children's schools or to job interviews. Be mindful of the stresses in your client's life before labeling some behaviors as fears or anxiety about change.

When there appears to be an obstacle to progress in the middle stage of treatment, such as a missed session, a worker can address this by simply saying, "I missed seeing you last week. Did anything happen?" If the client answers vaguely, or indicates that she didn't feel like coming, gently ask if anything happened in the previous session that upset her. What has she been thinking about the therapy? What has she been thinking about your working together? That last question will bring you to issues of transference, which are important to air in the middle stage of treatment. Examine for yourself if you have said or done anything that might have offended or hurt your client. Were you too quick to make an interpretation, too confronting, too unempathic? If you cannot come up with the answer yourself, ask the client, or your supervisor. Workers aren't perfect: They make mistakes. But transference reactions occur in spite of what we do. Perhaps you begin to remind your client of a significant person who was critical or judgmental. You can get at this material by asking, "Did I say or do something to remind you of someone in your past—someone in your family or a friend? What was that person like?" It is very important to distinguish transference reactions from reality. Exploring the transference will often help the client to make significant progress in present relationships. This is most obvious in couples therapy, when both partners begin to recognize that their strong reactions to spousal behaviors are often based on past anger or annoyances with parents. Exploring the reality—the real relationship—will help the worker to adjust to client needs. A client may be justifiably angry at a worker for numerous reasons. Perhaps she was inattentive, unempathic, preoccupied. Something as seemingly slight as answering the phone during a client's session may feel like a drop in empathy and produce a strong reaction. You may not hear the reaction right away, but subsequent sessions will provide clues. The skilled worker pays sharp attention during the middle phase to the client's verbal and nonverbal behaviors. It is completely appropriate to mention, for example, that the client seems less talkative, more edgy, or that something seems different. This is not to be confused with confrontation. Direct confrontation can be offensive and angering to a client, with the exception of those who have or are participating in recovery programs where confrontation is the norm. It is much better to gently comment that it seems hard for the client to talk about something, or to respond to your words, than to rush headlong with an interpretation such as "You are angry that I'm talking about your past." Interpretations often feel like wounds, especially if they are made too early in the work. And they can often be incorrect. It is more appropriate to explore and let the client come up with the meaning for herself. It is important to remember that what is crucial during this stage of therapy is that the client experience safety within the therapeutic relationship so as to be able to overcome the anxiety associated with change and take the necessary steps toward mastery (Wachtel, 1993).

Middle Phase Treatment Issues

My initial sense was that Dan needed a new relational experience—insight into how his past was impacting on his current life and tools in order to facilitate change. He complained of insomnia. Relaxation training seemed a good method to help him relieve stress. In our fifth session, I taught him a relaxation technique and put this on a tape that he played before bed. Also included on the tape were suggestions as to how he could manage stress. Dan played the tape religiously—it put him to sleep at night. I shared with him my knowledge of what his trigger was, his vulnerability, his Achilles heal. I did this within the context of my ever-present and conscious decision to make sure that Dan felt safe, respected, and nurtured in our relationship. I knew that once trust was established, I could repeatedly, and gently, remind Dan that he overreacts when he feels criticized, humiliated, or dismissed by someone in authority. I conveyed empathy and understanding by letting him know that these feelings originated very early, with his mother, and that was why his reaction was so powerful. In the beginning middle phase of treatment, I made these interpretations rather than use exploration to help him gain this understanding for himself because his extreme behaviors were getting him in trouble in his school. I also allowed him to ventilate, a technique that enables the expression of feelings and reactions, and he did this quite frequently. Mostly, Dan ventilated his anger. I used a behavioral intervention: I taught Dan some self-statements that he could use when he felt criticized or dismissed. Instead of telling himself things that fueled his anger as he had been doing (i.e., this idiot is out to humiliate me), I had him use statements such as "This isn't personal, the teacher doesn't know me, he's not trying to hurt me, I'm reacting because of my past, I need to stay focused on my goals, I want to succeed, if I get through this I can go to college and be on my own, I need to keep myself cool, reacting with anger only gets me in trouble." Dan memorized these, and added a few of his own that were positive in nature.

Another technique that I employed was advocacy. I intervened in the environment, a concept basic to social work practice that is often critical in working with adolescents whose behavioral problems can be misunderstood by people in authority who react punitively, unwittingly replicating past traumatic experiences. I wanted to minimize the opportunity for Dan to become stressed in school. Talks with the assis-

(continued)

Middle Phase Treatment Issues   **Continued**

tant principal about Dan's needs resulted in her hand-picking Dan's teachers for his fall semester. She selected teachers with experience who had good classroom management skills and nurturing styles. I told Dan that this wouldn't happen throughout his lifetime, and he had the responsibility, ultimately, of managing his emotions, but that, for now, he needed a chance to be successful and have a positive school experience. His job was to stay cool, get good grades, and prove that he was not a troublemaker. Dan was now looking to me as a source of support. Interestingly enough, he had started to decline the snacks that I brought for him. Psychologically, he didn't need my concrete demonstrations of feeding any more. He was being fed in other ways.

In continuing middle phase sessions, I reinforced his impulse control by appealing to his intellectual strengths. Recognizing and acknowledging his strengths helped shore up his adaptive capacities. Using the positive relationship, I began to bring up his mother more frequently in our conversations. Dan began to talk about his memories of his mother's abuse, and I shared with him my assessment of the origin of some of his difficulties with anger—how his traumatic past has impacted on his relationships with authority in the present. I initiated this conversation by saying, "You know, Dan, I think some of the anger you have now may have started when you were a younger boy and you felt confused and upset over how your mother was treating you . . . . What do you think?" About five months into the treatment Dan's mother called after a three-year hiatus. His initial reaction was rage—he wanted to meet her in person and ventilate his stored up anger—to abuse her as she had abused him. We discussed what he would need from her in order to let her back into his life. He was clear. He wanted an apology and some understanding as to why she had behaved so cruelly to him. And he wanted evidence that he could trust her—that she would be available to him on a consistent basis. I supported him in this, noting how logical and correct he was. Dan and his mother began to correspond by email, and she kept up her part of the bargain by writing every day.

Simultaneously, Dan began to reduce his sessions to bimonthly. My analytic mind conjured up thoughts of resistance. I speculated that Dan was getting closer to his mother and hence more fearful—something he did not want to think or talk about. Knowing his impulsivity, I felt worried. I stayed in contact with his school and learned that he was becoming more explosive again, picking fights with students and teachers. Clearly, he was under stress. In exploring the reduced sessions with Dan, I learned that his father was feeling the burden financially and that their insurance company was limiting his benefits. This was a reality that could not be ignored. Neither could the fact that Dan needed the help, and needed it on a consistent basis could also not be ignored. (Biweekly sessions are useful for problem-solving therapies, but we were now doing more in-depth work, and losing continuity). I decided that I would also use email to communicate with Dan between sessions and would be available to him via computer from my home to his. I also provided concrete help by asking his insurance company to consider reinstating his benefits. I spoke with Dan's mother by phone, because he was hopeful that, with my assistance, she would shed some light on the past abuse experience. It was my intention to help her to convince Dan that he was not to blame.

Dan and I did not talk about transference issues in the middle stage of treatment. I was working with the positive relationship—quite deliberately—and wanted to keep it so. Negative transferential reactions (i.e., Dan's anger at me) might have caused a rift in our relationship and that would not have been helpful. Dan needed to see me as his ally and supporter—and I could only provide that within a framework of trust and security.

The Ending Phase of Treatment

In long-term treatment, termination is not necessarily agreed upon beforehand but is an outgrowth of the therapeutic process that has reached an end. In today's managed care environment, endings may be influenced by insurance carriers who allow a limited number of sessions to reduce symptomatology and achieve clearly delineated objectives.

In these instances, workers generally contract for a definitive number of sessions and collaborate on identifying achievable goals. Often, sessions end before all goals are met. In those cases, the worker might try to make a community referral for continued care or help the client to take credit for the progress that has been made and extend advice as to how he or she might continue to work on his or her own. Sometimes the client's goals have not been met because of limited internal and/or external resources, and treatment has not been successful. If the client has not been able to change the exterior of her life because of inadequate resources, it is important to empathize with the client's sadness and to validate her reality. If progress has not been made because of some inner problems, the worker needs to gently point out that perhaps the client wasn't ready to take on the necessary changes, and to share your opinion of what internal roadblocks have made change difficult.

Termination can be planned or unplanned. Some clients leave unexpectedly, before the completion of the work. Often this can be due to the disorganization and chaos of the client's lives. Other times, it may be because of a dissatisfaction in the treatment that did not get addressed. If an unplanned termination occurs, it is helpful to reach out to the client and let her know that the door is always open. If the client cannot be reached by phone, the worker should write a note to that effect and also express well wishes. Clients need to feel that they will not be punished for premature endings, and that their actions will be understood within the context of their lives. Even the best planned termination can be fraught with difficulties. The loss of the worker is a loss, and often brings with it feelings of abandonment for clients, particularly if they have suffered other significant losses in their lives. Clients may react with anger, sadness, or with little reaction at all. As a worker, it is important to be able to listen, explore, and to empathize, but not to personalize. At times it will appear that there is a resurgence of problems when one is trying to end treatment. Or a new crisis may occur. This may present an opportunity for the client to continue the work through referral to someone else—but this is not a reason to hang on.

Workers need to let go when there are clear parameters to the treatment. If a referral needs to be made, it is important for the client to meet the new worker before you leave. When possible, try to facilitate the introduction. If the client comes back to you and reports that she doesn't like the new worker, that she's not as nice as you, be sympathetic but help the client to see that there might be a period of adjustment. You need to appear confident in the new worker's abilities in order to help the client with the transition. In the ending phase, clients might ask for your home phone number or if they can continue to contact you. This is against ethical practice, and it makes it harder for the client to let go. The best way to be of help is to review with the client the progress that has been made, crediting her with her capacity to be effective, and to remain hopeful about the future. Point out next steps—be they continued psychosocial intervention or concrete service needs. Final goodbyes can be ritualized by sharing a review of progress with the adult client, making a memory book with a child, or giving small gifts that are appropriate to the work accomplished (a small book of poems, for example). And while we are cautioned not to accept gifts from clients, it is important to be culturally sensitive. I frequently found that Latina mothers liked to express their appreciation of the help I extended to their children with a departing gift. Often this was a *pastilla* (a sweet). My cross-cultural students like to bring foods from their countries to our final practice classes. These are opportunities to give back and should be accepted in the spirit in which they are presented.

Ending with Dan

Dan and I did not have an ideal ending. His father pulled him out of treatment prematurely, claiming that the insurance benefits had run out. This became one more abrupt termination for Dan in his lifetime. The court took him away from his mother after he made numerous complaints of child abuse. While he was ostensibly happy to be removed from that traumatic situation, we know there can be ambivalence toward perpetrators in the traumatized child. And although Dan claims to have been angry at his mother all these years, he readily accepted her efforts to come back into his life. I was concerned that Dan would experience the termination as an abandonment, no matter how carefully planned. I also knew that Dan may have had to leave therapy in anger. Or there would be denial of my importance, so as to keep his powerful feelings of loss at bay. We were left with only one session to terminate. During that brief time, I pointed out the positive steps he had taken, the management of his anger, and his ability to use his intellect to see his situation clearly, when not clouded by issues of loss, abandonment, and humiliation. I pointed out that he might need to feel angry at me, because letting go in anger was easier than ending when you are really feeling good about someone. Dan said little. He kept reiterating that he didn't care, he only came to therapy because he was forced by the school. I used the transference and interpreted that it would be difficult for him to recognize me as an important person and to leave at the same time. Using the real relationship, I again stated that I was his ally, did care about him, and that I would be there for him if he needed me. I felt sad losing Dan and I worried about him. But sometimes the most one can do is to leave the door open and hope that the strength of the relationship will carry the client back to you in the future.

Summary

As our case material has illustrated, clients do not always move smoothly through the stages of treatment. Each phase presents a significant challenge.

Beginnings are critical, because they provide a model for what will follow. Even the most inexperienced of workers can compensate for a lack of knowledge and engage the client by being supportive and nurturing in the initial interviews. Middle stage issues present a different type of challenge, because it is during that time that the treatment may appear to be stagnated, without goals or focus. The worker and client may seem to be covering the same ground again and again, and the same difficulties may be occurring. You may feel that it is impossible for the client to change or that the environment does not support progress and growth. Often, clients are so overburdened by the harsh realities of their lives—poverty, illness, loss—that counseling appears to be last on their list of needs. Clients often terminate prematurely in the middle stage because they, as well as the worker, have become bored or frustrated. For a successful middle phase resolution, the worker must remain patient and confident. Your emotional availability and support may be very sustaining to your client, especially when setbacks occur. Eventually, perhaps when least expected, progress will occur, some goals will be achieved, and others will be abandoned in the light of new and changing realities.

Termination can be unpredictable. It can happen in a moment, as in the case of Dan. More often than not, terminations are difficult for students, who can experience the loss as sharply as does the client and can have difficulty letting go. Students frequently worry about what will happen to their clients once they have left the agency, knowing that they have had the luxury of investing a great deal of time and energy and that another worker may not. Even when one follows all the rules that apply to planned terminations, leaving ample time to talk about feelings of loss and uncertainty, the process may not run smoothly. Clients may want to avoid the pain and withdraw from treatment before feelings have been explored. The important thing is for the worker to credit the client for her effort and capacity to promote change and to acknowledge her ability to continue on without you.

On a final note, we want our students to understand that clinical competence requires continued learning, self-examination, and a willingness to take risks. One becomes a skilled practitioner with increased experience. By remaining open to learning from your clients, your mentors, and your mistakes, you will achieve this in time.

Learning Assignments _____

1. Working in pairs, take turns role-playing a first meeting with a client. Be sure to include a discussion of confidentiality. Evaluate your interviewing style and skills. Raise two or more questions about the interview for class discussion.

2. Write a process record of a first interview or any subsequent interview with a client. Consider the way in which the client presented herself to you. Consider the way in which you presented yourself to the client. What were your reactions to the client? What did you like about your interviewing style? What would you consider changing?

3. You have just met and introduced yourself to a new client as a student studying social work. The client pauses and then says the following: "I don't really want to work with a student—why did the agency assign me to a student? . . . I didn't ask to work with a student." How does this make you feel? Write down your response to the client.

References _____

Bordin, E. S. (1979). The generalizability of the psychoanalytic concept of the working alliance. *Psychotherapy, Theory, Research and Practice, 16*(3), 252–260.

DeLaCour, E. P. (1998). How has the therapeutic relationship changed in psychoanalytic psychotherapy? *Smith College Studies in Social Work, 68*(2), 171–183.

Freud, S. (1912). A note on the unconscious in psychoanalysis. In J. Strachey, Jr. (Ed.), (1953–1974), *The standard edition of the complete psychological works of Sigmund Freud* (Vols. 1–24, pp. 255–266). London: Hogarth Press.

Greenberg, J. R., & Mitchell, S. A. (1983). *Object relations in psychoanalytic theory.* Cambridge, MA: Harvard University Press.

Greenson, R. R. (1967). *The technique and practice of psychoanalysis.* Madison, CT: International Universities Press.

Monk, G., Winslade, J., Crocket, K., & Epston, D. (1997). *Narrative therapy in practice.* San Francisco, CA: Jossey-Bass.

Morrison, J. (1995). *The first interview.* New York: Guilford.

Natterson, J. M., & Friedman, R. J. (1995). *A primer of clinical intersubjectivity.* Northvale, NJ: Jason Aronson.

Saari, C. (1986). *Clinical social work treatment: How does it work?* New York: Gardner Press.

Safran, J., & Segal, Z. (1996). *Interpersonal process in cognitive therapy.* Northvale, NJ: Jason Aronson.

Wachtel, E. (1994). *Treating troubled children and their families.* New York: Guilford.

Wachtel, P. (1993). *Therapeutic communication.* New York: Guilford.

Weingarten, K. (1997). From "cold care" to "warm care": Challenging the discourses of mothers and adolescents. In C. Smith & D. Nylund (Eds.), *Narrative therapies with children and adolescents* (pp. 307–338). New York: Guilford.

4

The Psychosocial Study

The Product of Assessment

In this chapter we will discuss the psychosocial study. This assessment method consists of the following: (1) the data that has been gathered from the client and other relevant people and sources; (2) an assessment of the client's mental status and current level of functioning—including ego and environmental strengths; (3) the establishment of diagnostic criteria *(DSM-IV)*; (4) a theoretical framework that helps us to understand the collected data; (5) treatment goals; and (6) a method to evaluate the effectiveness of practice. Each of these components will be further explained in the following model. A sample psychosocial study of a child in a residential treatment center will illustrate this assessment method.

Preparing the Psychosocial Study

A Psychosocial Model Outline

Identifying Information. The leading paragraph in this section provides a general statement about who the client is. It may include information about the client's age, gender, race, ethnicity, religion, marital status, employment, resources (family, friends, finances, household members), and immigration status. Describe the client's appearance, noting dress and grooming, the quality of speech (hesitant, spontaneous, disconnected, pressured), and intelligence (average, below average, above average). The client's attitude toward the interviewer is also important—does she appear anxious, relaxed, angry, unfocused, or comfortable?

Referral Source. Who is the referring source? What does the referring source say about the client's problem? Is the client seeking treatment voluntarily or involuntarily? Does the client understand the reason for the referral?

Presenting Problem.   This critical paragraph requires a statement of the present problems that have led to the referral. It is the reason that the client has come to see you. You may want to include a statement incorporating the client's exact words in presenting her problem. This may be especially significant when the client's presenting problem differs from the referral source's interpretation of the client's presenting problem.

History of the Problem.   This section should tell the reader how the problem developed. Did the situation have a rapid onset, or is it chronic in nature? Describe the precipitating events, the course of the symptoms, and any previous attempts to solve the problem. If the client has had previous treatment for the problem, what was the length and frequency of that treatment, and what was its outcome? What was the client's response to the treatment? How did she feel about the therapeutic relationship? What are the circumstances under which the problem is currently manifested (home, school, employment)?

Previous Counseling Experience.   Discuss any previous counseling attempts and their outcomes. It is helpful for the interviewer to have a complete record of the client's experiences with counselors as well as the client's perception of whether the counseling was helpful.

Family Background.   Both the facts about the socioeconomic, educational, and occupational background of the family and some conceptualization of how the family members interacted should be included here. How does the client view her family, and how is she viewed by them? The genogram (McGoldrick & Gerson, 1985; McGoldrick, Gerson, & Schellenberger, 1999), a diagram of all members of the nuclear and extended family, can be a useful assessment tool in gathering this data. Genograms can be used in a variety of ways—for example, to illustrate a family structure, record relevant family information, or delineate significant family relationships. Another useful assessment tool is the ecomap (Hartman, 1978), which offers a visual representation of the family's connections with their environment. A model for a genogram and ecomap is presented in Chapter 11, pages 170 and 172.

Personal History.   This section may include a developmental history (with a child client) and information about prenatal care, birth, achievement of milestones (such as feeding, toileting, language, and motor development), and whether these milestones were achieved within normal time limits. Were there any complications? If assessing a child, include information about school and peer functioning, levels of achievement, and learning differences (for a thorough developmental history outline in assessing a child, see Webb, 1996, p. 76). The client's previous attempts to cope with problems should also be discussed. A vocational history including adaptation to jobs, bosses, and co-workers; recreational activities; and special interests should be noted. Is there current and/or past use of substances such as alcohol and drugs, including prescription medication? It is also important to have the client's sexual history (where appropriate), as well as information about any past physical, sexual, or emotional trauma.

Medical History.   A medical history helps to rule out the possibility of medical problems and/or organic factors that may be contributing to psychosocial difficulties and also focuses the client's attention on medical needs that may have been overlooked. It is essential that the client has had a recent medical examination.

Cultural History.   It is important to understand the presenting problem within the context of a relevant cultural framework. This would include issues of bicultural identity, generational differences in cultural identification, and degree of acculturation to U.S. society. The culturagram (Congress, 1994) is a useful tool that addresses the family's reasons for immigration; their length of time in the community; their immigration status (legal or undocumented); the ages of family members at the time of immigration; language(s) spoken; contact with cultural institutions; health beliefs; holidays and special events; family, education, and work values; and traumatic stressors and crisis events. A model culturagram appears in Chapter 5, page 68.

Spirituality/Religion.   Included in this section should be some discussion about the client's current or past religious affiliations or spiritual beliefs. It is important to differentiate between religion and spirituality. Spirituality is a personal sense of meaning or belief about one's life and the world. Religion is the way in which those beliefs are formalized, generally within a community context such as participation in a religious organization (Joseph, 1998). How do these factors help us to understand the client's perception of the events in her life, and how will this affect the counseling process?

Mental Status and Current Functioning.   The concept of ego functioning is critical to social work assessment. (For an excellent social work text on this theory, see Goldstein, 1995). Ego psychology is ideally suited to social work practice because of its emphasis on the environment, life roles, and developmental tasks, as well as on a person's inner capacities (Schamess, 1996). In the section on mental status and current functioning, the worker should include a discussion of the characteristic ego functions, mechanisms of defense, and any particular strengths or limitations—social, psychological, physical, or environmental. Also evaluate the client's motivation, ability to be consistent, degree of self-awareness, capacity for insight into her situation, and ability to follow through with treatment recommendations. The functions of the ego and their major components (according to Bellack and colleagues, 1973), are briefly listed in Table 4.1, on pages 48–49. See Table 4.2, on page 49, for a list of defense mechanisms.

TABLE 4.1 *Ego Functions*

Ego Function	Components
1. Reality testing	Distinction between inner and outer stimuli. Accuracy of perception of external events and inner reality testing.
2. Judgment	Anticipation of consequences of behavior. Extent to which a manifest behavior reflects an awareness of its probable consequences. Appropriateness of behavior.
3. Sense of reality	Extent of derealization, or depersonalization. Self-identity and self-esteem. Clarity of boundaries between self and the world.
4. Regulation and control of drives, affects, and impulses	Directness of impulse expression. Effectiveness of delay and control and the degree of frustration tolerance.
5. Object relations	Degree and kind of relatedness to others. The extent to which present relationships are adaptively or maladaptively influenced by or patterned upon older ones, and whether they serve present mature aims or past immature ones.
6. Thought processes	Memory, concentration, and attention. Ability to conceptualize. Extent to which thinking is unrealistic or illogical.
7. ARISE	Adaptive regression in the service of the ego. Relaxation of perceptual and conceptual acuity (and other ego controls).
8. Defensive functioning*	Extent to which defenses adaptively affect ideation and behavior. Success and failure of defenses.
9. Stimulus barrier	Threshold for stimuli. Effectiveness of management of excessive stimulus input.
10. Autonomous functioning**	Degree of freedom from impairment of primary autonomy apparatuses (e.g., sight, hearing, intention, language, memory, learning, motor function, intelligence). Degree of freedom from impairment of secondary autonomy (e.g., habits, complex learned skills, work routines, hobbies, interests).
11. Synthetic-Integrative functioning	Degree of reconciliation or integration of incongruities. Degree of active relating together of psychic and behavioral events, whether contradictory or not.
12. Mastery-competence***	How competent or effective one feels in mastering the environment.

*Defenses operate unconsciously to protect a person from anxiety by keeping intolerable or unacceptable impulses or threats from his or her conscious awareness. Defenses have both positive and negative aspects and are a necessary part of personality development. They become problematic when they are overused and thus distort reality, restrict ego functions, or interfere with further development. Included in Table 4.2 (p. 49) is a list of the major defenses of the ego and their definitions. (For a comprehensive discussion of defense and excellent examples, see Goldstein, 1995.)

**The functions that have primary autonomy include intellectual ability, perception, motor activity, and inborn capacities that facilitate the acquisition of language and make it possible to plan and initiate goal-directed behavior. Under ordinary circumstances the autonomous functions are not

TABLE 4.1 *Continued*

affected by conflict. The ego is capable of maintaining and further developing these functions during the various phases of development, provided that the social environment is "average and acceptable" (Hartman, 1939). The "fit" between an infant's inborn temperament and the caregiver's ability to understand and address the infant's unique ways of conveying need states is crucial in determining the infant's subsequent developmental course. When the child's genetic endowment is compromised, or when the social environment is less than average and acceptable, autonomous ego functions can be disrupted and the child experiences significant emotional distress and suffers from serious functional impairments (Schamess, 1996).

*** Mastery/Competence has to do with adaptation, the behavior that allows individuals to cope advantageously with the environments in which they live. Adaptation is desirable when it creates a more harmonious relationship between the individual and the external world. It is critical that psychosocial assessment includes information about the client's adaptive capacities and coping skills, as this tells us what strengths the client can summon to facilitate problem solving. An appreciation of the client's strengths and latent capacities makes it possible to approach treatment in an optimistic and respectful way—without losing sight of the underlying problems in ego functioning and adaptation. The concept of adaptation makes it unmistakably clear that individuals do not exist separately from their social and biological contexts. As a species, humans are not only capable of changing our own behaviors to suit a range of different environments, but are also capable of changing the environments in which we live, to better suit our wishes and needs.

Source: Information in this table adapted with permission from Bellak, L., et al. (1973). *Ego functions in schizophrenics, neurotics and normals.* New York: John Wiley & Sons.

TABLE 4.2 *Mechanisms of Defense*

Defense	Description
A. Introjection	Also known as incorporation, it literally means a taking in whole (with a secondary consequence of destroying the object).
B. Identification	This is a general process in which one takes over elements of another.
C. Denial	This involves a negation or lack of acceptance of important aspects of reality or of one's own experience that may actually be perceived.
D. Repression	More complicated than denial, it is when one makes unconscious and unwanted a memory, feeling, or fantasy.
E. Projection	This is a mechanism whereby consciously disowned aspects of the self are rejected, put outward, and attributed to others.
F. Displacement	This is a mechanism by which feelings or conflicts about one person or situation are shifted onto another.
G. Reaction Formation	This is similar to repression—it involves keeping certain impulses from awareness. The mechanism involves replacing the impulse in consciousness with its opposite.
H. Rationalization	This involves the use of convincing reasons to justify certain feelings or actions as to avoid recognizing their underlying unacceptable motive.
I. Intellectualization	This involves warding off unacceptable impulses and affects by thinking about them in a cerebral way, rather than feeling them directly.

The Mental Status Exam. The mental status exam is a way of organizing and recording information about the mental state of the client, according to guidelines established by medical schools in the United States (Taylor, 1981). A mental status exam helps the social worker to assess the quality and range of perception, thought, feelings, and psychomotor activity of a client so as to better understand how the client's behavior may be symptomatic of a mental disorder. It leads to establishing a diagnosis according to the criteria set forth in the *Diagnostic and Statistical Manual* (American Psychiatric Association, 1994), a classification system that divides mental disorders into categories with defining features (Jordan & Franklin, 1995). The following are the broad categories that are considered in the mental status exam:

1. **Appearance.** Is the client well groomed or disheveled? Is his manner of dress appropriate for the occasion of the interview? Is he flamboyant or bizarre?

2. **Attitude.** Is the client cooperative? Guarded? Suspicious? Aggressive or belligerent?

3. **Motor Activity.** Is the client calm or agitated? Does he have tremors, tics, or muscle spasms? Is he hyperactive?

4. **Affect.** This refers to the client's tone. Is it appropriate to the conversation? Is she, for example, talking about a sad event and smiling? Is her affect flat or blunted, apathetic, or labile—rapidly switching up and down. Is she expansive or constricted?

5. **Mood.** How does the client seem? Is the client depressed or anxious? Is there variability in her mood?

6. **Speech.** This refers to the client's tone of voice. Is it loud or soft, whiny or high pitched? Are there any unusual characteristics or affectations (such as an accent or a halting manner)? Is the speech rapid or pressured? Does he stutter?

7. **Thought Processes.** Do the client's thoughts flow logically? Are the thoughts organized or disorganized? Is the client coherent? Are there perseverations (repetitions of thoughts as if the client were stuck)? Does the client experience thought blocking (thought stopping or interfering thoughts), or loose associations (not following logically from one thought to another)?

8. **Thought Content.** Are hallucinations or delusions present? Does the client speak of being controlled by external sources? Is the content of her thoughts grandiose or bizarre? Is suicidal ideation present? Is the content circumstantial (the client demonstrates the loss of capacity for goal-directed thinking), or tangential (the client loses the main idea of the conversation and is unable to return to it)?

9. **Perception.** Is the client's view of reality correct, or are their distortions in her thinking? Is there evidence of depersonalization or derealization?

10. **Orientation.** Is the client oriented to time, place, and person? How is his memory for present as well as past events? (Does he forget what he ate for breakfast but recall childhood events?) How are his concentration level and

attention span? Is anxiety, a mood disturbance, or a learning disability responsible for the difficulty in focusing?

11. **Cognitive Function.** What is the client's general fund of knowledge? Is it intact? (This function can be tested by asking the client to count backwards serially by sevens.)

12. **Abstraction.** Is the client an abstract or concrete thinker? (To help you assess this function, ask her to interpret a proverb.)

13. **Judgment.** Are there any disturbances in judgment? Does the client understand the consequences of his behaviors, and to what degree?

14. **Insight.** Does the client have insight into her difficulties, or are there impairments (minimal, moderate, or severe) that lead her to deny them? Is the insight intellectual or does she have an awareness of motives and feelings on an emotional level?

Establishing the Diagnosis according to DSM-IV.   Now that the clinician has a clear picture of the client from his mental status evaluation, he is ready to establish a multiaxial diagnosis using the categories and codes described in the *Diagnostic and Statistical Manual of Mental Disorders* (American Psychiatric Association, 1994). Formerly, *DSM-IV* was in the province reserved for psychia-trists. Now, most agency social workers and other mental health professionals need to use the criteria set forth in the *DSM-IV* to diagnose their clients' symptoms. The *DSM-IV* is based on a medical model and is symptom driven. Some social workers object to its use because they feel it is not congruent with the strengths perspective of social work. However, there are times when it is necessary to have a clear picture of a client's symptoms. This information may help us to know whether a client is suffering from a mood disorder and whether depression or anxiety is interfering with a client's functioning. We may then elect to refer the client to a psychiatrist for a medication evaluation or recommendation for hospitalization. This data guides our choice of theory, which, in turn, guides our treatment plan. For example, depressed clients may benefit more from a cognitive approach than from a psychodynamic model. An anxious client might need stress-management techniques framed within the context of behavior theory. Information about a client's mental state can also inform us if psychotic processes are involved, if suicidal thoughts prevail, or if our client is a danger to others. And, as more of our work comes under the umbrella of managed care, we are required to diagnose from a medical model and to then alleviate symptoms in order for agencies to receive financial reimbursement. However, the major purpose of the *DSM-IV* is not for insurance reimbursement. It is to enable the practitioner to "come closer to fostering a connection between an accurate diagnosis and an effective treatment" (Abramovitz & Williams, 1992, p. 340).

The Multiaxial Diagnosis.
Axis I.   Here the clinician will place the principal diagnosis—the clinical disorder or other condition that may be the focus of attention—and its corresponding code.

There can be more than one diagnosis noted on Axis I as well as a principal diagnosis and a second diagnosis that may eventually be ruled out (R/O).

Axis II.   Personality disorders and mental retardation, and the corresponding codes are found on Axis II.

Axis III.   Axis III tells us about any physical disorders or general medical conditions that are present in addition to a mental disorder.

Axis IV.   Here we list psychosocial and environmental problems that contribute to the exasperation of the current disorder. The stressors can be positive (job promotion) or negative (job loss).

Axis V.   On this final axis one places a score according to a *global assessment of functioning scale* (GAF), which ranges from 0 to 100. This scale is a composite of social, occupational, and psychological functioning. The higher levels of functioning prior to illness have a better prognosis. Enter the number indicating the client's highest level of functioning for at least a few months during the past year. Also indicate the severity of the disorder—mild, moderate, severe, in partial remission (full criteria for disorder were previously met, but currently only some of the symptoms remain), or in full remission (no longer any symptoms but it is clinically relevant to note the disorder). Sometimes we are asked to separate scores for the client's past, present, and future functioning (level to be achieved in order for treatment to terminate).

Summary.   This section is the most difficult part of the psychosocial study to write, as it requires a high degree of conceptualization. All of the information that has been gathered is now pulled together within the context of a theoretical framework that helps us to understand the data and establish treatment goals. Theories can be value and culture driven (Turner, 1996, p. 12) and are harmful when used to label pathology, since they compromise the practitioner's commitment to empathy. Although they often resonate with the therapist's sense and use of self (Greenberg & Mitchell, 1983), we do not think theoretical models that guide practice should be selected on the basis of subjective appeal. The advanced practitioner draws upon a wide range of theoretical constructs to understand the client's story. He also uses empirical research findings to select the best model of treatment, and his own research design to test the effectiveness of the treatment as he undertakes the therapeutic work.

Recommendations and Goals for Treatment.   In this section the worker elaborates on the treatment goals that flow from the psychosocial summary and indicates the specific ways in which the theoretical model selected will be used to guide the treatment. It is also necessary to include the client's response to your recommendations (motivated, reluctant, needs to think about it, etc.)

and whether alternative models (perhaps models not provided by your agency) would also meet the client's needs. The duration and frequency of the treatment should be specified, as well as the treatment modality or modalities (e.g., individual treatment once a week combined with family sessions to be held on a monthly basis).

Plans to Evaluate.   Evaluation should be built into the treatment plan. Reimbursement guidelines often dictate that treatment goals and objectives be written in behavioral terms that can be measured quantitatively. It is also important to remember that some theoretical models and treatment goals may be less amenable to quantitative description. Qualitative evaluation methods can be substituted when appropriate and/or used in conjunction with the more traditional quantitative methods that may not be able to totally reflect a treatment goal(s).

The following case provides a model for the psychosocial study. It includes a mental status exam, and a diagnosis according to *DSM-IV.*

A Sample Psychosocial Study: The Case of Vincent, Age 7, a Traumatized Child

Identifying Information

Vincent W., age 7, is a small, active, alert, well-groomed, verbal, intelligent, and engaging African American Protestant child who has been in residential placement for one month. His mother voluntarily placed him in residential treatment following unsuccessful outpatient treatment in the community.

Referral Source

Vincent was referred by the Child Development Center at St. Mary's Hospital—which had been acquainted with Vincent and his family for the previous 18 months. Vincent was initially referred to the Center because of poor school adjustment and problems in academic achievement. The sources of information used in this report came from the records of St. Mary's Hospital and from Vincent's mother, and are believed to be fairly reliable.

Presenting Problem

Vincent was admitted to residential treatment from his mother's home because of behavioral problems at home and in school. Vincent was manifesting severe anxiety, hyperactivity, aggressiveness, and a low tolerance for frustration. He would hit, punch, and kick other children in his classroom, rip up his work when he became frustrated, and have frequent temper tantrums. Vincent also demonstrated this behavior with his mother, but not with his mother's boyfriend, who seemed to have better control over him. Vincent's mother was using physical punishment to contain him, and his aggressive behavior was escalating. She feared that if she did not have him leave the

(continued)

A Sample Psychosocial Study   Continued

home, she "would lose control and hurt him." Community supports did not appear strong enough to help her to parent Vincent appropriately given his high level of difficulty.

History of the Problem

Vincent's emotional and behavioral difficulties had a gradual onset. At age 4, when Vincent entered daycare, he was seen as very demanding, whining and pouting when his needs were not immediately met. At age 5, in kindergarten, Vincent was unable to sit and was disruptive in the large group. He often had to be taken out of the classroom and restrained to prevent him from hitting another child or destroying things. Vincent went to daycare after school, and on weekends he was cared for by a sitter, while his mother worked. There is no information regarding his adjustment in those settings.

Vincent had difficulty entering first grade and was unable to function well within the large classroom setting. Vincent's mother was frequently called to take him home when he became defiant and destructive. The school, recognizing Vincent's difficulties, referred the family to St. Mary's Child Development Center for an evaluation. The Center gave Vincent a complete medical, neurological, psychiatric, and psychological evaluation. Their diagnostic impression was "normal intelligence with a childhood behavior disorder." The mental status report stated, "Vincent appeared to be a well-dressed, 6-and-a-half-year-old black male who was immediately sociable. He was trying to be a clown, and seemed to have a short attention span. His mood seemed mildly sad and his affect appropriate. He showed considerable anxiety—which was manifested physically—when asked to perform. There seemed to be a moderate usage of denial and avoidance with other regressive adaptations at resolution. Vincent evidenced guilt over his "badness" and tried to seek disapproval and limit setting. His fantasies centered around not talking about things so as to avoid getting hurt. There were recurrent signs of an early depression. He perceives his family as fragile and is looking for a male role model with whom to identify. Vincent blocked most material that tended toward the negative feelings he has toward his mother." The medical report from St. Mary's noted no neurological abnormalities, and all findings were within the normal range. Some graphomotor difficulties were noted, and, academically, Vincent was behind the normal level for his age group in reading, spelling, and math. An expressive language difficulty was also noted.

Family Background

Mother.   Mrs. W. is a 22-year-old woman who is herself the product of a traumatic background. She is the older of two children, whose father died when she was quite young. She was raised by a strict and aloof mother who administered severe beatings and punishments. At age 15 she became pregnant with Vincent, and was pressured to marry Clark W., a violent man, who was three years older than she. They moved to a northern city so that he could find work. Mrs. W.'s preoccupation with Vincent's care after the birth allegedly infuriated her husband, and he became increasingly abusive toward her. Mrs. W. became pregnant with her second child when Vincent was a year and a half, and Mr. W.'s subsequent abuse toward her accelerated. When Vincent was 3 years old, Mrs. W.'s daughter died at the age of 18 months. The exact circumstances surrounding the death are unknown, but Mrs. W. holds her husband responsible. According to her account, their daughter ingested some bleach, whereupon Mr. W. beat the child for misbehaving. Mrs. W. was severely beaten when she attempted to take the child to the hospital. Vincent was a witness to all this. The baby was eventually taken to the hospital, but she was not admitted. She died the next morning. The couple separated one year later, and Vincent has refused to see his father since that time.

Father.   Clark W. is described as abusive and volatile. He currently resides with his girlfriend and their 2-year-old child. He is said to be involved in criminal or sublegal activities and does not pay child support. Vincent expresses no interest in seeing his father.

Boyfriend.   John S. has resided in the home for several years. He plans to marry Mrs. W. He is soft spoken and articulate and appears to provide care and support to Vincent. Vincent is very attached to him and refers to him as his father. Although Mr. S. seems to care for Vincent, he was not opposed to residential placement, and, when Vincent was at home, Mr. S. was unable to help to contain him.

Personal History

Vincent was an unplanned and unwanted child, born into an arranged marriage. There were no medical complications during Mrs. W.'s pregnancy, but Mrs. W. remembers labor as having been long, arduous, and extremely painful. Vincent weighed 8 pounds at birth, and Mrs. W. remembers that her first feeling about him was that she wanted him to "grow up." Developmental milestones were achieved within normal limits, with no unusual occurrences noted, except for delayed speech. Vincent has had numerous separations and losses during his first 7 years of life. At 6 months of age, Vincent was sent to live with his maternal grandmother in the South for approximately one year, and then returned to his mother for a brief period of time. After his sister's death, he was again placed in his grandmother's care. When he returned at 4 years of age, Mrs. W. was working long hours and asked a friend, described as an alcoholic who had difficulty managing her affect, to look after Vincent. At age 4 and a half Vincent entered daycare. His mother dates her difficulties with him to the death of his sister, but acknowledges that she was too distraught over her loss to do much about Vincent's poor behavior.

Medical History

Vincent's general health has been good and there have been no hospitalizations. His last complete physical examination was conducted at St. Mary's Hospital, prior to placement.

Cultural History

Vincent is an African American child born to a teenage mother who was forced into an arranged marriage with the 18-year-old father of her child. The couple left their familiar southern town and extended families to seek work in a northern city. One can assume that as a young African American family with few familial or economic re-

(continued)

A Sample Psychosocial Study   Continued

sources, Vincent and his parents faced hardships that may have strained their personal resources.

Religion/Spirituality.   The family is Protestant, and Mrs. W was an active member of the church in her southern community. She regrets having lost this affiliation when she moved to New York and aspires to become a more involved member of her congregation when time permits. Currently, she attends church only on holidays and special occasions. While not a highly religious person, she does believe in a higher power and finds comfort in prayer.

Mental Status and Current Functioning

(To best illustrate how the mental status exam is used in practice, we have incorporated the mental status indicators in bold type within the text.)

At the residential treatment center, Vincent remains anxious **(mood)**, active **(motor activity)**, and somewhat depressed **(mood)**. He seeks support from his social worker and reassurance from the other adults in his environment **(attitude)**. He comes to sessions well groomed and takes pride in his appearance **(appearance)**. His speech is clear but there is some difficulty with expressive language **(speech)**. In sessions he is variable **(affect)**, and a wide range of functioning and unevenness of development do exist. There are frequent shifts between age-appropriate behavior and more regressed and infantile behaviors. In play, Vincent is creative, imaginative, and purposeful **(orientation)**, and underlying themes of inadequacy and badness and fears of abandonment are repeatedly played out. With family dolls, he repeatedly submerges the girl doll in water and then brings her up to the surface of the sink. This repetitive play occurs in each session. He can be demanding, provocative, and at times genuinely obnoxious. His distractibility **(thought processes)**, emotional lability **(affect)**, and hyperactivity **(motor activity)** can generate considerable frustration in those who deal with him, and it is not always easy to avoid engaging in a power struggle with him. His reality testing is basically intact **(perception)**, as is his judgment **(judgment)**. Thinking is concrete **(abstraction)** and appropriate for his age. He seems to have some awareness of his provocative behavior **(insight)**, but an underlying sense of "badness," a need for punishment, impulsivity, and lack of control **(motor activity)** intrude upon his conscious efforts to be more conforming. His good intellect, creativity, and artistic sense **(cognitive function)** are strengths. He is an emotionally vulnerable child who is fearful of abandonment **(thought content)**. Vincent's regressive and maladaptive defenses do not seem adequate to ward off his instinctual impulses, and it seems that he is in a perpetual state of anxiety **(mood)**. Vincent refuses to talk about his sister's death and avoids the worker's attempts to bring the subject up in therapy. He accomplishes this by changing the subject or running around the room **(motor activity)**. When asked by the psychiatrist what he would like to be when he grows up, he remarked "I'm not going to grow up—I'll probably die soon anyway." Although Vincent cannot cope with his many internal conflicts, he does have a number of strengths. He is a likable child with a good intellect **(cognitive function)**. Vincent is warm and enthusiastic and has the ability to form relationships **(attitude)**.

DSM-IV Diagnosis:

Axis I   309.81 Post-traumatic stress disorder
          314.01 Attention deficit disorder/hyperactive-impulsive
Axis II V71.09 No diagnosis
Axis III Expressive language difficulty
Axis IV Removal from home—Severe parent–child conflict
          Domestic violence (suspected abuse by father)
          Death of sister (circumstances unclear)
Axis V (current) GAF 35

Discussion of *DSM-IV* Diagnosis

Although this would not need to appear in a psychosocial, we include it here to help you understand the rationale for the worker's multiaxial diagnosis.

Vincent is a traumatized child who meets the diagnostic criteria for post-traumatic stress disorder (PTSD). Diagnostic code: 309.81. The criteria for PTSD, according to the DSM-IV (1994), is as follows:

A. The person has been exposed to a traumatic event in which both of the following were present: (1) The person experienced, witnessed, or was confronted with an event or events that involved actual or threatened death or serious injury, or a threat to the physical integrity of self or others. (2) The person's response involved intense fear, helplessness, or horror. Note: In children, this may be expressed instead by disorganized or agitated behavior.

B. The traumatic event is persistently reexperienced in one (or more) of the following ways: (1) Recurrent and intrusive distressing recollections of the event, including images, thoughts, or perceptions. Note: In young children, repetitive play may occur in which themes or aspects of the trauma are expressed. (2) Recurrent distressing dreams of the event. Note: In children, there may be frightening dreams without recognizable content. (3) Acting or feeling as if the traumatic event were recurring (includes a sense of reliving the experience, illusions, hallucinations, and dissociative flashback episodes, including those that occur on awakening or when intoxicated). Note: In young children, trauma-specific reenactment may occur. (4) Intense psychological distress at exposure to internal or external cues that symbolize or resemble an aspect of the traumatic event. (5) Physiological reactivity on exposure to internal or external cues that symbolize or resemble an aspect of the traumatic event.

C. Persistent avoidance of stimuli associated with the trauma and numbing of general responsiveness (not present before the trauma) as indicated by three or more of the following: (1) efforts to avoid thoughts, feelings, or conversations associated with the trauma; (2) efforts to avoid activities, places, or people that arouse recollections of the trauma; (3) inability to recall an important aspect of the trauma; (4) markedly diminished interest or participation in significant activities; (5) feeling of detachment or estrangement from others; (6) restricted range of affect; (7) sense of a foreshortened future (e.g., does not expect to have a career, marriage, children, or a normal life span).

(continued)

A Sample Psychosocial Study   Continued

    D. Persistent symptoms of increased arousal (not present before the trauma) as indicated by two or more of the following: (1) difficulty falling or staying asleep; (2) irritability or outbursts of anger; (3) difficulty concentrating; (4) hypervigilance; (5) exaggerated startle response.

    E. Duration of the disturbance (symptoms in Criteria V, C, and D) is more than 1 month.

    F. The disturbance causes clinically significant distress or impairment in social, occupational, or other important areas of functioning.

        Specify if acute (duration of symptoms is less than 3 months) or chronic (duration of symptoms is 3 months or more).

        Specify (delayed onset) if at least 6 months have passed between the traumatic event and the onset of the symptoms.

Diagnostic Rationale

Vincent has witnessed physical abuse and the death of his sister within the context of domestic violence. He seems to be specifically reenacting his sister's death in traumatic play (Gil, 1991) as he repetitively drowns the girl doll in the sink and tries to rescue her by bringing her to the surface of the water. This qualifies him for a PTSD diagnosis based on Criteria A and B. For Criteria C, Vincent shows persistent avoidance of stimuli associated with the trauma by (1) refusal to have conversations about it, (3) inability to recall aspects of it, and (7) sense of foreshortened future (he doesn't think he will live to grow up). To further make a case for PTSD as a principal diagnosis based on the final criteria, for Category D it could be said that Vincent displays both irritability and outbursts of anger, as well as difficulty concentrating. The duration of Vincent's symptoms has been several years, indicating that there is chronicity involved. This would rule out considering a diagnosis of adjustment disorder with mixed anxiety and depressed mood (309.28), despite his two outstanding symptoms of anxiety and depression.

    The second Axis I diagnosis of attention deficit disorder/hyperactive-impulsive (314.01) accurately describes Vincent's current behavior and is based on Vincent's meeting the minimum criteria of at least six symptoms for the disorder in the area of hyperactivity and impulsivity (American Psychiatric Association, 1994). These symptoms are:

    A. (1) Hyperactivity

        (a) often fidgets with hands or feet or squirms in seat

        (b) often leaves seat in classroom when remaining seated is expected behavior

        (d) often has difficulty playing or engaging in leisure activities quietly

        (e) often is "on the go" and acts as if driven by a motor

      (2) Impulsivity

        (h) often has difficulty awaiting turn

        (i) often interrupts or intrudes on others

    B. Some hyperactivity-impulsivity or inattentive symptoms that caused impairment were present before age 7 years

C. Some impairment present in two or more settings (home and school)

D. There must be clear evidence of clinically significant impairment in social, academic, or occupational functioning (American Psychiatric Association, 1994)

Vincent has lived in a very uncertain environment for many years, with multiple losses and multiple changes. Young children lack the ability to verbalize what they are feeling; Vincent may be expressing anxiety through motoric behavior, thus giving the appearance of ADHD. Vincent should have the opportunity to be observed over time in his new setting, to see if his impulsivity and hyperactivity abate once he feels more tranquil and less overwhelmed.

On **Axis II,** Vincent was not given a diagnosis. As Axis II is reserved for mental retardation (Vincent is not retarded) and personality disorders (not used with children under age 12), the worker correctly entered "no diagnosis" on Axis II. She used the V 71.09 code because the absence of a code might indicate that the worker neglected to make a diagnosis.

On **Axis III,** there is noted an expressive language difficulty. This information was part of Vincent's referral material from St. Mary's Hospital.

On **Axis IV,** the worker has noted removal from home, severe parent–child conflict, domestic violence, and the death of his sister as psychological stressors for Vincent. His current GAF score is 35 on a scale ranging from 0 to 100, which gives him a low rating for overall functioning. Persons falling between 31–40 show either some impairment in reality testing or communication, or major impairment in several areas, such as work or school, family relations, judgment, thinking, or mood. For Vincent, it would seem that the severe impairment in school and family relations justifies this low GAF score. The social worker has not been asked to predict a GAF score needed for discontinuation of placement, but Vincent would probably need to be functioning in a range above 50, showing moderate to mild symptoms, before discharge to outpatient treatment could take place.

Conclusion

Vincent's past and current functioning can be best understood within a multidimensional framework that combines treatment principles from object relations, and cognitive and behavioral theories (see relevant chapters in this text). From a psychodynamic perspective, Vincent's history suggests the coexistence of both trauma and attachment disturbances.

Vincent had multiple caretakers from the age of 6 months when he was sent to live with his maternal grandmother in the South. He was returned to his mother at 18 months, placed with questionable babysitters (one suspected of alcoholism) and finally placed in daycare. These events can be understood within the cultural context of the African American family where kinship care is customary when parents are working to support the family. They also may be seen as an accommodation to his mother's needs: She was attempting to separate from an abusive husband (Vincent's father) and find active employment, all the while grieving the death of her daughter. Vincent witnessed the physical abuse directed at his mother and his sister. We might speculate that he was also the victim of physical abuse, although we have no corroborating evidence.

(continued)

A Sample Psychosocial Study   **Continued**

Cognitive mechanisms such as Vincent's self-blame are often correlates of depression and low self-esteem, illustrating how the cognitive and affective consequences of trauma reinforce one another (James, 1989). Vincent also evidences destructiveness, identification with the aggressor, and feelings of loss and betrayal characteristic of children who have experienced trauma at an early age. There are developmental deficits as well. These include difficulties with trust, an inability to curb his aggression, lack of more mature defenses, and signal anxiety. Vincent's behavior therefore needs to be understood within the context of his attempts to deal with trauma that he is unable to cognitively or affectively process. This dramatically affects Vincent's ability to cope and master new experiences and expectations. Vincent's repetitive drowning and rescuing of the doll is of serious concern as it represents post-traumatic play (Gil, 1991). Vincent's unsuccessful attempt at mastery of his sister's death leaves him feeling vulnerable and helpless and clearly signals that attention must be focused on this particular trauma. In addition, Vincent worries that his mother will not take him home and that she will disappear from his life altogether. (She threw out his bedroom furniture once he left home, claiming that she needed the room for her study.)

Recommendations and Goals for Treatment

The goal of residential treatment is to bring Vincent's behavior under control so that he will be able to return home and attend school in his community. This will be accomplished through psychodynamic, cognitive, and behavioral therapy that will help Vincent to begin to address and work through his past traumas, while helping him to develop the social skills and behavioral controls that will aid his adjustment at home and in school. The treatment plan for Vincent and his family includes

(1) Providing a safe, supportive context to grieve.

(2) Using play therapy (as opposed to talk therapy) to help Vincent work out his feelings about the death of his sister. Vincent's traumatic play must be carefully interpreted so that he can experience some resolution to this conflict. The worker should talk to Vincent about what the "dolls" are feeling and thinking when he attempts to drown them in the sink. Working in this off-target way helps children to gain some safe distance from highly charged material.

(3) Addressing Vincent's internalized self-blame (his inner sense of badness) by clarifying the circumstances of his sister's death and the reasons for his separation(s) from his mother (family), in order to change the cognitive distortions associated with these events.

(4) Working with Vincent on behavioral strategies to cope with his anxiety and fear.

(5) Educating staff and primary caretakers in behavior management techniques that recognize Vincent's behaviors as manifestations of his past trauma. This would include structure, support, and firm, but empathic, limit setting.

(6) Giving Vincent the opportunity to form relationships with positive male role models, particularly an African American male(s), with whom he can identify.

(7) Providing a highly structured classroom setting where there are opportunities for Vincent to feel empowered. He also needs outlets for his creativity and physical energy and an accepting noncritical approach to learning.

(8) Outreach and involvement with his mother and her boyfriend that is educational and supportive, so that his mother and her boyfriend can be a resource for Vincent when he leaves the residential treatment center.

(9) Placement not to exceed one year, with plans to transfer him to home and a community school.

Plans to Evaluate

1. A behavioral token economy should be set up with the teacher and with Vincent's cottage parents. The social worker will show them how to implement this. Vincent will earn points for good behavior that can be cashed in for privileges at the end of each week. Vincent and the staff will develop a list of these privileges. The staff will monitor his response by tracking three target behaviors—hitting other children, following commands, and temper tantrums. The monitoring of these three target behaviors will begin immediately, and the intervention will take place after one week.

2. The social worker will request feedback about Vincent's behavior from Vincent's mother following each home visit. This feedback will be documented in her record. The worker will specifically ask about Vincent's adjustment in behavioral and attitudinal terms.

3. The social worker will collect feedback on the above indicators from the cottage parents and the school following each home visit.

4. The social worker will interrupt Vincent's posttraumatic play through direct interventions that will allow him to consider other options in his play. For example, the social worker can comment on the child's play, take a particular role in the play, or get involved in the play. This intervention should begin immediately, and its effectiveness should be evaluated after each play therapy session, in order to determine the extent to which Vincent has moved away from his posttraumatic play.

5. A followup meeting will be held in 3 months to discuss the results of the intervention plan.

Source: Case material supplied by Helen Solomon.

Summary

In this chapter, we have illustrated how the psychosocial study, a method of gathering the facts about the client and his situation, leads to the development of a diagnosis that then informs our treatment plan. Mary Richmond, quoting Dr. Richard Cabot, wrote "In social study you open your eyes and look, in diagnosis you close them and think" (Richmond, 1917, p. 347, in Woods & Hollis, 1990). To best demonstrate how the worker both looks and thinks, we presented the case of

Vincent. This case example incorporates both the facts of Vincent's young life that led to his placement away from home and the worker's dynamic interpretation of those facts. We added the knowledge of the components of the mental status exam to help Vincent's worker frame her diagnosis according to the *DSM-IV*. Our final product also includes treatment recommendations, goal setting, and a method of evaluating whether those goals have been met. We acknowledge that preparing a psychosocial study of this magnitude takes considerable time. However, we firmly believe that, when the worker is given the opportunity to think critically about the case before her, the final product is well worth the effort.

Learning Assignments

1. Develop a psychosocial assessment of a client following the outline in this chapter. What parts of the assessment have you found easiest or most difficult to write? Consider what additional skills or readings you may need to write the entire psychosocial assessment.

2. Working in small groups, practice writing a mental status assessment on one or more client(s) who were presented by students in your group.

3. Working in small groups, consider what theory or theories might be applicable in understanding or working with one or more client(s) presented by students in your group. Discuss your treatment goals and how you would evaluate whether these goals have been reached.

References

Abramovitz, R., & Williams, J. (1992). Workshop 2: The pros and cons of the diagnostic and statistical manual for social work practice and research. *Research on Social Work Practice, 2*(3), 338–349.

American Psychiatric Association. (1994). *Diagnostic and statistical manual of mental disorders* (4th ed.). Washington, DC: American Psychiatric Association.

Bellack, L., et al. (1973). *Ego functions in schizophrenics, neurotics and normals.* New York: John Wiley & Sons.

Congress, E. P. (1994). The use of culturagrams to assess and empower culturally diverse families. *Families in Society, 75*(9), 531–539.

Gil, E. (1991). *The healing power of play: Working with abused children.* New York: Guilford.

Goldstein, E. (1995). *Ego psychology and social work practice.* New York: The Free Press.

Greenberg, J., & Mitchell, S. (1983). *Object relations in psychoanalytic theory.* Cambridge, MA: Harvard University Press.

Hartman, A. (1978). Diagrammatic assessment of family relationships. *Social Casework, 59,* 465–476.

Hartman, H. (1939). *Ego psychology and the problem of adaptation.* New York: International Universities Press.

James, B. (1989). *Treating traumatized children: New insights and creative interventions.* Toronto: Lexington.

Jordan, C., & Franklin, C. (1995). *Clinical assessment for social workers.* Chicago: Lyceum.

Joseph, M. V. (1998). Religion and social work practice. *Social Casework: The Journal of Contemporary Social Work, 69,* 443–452.

McGoldrick, M., & Gerson, R. (1985). *Genograms in family assessment.* New York: Norton.

McGoldrick, M., Gerson, R., & Shellenberger, S. (1999). *Genograms: Assessment and intervention.* New York: W. W. Norton.

Richmond, M. (1917). *Social diagnosis* (p. 347). New York: Russell Sage Foundation.

Schamess, G. (1996). Ego psychology. In J. Berzoff, L. Melano Flanagan, & P. Hertz (Eds.), *Inside out and outside in: Psychodynamic clinical theory and practice in contemporary and sociocultural contexts* (pp. 68–103). Northvale, NJ: Jason Aronson.

Taylor, M. A. (1981). *The neuropsychiatric mental status examinations.* Jamaica, NY: Spectrum.

Turner, F. (Ed.). (1996). *Social work treatment: Interlocking theoretical approaches* (4th ed.). New York: The Free Press.

Webb, N. B. (1996). *Social work practice with children.* New York: Guilford.

Woods, M. E., & Hollis, F. (1990). *Casework: A psychosocial therapy* (4th ed.). New York: McGraw Hill.

5

Cross-Cultural Practice

Cross-cultural counseling challenges therapists to examine their culture-bound attitudes and beliefs about which values, customs, and behaviors they consider sensible and acceptable. Cross-cultural therapy is unique in the way that the dynamics of power and powerlessness and those of cultural identity or ethnicity transact and profoundly affect the course of treatment (Cartec, 1995; Pinderhuges, 1984). This type of practice demands that the clinician be able to examine her own cultural group and the ways in which it has contributed to discrimination and prejudice. Cross-cultural counseling requires understanding the value systems of families from other cultures and how those values influence the behavior of the family members.

In this chapter we discuss some of the competencies that clinicians are required to have in order to work with clients of various races and cultural backgrounds. These skills are illustrated through two case examples: (1) counseling a Vietnamese adolescent who was destructively acting out in the community and (2) treatment of an African American woman who was in conflict over her racial identity and cultural allegiance.

Racial Identity Development

North American society, in spite of its cultural diversity, still has a good deal of racial segregation. White people, in particular, have very little firsthand knowledge about life in nonwhite cultures and communities. Several authors discuss the concept of white racial identity development as pivotal in the development of cross-cultural therapeutic skills (Hardiman, 1982; Helms, 1984; Ponterotto, 1988; Sabnani, Ponterotto, & Barodovsky, 1991). We think it is important to highlight this model since the majority of students in schools of social work come from the dominant white culture of our society. Five stages of white identity development are depicted in the literature. These stages are not linear—individuals may move through different stages at varying times, as they make choices that cause them to either regress or advance. In the first stage of this model, the white person lacks awareness of herself as a racial being. In the second stage, the person has acquired some knowledge regarding race, including the significance of one's whiteness in U.S. society, either through involvement with members of other racial groups or through multicultural training. The third stage is characterized by feelings of guilt and possible rejection of internalized racist beliefs. In the fourth stage, the person retreats back into white culture perhaps as a result of hostility and/or fear. The last stage involves an internalization of white racial identity and a healthy recognition of and respect for cultural differences. It is extremely important that the white cross-cultural therapist be aware of her current stage of development, so as to be able to examine the assumptions and feelings engendered by working with clients whose backgrounds may be different.

Which Psychotherapeutic Models Work Best?

There are various recommendations in the literature regarding which psychotherapies are effective in cross-cultural practice (see, for example, Atkinson, Thompson, & Grant, 1993), and considerable disagreement exists. Opinions on what is therapeutic range from psychotherapies that focus on intrapsychic change—the abandonment of therapy in favor of social action to promote change—and approaches that would include attention to both oppressive external environments and destructive personal behavior (Ivey, Ivey, & Simek-Morgan, 1997; Sue & Sue, 2003). Psychoanalytic therapy traditionally has been considered inappropriate for African American clients and clients of lower socioeconomic status (Helms & Cook, 1999), a view that could be interpreted as biased. Cognitive-behavioral approaches, however, due to their emphasis on structure, have been recommended for all clients regardless of racial, cultural, or socioeconomic conditions. Client-centered therapy has been advocated for traditional Japanese clients because the interventions are indirect (Hayashi, Kuno, Osawa, & Shimizu, 1992). Also due to the indirectness of its interventions, client-centered therapy is not recommended for Latino clients (Ruiz, 1995; Velasquez, 1997). In general, it appears that therapists' training experiences, as well as their racial and cultural perspectives, shape their thinking about what approaches work best with different racial and cultural groups. Our thinking is that most of the time, *all* of the major theoretical orientations on which clinical practice is based can be adapted to work with clients of various racial and cultural groups. It is not the therapist's theoretical orientation, per se, but instead the cultural and racial sensitivity, ability to set goals commensurate with the client's level of acculturation, and selection of a modality that is tailored to the client's needs that makes for effective cross-cultural practice. The literature refers to effective cross-cultural practice as culturally competent practice (Nwachuku & Ivey, 1991; Sue, 1990; Sue, Arredondo, & McDavis, 1992). We also feel that there are times when culturally specific practice is indicated (Sue, 1990). This includes attention to the development and use of theoretical and conceptual models of practice specific to the client's cultural group.

Cross-Cultural Assessment

A cross-cultural clinical assessment requires that the client be understood according to the norms of the client's culture and the variations that exist within every culture. In addition to confronting racial and cultural bias, therapists need to have knowledge about the client's cultural group, including what is normative and what is deviant. Given the sheer numbers and diversity of cultures represented in our society, particularly in urban America, this is a daunting task. Obviously, clinicians will not be experts or equally well informed on every race and culture. What is important is the worker's willingness to learn. While there is a fairly comprehensive body of literature that one can draw information from, listening to the client's experience in an open and nonjudgmental way may be the best way to learn.

Ten Elements of Cross-Cultural Practice

Locke (1992) introduced ten significant cultural elements that need to be considered in cross-cultural clinical practice. The degree of a client's acculturation—the extent to which a racial/ethnic minority group has adopted the beliefs, values, customs, and institutions of the dominant culture—is primary. The other important factors are poverty, history of oppression, language and the arts, racism and prejudice, sociopolitical factors, child-rearing practices, religious practices, family structure, and values and attitudes. Workers also need to assess whether a client's problems stem from internal or external dynamics, particularly since oppression and racism are so predominant in our society. Newer immigrant groups raise different concerns than African Americans, for example, who have been present in this country since the arrival of early European Americans.

Atkinson, Thompson, and Grant (1993) delineate seven important roles for cross-cultural therapists (see Figure 5.1). The first is that the therapist acts as an adviser to clients regarding potential problems they may encounter as minority immigrants. Next, the therapist must be an advocate who works on behalf of clients who are having problems related to oppression and discrimination. The therapist must have a knowledge of clients' indigenous support systems and be able to facilitate the development of new ones in the clients' present cultural environments. This includes consideration of indigenous healing methods that may be important adjuncts to the help being offered by the therapist. Another important role for the cross-cultural therapist is that of consultant—helping clients (and others in their lives) find ways to work toward reducing discriminatory practices in the community. This is closely aligned to the role of change agent, in which the therapist tries to effect changes in those conditions in the social environment that contribute to social injustice. The role of counselor is one that is aimed toward preventing intrapsychic problems from occurring, and the role of psychotherapist aims at treating intrapsychic problems.

Atkinson, Thompson, and Grant (1993, pp. 264–270) delineated seven important roles for cross-cultural therapists:

1. Adviser to clients regarding potential problems they may encounter as minority immigrants.
2. Advocate who works on behalf of clients who are having problems related to oppression and discrimination.
3. Person having knowledge of the client's indigenous support systems and the ability to facilitate the development of such systems in the client's new culture.
4. Consultant helping clients (and others in their life) find ways to work toward reducing discriminatory practices in the community.
5. Change agent trying to effect changes in those conditions in the social environment that contribute to social injustice.
6. Counselor aimed toward preventing intrapsychic problems from occurring.
7. Psychotherapist aimed at treating intrapsychic problems.

FIGURE 5.1 *Seven Important Roles for Cross-Cultural Therapists*

Clinical Example of Culturally Competent Practice

The following example of social work with a Vietnamese adolescent is based on a constructivist framework (see Chapter 11, Narrative Therapy). It illustrates what we believe to be central to cross-cultural practice: (1) that some therapeutic models can be adapted to work with a client of a different race and culture, and (2) that culturally competent practice requires an openness to learning about one's own cultural assumptions as well as those of the client. A culturagram (Congress, 1994) is included in Figure 5.2 (p. 68).

Case Study

Pan, a 17-year-old Vietnamese adolescent, was referred to a residential treatment facility by the Department of Youth Services. Pan had been committed to the Department of Youth Services on several charges, including two counts of possession of a firearm, possession of heroin and marijuana with intent to distribute, and larceny of a motor vehicle. The social work student, a white woman from a middle-class background, understood that for she and Pan to be an effective cross-cultural team, it was necessary to pay attention to what was important to him and to listen carefully so as to learn what was considered normative or deviant in his culture. Having no firsthand experience with people from the Vietnamese culture, she turned to the literature and learned that a constructivist perspective was considered well suited for work with Asian clients. This approach enables the therapist to "identify idiosyncratic variations within a culture as well as those culturally embedded behaviors presented by clients of diverse ethnoracial backgrounds (Lee, 1996, p. 190). Constructivism is a conceptual framework, and a basic tenet of treatment from this perspective is the use of narratives

(continued on p. 69)

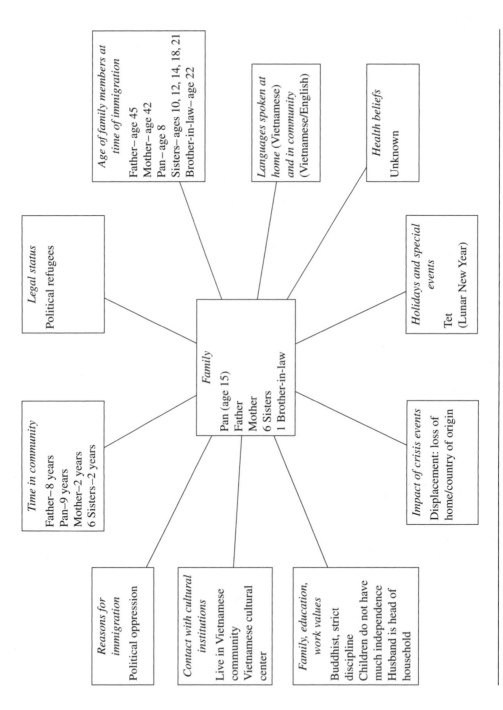

FIGURE 5.2 Culturagram—Pan and His Family
Adapted from Congress (1994).

Case Study **Continued (from p. 67)**

or stories. Narratives are reformulations of memories in a client's life that change over time and through dialog with the therapist, who balances questions with attempts at clarification as the client tells her story. A complete discussion of narrative therapy is presented in Chapter 11. Briefly stated, narrative therapy emphasizes the need to learn as much as possible about the client's problem within the context of the social and environmental forces surrounding it. In this way, clients are presented with the opportunity to explore various aspects of the presenting problem(s). Narrative therapy also helps to reveal any cultural assumptions that may have contributed to the definition of the problem (White, 1991; White & Epston, 1990).

Case

Pan was born in a poor, primitive village outside Saigon three years after the end of the Vietnam war. He was the youngest of eight children and the only male. Pan's father left for the United States when Pan was 7. Pan, a married sister and her husband, and the youngest sister left to join their father the following year, leaving their mother and the others behind. The journey from Vietnam was treacherous, and the overcrowded boat nearly capsized several times. Before permanently relocating in a northern city, Pan and his family lived in refugee camps for two years where only Vietnamese was spoken. When at last he joined his father, Pan began to attend a public school and was exposed to a life very different than that of his cultural origins. At home, Vietnamese continued to be spoken; the family only associated with other Vietnamese families and insisted that Pan do the same. By the time he was a teenager, his mother and other sisters had joined him in his new homeland, making it even more difficult for the family to assimilate since his mother and other sisters had no knowledge of English, and his father, hard at work, was rarely at home. Torn between love for his family and conflict with their old-world values and paternalistic ways, Pan began to associate with an Asian gang who accepted him, cared for him, and seemed knowledgeable about his new country. His family, upon learning of this, were ashamed and embarrassed and demanded that he leave their home. Pan became depressed and started to burn himself with cigarettes. His drug and gang involvement intensified, resulting in his being hospitalized for a heroin overdose.

In examining the life experiences of southeastern refugees, Harper and Lantz (1996) underscore the need to examine problematic events "before, during, and after" their flight to America. Listening to Pan helped the worker to understand that before immigrating to America his family lived in abject poverty, his father was the unquestionable authoritarian head of the household, and Pan, the only male child, was severely beaten for misbehavior, while his sisters were not. Prior to immigration, an older sister committed suicide rather than tell the family that she was pregnant, with no hope of marriage to the father of her child.

The student understood Pan's need for a family to love and accept him within his new cultural context and that, in his mind, the gang affiliation provided just that. The gang leader was authoritarian, as was Pan's father, and Pan did as he commanded, which included drug trafficking and drug use. While this "new family" clearly exploited Pan, they also financed his legal fees when he was initially committed to the Department of Youth Services.

Case Study   Continued

Process Recording

The following excerpt from treatment illustrates how the worker tries to understand what is culturally specific to Pan's experience, and what might be deviant.

Pan: My father used to hit me in Vietnam; he used to hit me a lot.
Worker: Can you tell me more about that?
Pan: He hit me because I was bad; he made me lie down on the floor and he hit me.
Worker: Tell me, Pan, what is your sense of why this was happening?
Pan: Well, usually my father hit me when he was drinking and then he would get angry. He wouldn't stop hitting me even when I cried.
Worker: So, drinking caused your father to act in ways that he might not otherwise behave . . . . Am I getting this right? Did he also hit you when he wasn't drinking?
Pan: Sometimes, if I did something bad . . . but he usually hit me a lot when he was drunk—and usually for no reason.
Worker: Did he stop hitting you when you cried when he wasn't drinking?
Pan: Yes, because he would be afraid of hurting me.
Worker: So, drinking made your father so angry that he wouldn't stop hitting you even when you cried because he was hurting you?
Pan: That's right.
Worker: Did this confuse you as a young child . . . maybe even now? It seems that your father sometimes hit you because he cared about you and it was his way of getting you to obey. And this type of discipline is customary among Vietnamese families, am I right?
Pan: Yes.
Worker: But then there were times when your father was drinking and hitting you for no reason or for reasons you couldn't connect with caring. Is this what made you begin to feel that you must be the problem, instead of your father's drinking? Is this what made you feel that you were bad?
Pan: I got to believe I was always bad even when I wasn't. But maybe some of the problem was my father's drinking.
Worker: The important thing to remember is that you weren't always bad. What's confusing is that your father cared about you but may have also mistreated you when he was drinking.
Pan: Yeah, well I could never look at it in any way besides I was bad and he didn't care about me . . . but I could never say anything to my family about this because we don't talk about these things. It's the way.
Worker: I understand . . . and it's important for you and I to talk about these things, even though it may be difficult to talk to a stranger about this . . . especially when you were not able to talk about it within the family.

The student acts as a "participant observer" (Anderson & Goolishian, 1988, p. 384), questioning Pan about cultural practices to help to clarify his confusion (and her own) as to whether his father acted out of harshness or caring. She offers clinical impressions tentatively and with the understanding that they may be influenced by her own personal and cultural values. She tries to locate the problem outside of Pan or his father by introducing "drinking" as the variable that may have separated the normative from the deviant forms of discipline within Pan's Vietnamese culture. Later in the treatment the student tries to help Pan attend to the conflicts in his family about acculturation.

Pan: My family hates my long hair—they think it means I am bad.
Worker: Why is that?
Pan: Because all good people in Vietnam have short hair.
Worker: So if you had short hair, your family would think of you in a better way?
Pan: That would be a beginning. They would also want me to show respect and not get into any trouble.
Worker: What else would your parents want you to do?
Pan: They want me to hang out with Vietnamese people like they do.
Worker: It sounds like you and your parents have different thoughts about life in America. You seem to want to make some changes but your family would like you to keep to your cultural ways. That often happens in families with teenage children who come to the United States.
Pan: Really? I thought it was just my family thinking I was bad again.
Worker: Well, understanding each other's point of view is important.
Pan: I can't talk to them about this. They would say I was being disrespectful.
Worker: Well, then how can you get them to see you in the way you would like to be seen? Do you think getting in trouble with the law will help them view you in a positive way?
Pan: No. I think they will see me in a good way if I get a job.
Worker: That may be a good first step.
Pan: Sometimes I feel confused about everything.
Worker: I'm sure you do and that is understandable. You've gone through a lot of changes these past several years and so has your family. I think some of these struggles have to do with coming from a different country. It takes a while to adjust to a new place. What do you think about this?

In this segment, the student worker attempts to understand and value Pan's Vietnamese culture as well as his personal struggle to fit in and be accepted in a new culture. Our last excerpt, a termination session, shows Pan's beginning understanding of his relationship with his family within its cultural context.

Worker: Now that you are ready to move on to your next program, what do you think you have learned about yourself here?
Pan: I learned that even though I made a lot of mistakes, I was not born a bad kid.
Worker: What have your learned about your family, Pan?
Pan: Well, my dad had some problems. . . . I don't think he felt good about not being able to take care of our family in Vietnam. I think he took some of his frustrations out on me because I was the only boy. He wouldn't hit my sisters.
Worker: You are recognizing that some problems in your family had nothing to do with you and that some of your father's problems were caused by struggles he faced both in Vietnam and here after your family moved.

(continued)

Case Study   Continued

> *Pan:*   I think they did what they could. My father made mistakes. But I think my family wanted the best for us. After all, that's why they left Vietnam to begin with. I was always so angry. I don't feel so angry any more.
>
> *Worker:*   What are your goals now, Pan?
>
> *Pan:*   I want to get a job and show my family that I am doing the right things. I hope they will start talking to me when they see that.
>
> *Worker:*   I hope so too, Pan. We both worked hard to get you where you are now and I will always remember you. I have a gift for you so you can remember how much you have learned here. It is an amethyst stone. The stone and the color purple mean sobriety. So when you are feeling unsure of yourself I want you to rub this stone and remember you are a great Vietnamese spirit with a goal to reach.

Conclusion

Some of the issues faced by the Vietnamese population have been cited in the literature and include survivor's guilt, sense of obligation to rescue family members left behind, adjustment of roles within the family, and intergenerational conflict caused by differential acculturation and social misunderstandings between refugees and members of the dominant culture left behind (Bemak, Chung, & Bornemann, 1996; Chung, Bemak, & Okazaki, 1997; Timberlake & Cooke, 1984). Tu (1985) notes that the suffering of an individual family member was second to the importance of the family name. As Pan began to construct a new narrative, he came to recognize that his family had tried to act in his best interest by talking with him about how his behavior would affect his future, letting him live with a family friend, bringing him to the hospital after a heroin overdose, and ultimately, allowing him to feel the full weight of the court by his commitment to the Department of Youth Services. Narrative therapy within the context of culturally competent practice helped Pan to reconstruct his life story so that he no longer blamed himself or his family. In the story that he and the worker created, Pan gained an increased understanding of his family and the difficulties that they faced living through the Vietnam war and their journey and life in refugee camps in America. Now Pan had a more accurate view of the realities of his life and of theirs and a greater appreciation of his family's concern for him. This new narrative has helped Pan to become closer to his family and to his origins.

Source: Adapted from Lesser & Eriksen (2000).

Clinical Example of Culturally Specific Practice

Our next case explores issues of racial identity development, biculturalism, and the effects of cross-racial counseling. In this case example, the worker bases her interventions on a racial identity treatment model because it is specific to the needs of the client and her culture and also relates to the manifest issues of racial stress that emerged during the course of treatment. The clinician is a white, middle-class social worker who came from working-class roots. The client is a professional, middle-class African American woman from a similar social class.

Does Race Affect the Helping Process? There is no conclusive evidence that racial dissimilarity impairs treatment outcome (Davis & Proctor, 1989). Devore and Schlesinger (1996) debate the pros and cons of having clients and therapists of the same race and background. Certain clients with traumatic backgrounds may not be able to work with therapists who are similar to those who perpetrated the original trauma and should not be made to do so. However, we believe that sensitive, skilled social work clinicians can work effectively with clients of different racial backgrounds if the issue of race is openly discussed within the context of the therapeutic relationship. Addressing one's own cultural assumptions and confronting racial biases is no mean feat. Since racism is so pervasive in our society, one tends to "breathe it in, like smog" (Tatum, 1993). Most white and black therapists have little or no formal training in treatment of nonwhite clients (Sue & Sue, 2003). Frequently, clinicians working with a client of a different race mistakenly take a colorblind stance, believing that there are no differences between themselves and their clients. Color blindness obscures the therapist's view of who the patient is. Color has to be acknowledged since many of the social tensions, fears, angers, and resentments attached to power imbalances between the dominant and devalued societal situations can affect the treatment process (Greene, 1986; Hall, 2002; Walker, 1996).

A Black Identity Development Model. Cross (1971, 1978, 1991, 1995) proposes a model of black racial identity development that is particularly useful in understanding the dynamics of black women in white communities. The five stages of this model are identified as follows:

- Pre-Encounter
- Encounter
- Immersion/Emersion
- Internalization
- Internalization/Commitment

In the Pre-Encounter phase, the black woman has absorbed many of the beliefs and values of the dominant white culture, internalizing negative black stereotypes that may be unconscious. Denial helps her to selectively screen out-of-awareness information that affirms she cannot really be a member of the dominant racial group (Helms, 1984), and she thus seeks assimilation and acceptance by the white society.

Crisis events such as social rejection by whites precipitate movement into the Encounter phase, where the black woman is forced to focus on her identity as a member of a group targeted by racism. In the Immersion/Emersion stage, she surrounds herself with visible symbols of racial identity, making everything of value black or relevant to blackness. In the Internalization and Internalization/Commitment stage, the woman is ready to build coalitions with members of other oppressed groups and has a general sense of commitment.

Sue and Sue (2003) propose a similar five-stage process:

- Conformity
- Dissonance
- Resistance/Immersion
- Introspection
- Integrative Awareness

Stage one, Conformity, is characterized by self-deprecating and group-deprecating discriminatory attitudes toward minorities and an appreciation of the dominant group. In stage two, Dissonance, there is a conflict between these attitudes. Resistance and Immersion are characteristic of stage three. In stage four, Introspection, there is conflict between responsibility and allegiance to one's own minority group versus notions of personal independence and autonomy. In the final stage, Integrative Awareness, a person has gained an inner sense of security and appreciation of the unique aspects of his culture as well as those of the dominant group. Conflict is resolved, there is more control, flexibility, positive self-esteem, racial pride, and sense of autonomy. The client becomes bicultural and is able to enjoy the benefits of both the dominant white society and that of his or her own—without a loss of personal integrity. As with other identity development models, these stages of racial development are not discrete, and movement may be more spiral than linear.

Case Study

The Case

Carol, a 28-year-old African American woman, grew up in a small southern town. Her family had great expectations of their only child. Her mother was the only one of thirteen children who went to college—her siblings either worked in the steel mills or were day workers. Her father was a government employee. After high school, Carol elected to attend a black women's college, and, while there, she gained admission on a master's level to a prominent eastern university, where she earned an advanced degree. Although she achieved, she felt it was a matter of luck and that she was seen as a "token" by her predominantly white classmates. She performed well and was recruited by a prestigious New York corporation upon graduation. In spite of her accomplishments, Carol was unhappy. She felt isolated in a large city and misunderstood by family and friends back home. Plagued with self-doubts, feelings of being alienated from family and friends, and conflicts at work, she entered treatment. This process continued over two years, during which time Carol began to resolve conflicts related to divided loyalties.

The Initial Phase of Treatment

The only woman of color at her prestigious firm, and brighter and more experienced than many of her colleagues, Carol, in the early stage of treatment, had talked of her discomfort in asserting herself. Recently, she had been invited to become a member of the Board of Directors of a major international corporation but her own company refused to support this initiative. While they stated that it was a matter of policy, Carol was not convinced. She felt that the issue had to do with race, and she felt angry, vulnerable, and exposed. This brought up earlier memories of childhood in her small southern town.

The following process recording is taken from an early interview.

Carol: I saw this movie on TV the other night—it's old and very famous, called *Imitation of Life*. Did you see that?

Worker: No, I have not. Would you like to tell me about it?

Carol: It's about a black girl who wants to be white. She passes, but pays a big price. She has to leave her family, and she's always afraid that she'll be found out and rejected and have nowhere to go. In high school I remember thinking that it would be easier if I were white or not there at all. I felt invisible. I got good grades. I looked good because my mother always dressed me well. The school was mainly white—my parents wanted me to have the best education possible so they sent me to parochial school. I had a friend named Betsy. She was very pretty and popular, and I thought that if I were with her people would like me. My mother chastised me, told me I was acting like I thought I was white. I told her that our school didn't recognize color, that we were all the same. She told me I was kidding myself, that color was always an issue. One day Betsy's cousin from New York came to visit. When she saw me, she refused to play with me because I was black. . . . Betsy went off with her and left me standing there.

Worker: That must have been very painful.

Carol: I was so startled I couldn't speak. I wanted to run and hide. I didn't say anything. And I feel that way now—I lose my voice at work when I feel I'm not being seen for who I am. I make all this money and yet I feel I don't deserve it. So I keep to myself; I don't socialize.

Worker: And that's very lonely.

Carol: Yes, but at least I don't have to feel like a fraud. I don't fit in anywhere—not in the white world or the black world. I feel like I live life on the fence.

Worker: Can you talk about the pain?

Carol: Have you ever seen the movie *Splendor in the Grass*? I feel like Dini. She's this pretty girl in a small town. Her parents are extremely strict, and she falls in love with this great-looking guy, has sex, and later has a nervous breakdown. She recovers and then moves away. She becomes really affluent after leaving her small town, but when she returns to find her former lover married with kids, as if nothing has changed; she wonders what she's really left behind, and if she's really happy.

Worker: So you feel as though you are living in two worlds.

Carol: I feel I could be Dini and have a breakdown. Sometimes I feel like I live on the edge. It's so hard to pull myself together.

Worker: Are you wondering whether you'd be happier back home?

Carol: At least I'd feel a sense of belonging.

Worker: It sounds like your present situation at work has brought back feelings you had as a young girl when you were trying to find an identity that felt right for you. And that struggle continues to this day.

(continued)

Case Study   Continued

In this interview, Carol struggles with living on the boundaries of two separate cultures. Rather than betray a part of her identity to live in the dominant culture, she isolates herself from both, which leaves her pained and alone. It is also evident that she has not internalized her success, but rather feels fraudulent in her white world of work. This is a common theme among professional women of color—the more successful they become, the more alienated they may feel from their ethnic and racial communities (Comas-Diaz & Greene, 1994). Having absorbed many of the beliefs of the dominant white culture, Carol appears to be in the early stages (Pre-Encounter/ Conformity) of racial identity development. While there is conflict characteristic of the dissonance stage (Sue & Sue, 2003), she retreats from both cultures rather than suffer the pain of confrontation.

What has been missed in this early stage of counseling is any discussion of the cross-racial helping relationship. The worker appears colorblind, a stance that enables her to avoid heated racial issues. As a white woman, she feels inadequate dealing with issues of racial identity with an African American woman and thereby misses the opportunity for an honest discussion of racial differences.

Powerful countertransference issues prevented the worker from discussing race. There were certain similarities between worker and client—both had crossed class boundaries to achieve success. In fact, Carol's salary was more than double that of the worker, making it difficult for the worker to view Carol as a victim of discrimination and herself as a woman of privilege. Within the framework of the white identity development model, the worker would be in stage one. She doesn't recognize herself as a racial being, and this contributes to her inability to see the differences between herself as a white woman and Carol as a black woman. Her failure to recognize these differences caused the worker to unwittingly replicate, within the therapeutic relationship, the normative unbalanced power relationship that exists between blacks and whites in this society (Greene, 1986).

The Middle Stage of Treatment

As treatment progressed, Carol spoke more openly of her conflicting loyalties and just how wide the gap between her past and present had become. She described how angry she was at her parents for pushing her to enter the white world, yet denigrating her when she assimilated at the expense of her own cultural heritage. The following process recording from the middle stages of treatment illustrates her continued struggle with racial identity development.

Carol: January 15th was Martin Luther King Day and I went to work. A group of colleagues asked me why, and I didn't know how to answer. It made me stop and think. Why did I work? My Jewish colleagues take time off for the Jewish holidays.

Worker: How do you feel about this? What did Martin Luther King Day mean to you?

Carol: I don't know (shifts uncomfortably). I can tell you something else that happened. I belonged to this group of professional black women at my previous job. When I left, I didn't keep up the contact. Recently, I ran into one of the women.

She was angry at me—she said we had to stick together. I felt uncomfortable. I am very busy, yet I did get in touch with a former white colleague recently. So now I feel torn.

Worker: Sounds like you feel a conflict of loyalties.

Carol: Exactly . . . because the more I continue to advance, the wider the racial gap becomes. I go to this upscale university, and my 16-year-old cousin back home has three kids and is still not married. Yet I don't want to work in the ghetto. I realized that if it weren't for Martin Luther King and the struggle of the 1960s, I wouldn't be where I am now—I'd probably be where my cousin is.

Worker: Still others like your cousin have not had success, and you have some mixed feelings about where this leaves you.

Carol (crying): I feel so guilty. It's awful. My parents didn't achieve as much because they didn't have the opportunities, but I just want to live my life. Sometimes I feel that it means forgetting that I'm black. And yet at work, I feel very black.

Worker: Can you talk about your feelings about being black?

Carol: Well, right now it's a burden. Sometimes I'm proud to be black, but many people still think that blacks are inferior. I don't, but then again you have to question why black people have never been able to rise above the slavery issue. It's all mixed up within me. Sometimes I feel that all I've done, I've done for my parents. At other times, however, I feel as though I am leaving them behind.

Worker: Carol, is it difficult for you to talk about these issues with me? I'm wondering if you're concerned about whether a white woman can understand your feelings. Do you feel you might receive more understanding from a black therapist?

Carol (crying): In some ways it is difficult to talk to you but I would like to tell you about my experiences. In all the time I have spent with white people, I feel I have never really been honest about who I am. Sometimes, I don't even know who I am. It's important for me to be honest with you and for you to be able to hear what I have to say. Working with you gives me a chance to practice being a black woman in a white world—but in a real way.

Worker: I can't pretend to fully understand your experiences as a black woman, particularly with regard to the obvious racism you experienced, but I do want to hear about them. I also promise I will do my best to examine my own prejudices as a white woman in our society and hope you'll let me know if you feel that they are reflected in my words to you, or if you feel that I am not hearing you.

In this interview, Carol has moved more solidly into the Dissonance stage of racial identity development by demonstrating a conflict between appreciation and deprecation in her attitude toward her minority culture (Sue & Sue, 2003). However, vestiges of the Pre-Encounter phase (Cross, 1991) are apparent in her negative stereotypical thinking about blacks and her continual strivings toward acceptance by the white culture. The denigration of her own ethnic group is used as a defense against internalized racism (Greene, 1993) and also allows her to feel superior—which enhances her flagging self-esteem. This denigration also engenders guilt, as it further separates her from her family and heritage. The worker is more comfortable raising the issues of racial difference at this stage of treatment, and cross-cultural mutuality (Coll, Cook-Nobles, & Surrey, 1995) seems possible.

(continued)

Case Study   Continued

The worker appears to be in stage two of white identity development wherein her recognition of her whiteness and its effect on understanding the black experience in American society is expanded. In acknowledging that she may not be able to fully understand Carol's experience as a black woman, the worker begins to hear the experiences of racism and discrimination that Carol has endured in the white world. While raising the issue of referral to a black therapist seems appropriate, it also reflects the worker's anxiety about her adequacy in dealing with issues of race.

The worker, somehow feeling caught between "oppression and humanity" (Atkinson et al., 1993), was now in conflict over whether to connect with Carol as a black woman or to retreat back into white culture. Carol's honest response sparked the worker to disclose her fear of not being effective because of their racial differences. This became a turning point in their relationship and opened up the possibility of authentic and mutual exploration of racial issues. As the worker was able to do this, she clearly moved into a white identity that enabled a respectful exchange regarding racial difference.

Conclusion

At the point of termination, Carol had gained acceptance and security living a bicultural existence. She started to visit her family back home more frequently. Cross-racial therapists need to be aware of the importance for black women to stay connected to their families (Boyd-Franklin, 1989) and should not push their clients toward separation and autonomy—a value of our dominant white culture.

Carol joined a professional black women's group and made some important personal connections, building new networks and a support system that became, in time, her extended family. After many years of cross-racial dating, she entered into a relationship with an African American man who shared many of her experiences and values. Together they socialized with business colleagues at their predominantly white corporations and enjoyed increased comfort and social mobility. It is in this stage of Integrative Awareness (Sue & Sue, 2003) that conflict is resolved. Carol, strengthened by her ties to both the black and white communities, felt increased self-esteem and racial pride and found new resources to replace her emptiness and pain. Carol was no longer feeling marginalized—living on the boundaries of two distinct cultures. Rather, the bicultural experience had become a source of empowerment, with resources coming from both cultural contexts. No longer splitting off a part of her identity, Carol finally began to feel whole.

Source: Adapted with permission from Cooper, M., & Lesser, J. (1997, Fall). How race affects the helping process: A case of cross racial therapy. *Clinical Social Work Journal, 25*(3), 323–335.

Summary

Cultural competency is a requisite condition for good clinical practice. The current draft of the Educational Policy and Accreditation Standards (CSWE, 2000) makes the development and application of culturally competent practice one of the defining principles of the social work profession (p. 6). Social workers from all backgrounds need to be trained to understand the value systems of other cultures and to confront their own biases in dealing with clients who are different. The effects of racism are pervasive and insidious in a person's life. An atmosphere of trust and comfort, where sensitive issues can be examined and processed, needs to be created with all clients. When the social worker stretches to understand the client's racial and cultural experiences, he becomes more authentic and truly empathic. It is then that the therapeutic relationship provides the context in which growth may occur.

Learning Assignments

1. Examine your readiness for cross-cultural work. Consider your own cultural background and how it may influence your work as a clinical social worker. Reflect on any messages you may have received about your cultural background from the larger society.

2. Select one of your clients who is from a different culture. Read relevant literature pertaining to your client's culture, especially if you are not familiar with it. Consider the ways in which your client's culture may influence which theory you choose to guide your practice. What aspects of the client's cultural strengths or lifestyle are relevant to your work together? Identify strengths from the client's culture that could be incorporated into the therapy.

3. Working in small groups, examine a process recording for latent content that may pertain to the cross-cultural therapeutic relationship. Can you identify any? If so, describe your understanding of the content and how/whether you would discuss it with the client. If so, why? How will your client's culture affect your working relationship?

4. Imagine a client has just told you he would like to work with someone who is more similar to himself and who could understand him better. How does this make you feel? What would you say to the client? Working in pairs, role-play this situation and then share your responses with the class.

References

Anderson, H., & Goolishian, H. (1992). The client is the expert: A not-knowing approach to therapy. In S. McNamee & K. J. Gergen (Eds.), *Therapy as a social construction* (pp. 25–39). Newbury Park, CA: Sage.

Atkinson, D. R., Thompson, C. E., & Grant, S. K. (1993). A three-dimensional model for counseling racial/ethnic minorities. *The Counseling Psychologist, 21*(2), 257–277.

Bemak, F., Chung, R. C.-Y., & Bornemann, T. (1996). Counseling and psychotherapy with refugees. In P. Pedersen, J. Draguns, W. Lonner, & J. Trumble (Eds.), *Counseling across cultures* (4th ed., pp. 243–265). Thousand Oaks, CA: Sage.

Boyd-Franklin, N. (1989). *Black families in therapy: A multi-systems approach.* New York: Guilford.

Carter, R. T. (1995). *The influence of race and racial identity in psychotherapy.* New York: John Wiley & Sons.

Chung, R. C.-Y., Bemak, F., & Okazaki, S. (1997). Counseling Americans of Southeast Asian descent. In C. C. Lee (ed.), *Multicultural issues in counseling* (2nd ed., pp. 207–231). Alexandria, VA: American Counseling Association.

Coll, C. G., Cook-Nobles, R., & Surrey, J. (1995). Diversity at the core: Implications for relational theory. *Work in Progress, 75.* Wellesley, MA: Wellesley College, The Stone Center.

Comas-Diaz, L., & Greene, B. (1994). *Women of color and mental health.* New York: Guilford.

Congress, E. P. (1994). The use of culturagrams to assess and empower culturally diverse families. *Families in Society, 75*(9), 531–539.

Council on Social Work Education. (2000, September). *Educational policy and accreditation standards.* Draft for public comment.

Cross, W. E., Jr. (1971). The negro to black conversion experience: Toward a psychology of black liberation. *Black World, 20*(9), 13–27.

Cross, W. E., Jr. (1978). The Cross and Thomas models of psychological nigerescence. *Journal of Black Psychology, 5*(1), 13–19.

Cross, W. E., Jr. (1991). *Shades of black: Diversity in African-American identity.* Philadelphia: Temple University Press.

Cross, W. E., Jr. (1995). The psychology of Nigrescence: Revising the Cross model. In J. G. Ponterotto, J. M. Casas, L. A. Suzuki, & C. M. Alexander (Eds.), *Handbook of multicultural counseling* (pp. 93–122). Thousand Oaks, CA: Sage.

Davis, L. E., & Proctor, E. K. (1989). *Race, gender and class.* Englewood Cliffs, NJ: Prentice Hall.

Devore, W., & Schlesinger, E. G. (1996). Ethnic-sensitive social work practice (4th ed.). Boston: Allyn and Bacon.

Greene, B. A. (1986). When the therapist is white and the patient is black: Considerations for psychotherapy in the feminist heterosexual and lesbian communities (pp. 41–65). In D. Howard (Ed.), *The dynamics of feminist therapy.* Haworth Press.

Greene, B. (1993). Psychotherapy with African American women: Integrating feminist and psychodynamic models. *The Journal of Training and Practice in Professional Psychology, 7*(1), 49, 65.

Hall, M. F. (2002). Race, gender, and transference in psychotherapy. In J. Magnavita (Ed.), *Comprehensive handbook of pschotherapy Vol. 1* (pp. 565–587). New York: John Wiley & Sons.

Hardiman, R. (1982). White identity development: A process oriented model for describing the racial consciousness of white Americans. *Dissertation Abstracts International, 43,* 104A. (University Microfilms No. 82-10330).

Harper, K. V., & Lantz, J. (1996). *Cross-cultural practice: Social work with diverse populations.* Chicago: Lyceum Books.

Hayashi, S., Kuno, T., Osawa, M., & Shimizu, M. (1992). The client-centered and person-centered approach in Japan: Historical development, current status, and perspectives. *Journal of Humanistic Psychology, 32*(2), 115–136.

Helms, J. E. (1984). Toward a theoretical model of the effects of race on counseling: A black and white model. *The Counseling Psychologist, 12,* 153–165.

Helms, J., & Cook, D. (1999). *Using race and culture in counseling and psychotherapy.* Boston: Allyn and Bacon.

Hersen, M., Kazdin, A. E., & Bellak, A. S. (1983). *The clinical psychology handbook.* New York: Pergamon Press.

Ivey, A. E., Ivey, M. B., & Simek-Morgan, L. (1997). *Counseling and psychotherapy: A multicultural perspective.* Englewood Cliffs, NJ: Prentice Hall.

Lee, M. Y. (1996). A constructivist approach to clients' help-seeking process: A response to cultural diversity. *Clinical Social Work Journal, 24,* 187–202.

Lesser, J. G., & Eriksen, H. (2000). Brief treatment with a Vietnamese adolescent: Integrating self psychological and constructionist models. *Crisis Intervention, 6*(2), 29–39.

Locke, D. (1992). *Increasing multicultural understanding.* New York: Sage.

Nwachuku, U. T., & Ivey, A. E. (1991). Culture-specific counseling: An alternative training model. *Journal of Counseling and Development, 70,* 106–111.

Parham, T. A., & McDavis, R. J. (1987). Black men and endangered species: Who's really pulling the trigger. *Journal of Counseling and Development, 66,* 24–27.

Pinderhuges, E. (1984). Teaching empathy: Ethnicity, race and power at the cross-cultural interface. *The American Journal of Social Psychiatry, 4*(1), 5–12.

Ponterotto, J. G. (1988). Racial consciousness development among white counselor trainees: A stage model. *Journal of Multicultural Counseling and Development, 16*(4), 146–156.

Ruiz, P. (1995). Assessing, diagnosing, and treating culturally diverse individuals: A Hispanic perspective. *Psychiatric Quarterly, 66,* 329–341.

Sabnani, H., Ponterotto, J., & Borodovsky, L. (1991). White racial identity development and cross-cultural counselor training: A stage model. *The Counseling Psychologist, 19*(1), 76–102.

Smith, E. M. J. (1985). Ethnic minorities: Life stress,

social support and mental health issues. *The Counseling Psychologist, 13,* 537–579.

Sue, D. W. (1990). Culture-specific strategies in counseling: A conceptual framework. *Professional Psychology, Research and Practice, 21*(6), 424–433.

Sue, D. W., Arredondo, P., & McDavis, R. J. (1992). Multicultural counseling competencies and standards: A call to the profession. *Journal of Multicultural Counseling and Development, 20,* 64–88.

Sue, W. S., & Sue, D. (2003). *Counseling the culturally different: Theory and practice* (4th ed.). New York: John Wiley & Sons.

Tatum, B. D. (1993). Racial identity development and relational theory: The case of black women in white communities. *Work in Progress, 63.* Wellesley, MA: Wellesley College, The Stone Center.

Timberlake, E., & Cooke, K. (1984, July). Social work and the Vietnamese refugee. *Social Work, 29,* 109–113.

Tu, W. M. (1985). Selfhood and otherness in Confucian thought. In A. J. Marsella, G. K. DeVos, & F. O. K. Hsu (Eds.), *Culture and self, Asian and western perspective.* New York: Tavistock Publications.

Valdes, M. R. (1983). Psychotherapy with Hispanics, *Psychotherapy in Private Practice, 1*(1) 55–62.

Velasquez, J. M. (1997). Puerto Ricans in the counseling process: The dynamics of ethnicity and its societal context. In C. C. Lee (Ed.), *Multicultural issues in counseling* (2nd ed., pp. 315–330). Alexandria, VA: American Counseling Association.

Walker, M., Miller, J. B. (2001). *Racial Images and Relational Possibilities. Work in Progress* TP 2, Wellesley, MA: Wellesley College, The Stone Center.

White, M. (1991). Deconstruction and therapy. *Dulwich Center Newsletter, (3),* 21–41.

White, M., & Epston, D. (1990). *Narrative means to therapeutic ends.* New York: Norton.

6

Object Relations Theory
A Relational Psychodynamic Model

Object relations theory emerges from Freudian psychoanalytic theory and ego psychology and includes a wide range of contributions from both American and British psychoanalysists. Detailed descriptions can be found in many books on psychoanalytic theory, and the reader should refer to these books to obtain a historical perspective (see, for example, Bacal & Newman, 1990; Greenberg & Mitchell, 1983; & Pine, 1990). This chapter highlights the major contributors from the British object relations school because of its pioneering attempt to connect the intrapsychic and the interpersonal worlds. The concept of internal and external "objects" to social work helps us to understand and treat abused children and adult survivors of childhood abuse.

Object relational theory is dense, and the wording may appear outdated. The theory still clings to the word "object," which is mechanistic and understandably distancing. The word, however, does have historical significance in psychoanalytic psychotherapy. It was coined within the context of Freudian drive theory when the focus was not on relationships but instead on "objects" that satisfied biological needs. Although the term is anachronistic, it is important to remember that early psychoanalytic theorists were pioneers in their time, crafting from numerous clinical encounters an understanding of early childhood interactional experiences that have withstood the test of time, if not of language.

The Work of Melanie Klein

The Internal Object: The Subjective Experience

Melanie Klein is considered to be the first to offer a complete object relations theory. She introduced the concept of the "internal object" (Bacal & Newman, 1990; Klein, 1964; Segal, 1974), which is the subjective experience of the infant based on her interactions with significant external objects in the environment. Klein believed that the infant, from birth, had an elaborate fantasy life, not based on the reality of the environment. These fantasies were destructive and guilt inducing, and because they were not tolerable to the infant, they were projected outward—particularly onto caretakers. With this theory, Klein retained an allegiance to Freudian intrapsychic drive theory, but also created a bridge to a later object relational theory that gave primary importance to the infant's actual experience of the surrounding environment.

Splitting and Projective Identification

Melanie Klein introduced the concepts of splitting and projective identification. Projective identification is motivated by the self's need to be rid of unwanted or dangerous aspects. A part of the self is split off and fantasized as being put into an external object (the other person). This is done to control the object and so prevent it from doing further psychical harm. This process of splitting (keeping apart two contradictory feelings states, such as love and anger) (Goldstein, 1995), then leads to an identification by projection; that is, the object becomes an extension of the self. As a consequence of projective identification, persecutory fears (of the external object) result (through identification with the bad parts of the self). Klein felt that good parts of the self were also projected, motivated by the need to establish the object as good by identifying it with the good aspects of the self. However, projecting either a good or bad part of the self can potentially weaken the ego and lead to an impoverishment of the self.

The Internal Object and Child Abuse

With social work's emphasis on the person in the environment, it would be easy to dismiss Melanie Klein's work—as it is so replete with inner objects and bizarre fantasies. Nonetheless, Klein's theory of the internal object and its subsequent development by other object relational theorists has been of great value, particularly in social work practice with vulnerable client populations. Klein provided insight into how many of our clients' internal experiences of objects from the past can influence, if not dominate, their worlds, distorting current relationships and seriously compromising their self-esteem. We see this most vividly in our work with abused children who are unable to detach from the abusive parent and who often experience even well-meaning caregivers as potentially dangerous. They then engage in behaviors that would seek to confirm a vision of their own inner badness, often leading to rejection by the well-intentioned adult. The concept of the internal object provides a guide in the complex treatment that these children require to overcome their early experiences.

The Internal Object and Internalized Oppression

Melanie Klein's concept of the internal object has been expanded to include wider sociological phenomena. Gainor (1992) applies the concept to the discrimination experienced by black women as members of a minority group in our society. She cites Pheterson (1986, p. 148) in suggesting these women may suffer from an "internalized oppression," which is defined as "the incorporation and acceptance by individuals within an oppressed group of the prejudices against them within the dominant society." These women then experience feelings of self-hatred, an inability to trust those similar to themselves, and a sense of powerlessness in confronting the sources of the oppression.

The Work of Ronald Fairbairn

The Internalized Bad Object: The Environmental Influence

Ronald Fairbairn (1952) was influenced by Melanie Klein's theory of the internal object. However, unlike Klein, Fairbairn regarded internal objects as reflections of real experiences with people, not of fantasies. Fairbairn considered the internal object to be a source of psychopathology. Briefly stated, Fairbairn believed that the child could not allow himself to think of his caretakers as bad, as it would threaten his sense of security. Instead, he takes the bad object into himself. (He internalizes it.) Thus, he protects himself from the reality of an externally bad environment and creates a reality of a tolerable environment. Fairbairn also highlighted the clinical importance of recognizing that the child (and later, the adult) experiences shame through his associated relationship with the bad object. Clinical symptoms are manifestations of the child's attempts to rid himself of internal bad objects without really losing them, because, in the child's mind, bad parents are better than no parents at all. The child manages the conflict associated with separating from the important object (i.e., caretaker) by this process of internalization.

Introjection and Self-Blame

Introjection (another concept introduced by Melanie Klein that is important in understanding abused children) of the bad object leads to self-blame. Self-blame occurs because the confused child needs to have some cognitive control over the abuse. How else could she understand that the person she needs and loves could hurt her? Self-blame is only a temporary coping mechanism, however, because it leads to depression and low self-esteem. The child needs to see that the caregiver is responsible for the abuse, not the child. If the abused child persists in the belief that she is responsible for the abuse, she will not be able to leave the relationship.

Trauma Bonding

Fairbairn's work on the internalized bad object laid the foundation for understanding the concept of trauma bonding in contemporary child abuse treatment.

A trauma bond is the internalized set of expectations and cues that a child develops when an adult intermittently harasses, beats, threatens, or abuses the child (DeYoung & Lowry, 1992; Dutton & Painter, 1981). These bonds allow the child to defend against abusive acts while feeling and remaining safe. These cues motivate the child to behave in ways that are acceptable to the abusive adult. The child thus accommodates to the situation but suffers from anxiety, muted affect, cognitive constrictions, and overcompliance. These behaviors, in addition to the obvious power imbalance inherent in abusive relationships, result in the child's increased feelings of low self-esteem. Paradoxically, the child develops a strong affective bond to the abusive person. Because of the child's obvious need for the relationship, treatment is complicated (James, 1989, 1994). Separation from that person can intensify the bond, increase idealization of the relationship, contribute to the victim's sense of psychological powerlessness, and result in an inability to form another primary relationship. James (1989) cautions that a child–parent relationship must not be evaluated on the basis of connection alone—the connection may be a strong trauma bond and not a secure attachment relationship.

The Work of Harry Guntrip

The Internalized Good Object (*ego devlpmt*)

Harry Guntrip (1969, 1971) elaborated on Fairbairn's ideas and focused on the importance of the object in ego development. He felt the "self" was at the core of the individual and at the center of psychoanalytic theory. This self was thought to grow in the context of meaningful personal relationships. This thinking bridges the gap between object relations theory and self-psychology (see next chapter). It is through the experience of a good object (relationship) that the child discovers herself as a person and ego development proceeds firmly and with self-confidence.

Object Loss and Ego Weakness

When external objects (relationships/the environment) significantly fail to respond to the child's needs, the surviving ego—the essence of the true self—experiences fear and shame and must retreat. This leaves the child unable to have strong feelings for another person, since the presence of that person triggers the wounded child's defenses, resulting in an emotional withdrawal that may include coldness, hostility, and lack of interest. These individuals sometimes fear positive relationships more so than negative ones because there is greater likelihood of feeling smothered or overwhelmed by the good experience, thus losing oneself in the process. Guntrip (1969, p. 288) referred to the way in which persons manage these relationships as the "schizoid compromise." The individual struggles to have a relationship in such a form that it does not involve full emotional connection, by being both in and out of a relationship simultaneously.

The Work of Donald Winnicott

The Internal Object(s) and Interpersonal Relationships

Winnicott (1965), a pediatrician, focused on the mother–child relationship. The mother, in a state of "primary maternal preoccupation" provides a "holding environment" that enables the child's psyche to grow. Her caring functions toward her infant were considered to be the most significant determinants of psychological health. Although Winnicott rendered a heavy burden to mothers in his theoretical formulation of the primacy of the mother as caretaker, he also coined the term "good enough mother" to describe mother as a caretaker with human faults and failings. Mother did not have to be perfect, just "good enough" to recognize and respond to the wide range of the infant's biological, psychological, and social needs while not harming her infant in any way. Winnicott felt that the "true self" of a person (Winnicott, 1965) emerges as a result of this relationship with a "good enough mother" who was able to give the infant a sound start in ego development by providing "ego coverage." Thus, personal object relationships are the starting point of all human life and all subsequent relationships. Like other object relational theorists, Winnicott felt that caretaker functions are internalized by the child and become the building blocks for psychic structure.

The Transitional Object

Winnicott was interested in how children experienced simultaneous separateness from and connection to the outside world. He introduced the concept of the "transitional object," which described how infants and young children use inanimate objects such as blankets, articles of clothing, and stuffed animals, to hold on to images of important others while not in their presence. These objects must retain their original form. If they are washed, or torn pieces are sewn or replaced, they no longer contain their original qualities—those that felt like mother—and the child becomes distressed.

The Interpersonal School

The Significance of the Therapeutic Relationship

Henry Stack Sullivan (1953), writing contemporaneously with the object relational theorists, introduced an interpersonal theory of human development that also emphasized an important theoretical shift from drive theory (Freud, 1905/1953, 1915/1957) to an interactional theory that looked at the relationship between the caretaker and the developing child. Sullivan can be credited as an early theorist in changing the conceptual framework of the therapeutic relationship, making it a more collaborative, interactional process. He felt that the greatest source of knowledge about the patient occurred in the interaction between the therapist and the patient. He introduced the concept of the therapist as a participant observer, working within the context of a "detailed inquiry" (DeLaCour, 1996, p. 208). The detailed inquiry raised questions about the patient's history and current problems. The information obtained would then help the therapist present himself as different from the original primary figure in the patient's life. Sullivan clearly stated that the therapist had a role in the patient's transference distortions and that these were not solely determined by the patient's childhood experiences. He redefined the role of the therapist and reformulated the psychoanalytic concept of anxiety, viewing it not as an intrapsychic process, but as a result of interactions between two people. Sullivan noted that patients avoid certain clinical material in an attempt to preserve self-esteem. The therapist's role is to lessen the patient's anxiety by establishing himself as a respectful, sensitive person.

Object Relations Theory and Brief Treatment

Strupp and Binder (1984) developed a model of time-limited dynamic psychotherapy (TLDP) that is rooted in an object relations framework. Within this model, the focus is on the maladaptive relational problems that a person has learned in the past, maintains in the present, and could potentially reenact in the therapeutic relationship. TLDP uses the relationship between the therapist and the patient to discuss and change the ways in which the patient interacts. Strupp and Binder's "cyclical maladaptive pattern" (CMP) is an organizational framework for understanding the presenting problem, determining treatment goals, and guiding clinical interventions. The CMP is comprised of four categories. The first category, *acts of the self,* includes the thoughts, feelings, motives, perceptions, and behavior of the patient that are interpersonal in nature. The second category, *expectations of others' reactions,* focuses on how the patient imagines others will react in response to his interpersonal behavior. *Acts of others toward the self* is the third category, and it focuses on the actual behaviors of other people as observed and interpreted by the patient. The fourth category is *acts of the self toward the self.* This category includes all of the patient's behaviors or attitudes toward herself. The clinician also considers his own reactions to the patient as they work together. The following case illustrates how object relational, time-limited dynamic psychotherapy was used in a 25-session treatment with an adult survivor of severe physical abuse.

Case Example: Object Relational Therapy
USING THE PRESENT TO TRANSCEND THE PAST

Client Information

Jane is a 29-year-old single white female treated for depression in a community mental health clinic. The client came for help because a recent breakup with her boyfriend triggered memories of severe childhood paternal abuse. As a result, Jane had difficulty

(continued)

Case Example: Object Relational Therapy   Continued

sleeping and could not concentrate at work. Most recently, Jane was very frightened that "someone would break into her apartment and hurt her." She also reported that although she "knows it's not real," she sometimes "feels as though she can hear the loud voice of her father threatening her." When this occurs, she plays loud music to distract herself and "drown out his voice."

History of Presenting Problem

Jane had been involved in a relationship with this recent boyfriend for approximately two years, and they had been living together for the past fifteen months. Jane describes the relationship as a "stormy one." Her boyfriend had been highly critical and demeaning, and on several occasions he had "pushed her around." Jane reported that he told her this happened because "she made him reach that point," and although she objected, she "believed this was true." Jane also described chronic, conflictual relationships with women roommates in which she felt exploited and disrespected. On a number of occasions, her possessions were taken without her permission and her roommate(s) spoke "rudely" to her. These tense living arrangements contributed to her decision to move in with her previous boyfriend although Jane did recognize that he was verbally abusive.

Family and Social History

Jane is the youngest of three children from a working-class Irish American family. Her mother had been hospitalized for psychiatric problems on several occasions. The first hospitalization was for two months and occurred shortly after Jane's birth. Because of her mother's emotional problems, Jane's abusive father became her primary caretaker. Jane reports one vivid memory of being stripped to her waist by her father, beaten with a belt, and hung from her feet. Jane remembers her father waking her up in the middle of the night when he was intoxicated and yelling at her for not doing household chores. Her father's abusive behavior escalated when she was a teenager. It was during this difficult time that Jane began to use drugs and alcohol "just to get away from it all." Jane left home at the age of 20—at which time she stopped abusing substances. She had two relationships with men, and both were abusive.

Case Assessment

Time-limited dynamic psychotherapy based on object relation constructs provides a conceptual framework that helps us to understand the impact of Jane's early childhood trauma on her adult life. Jane's current interpersonal problems were assessed within the context of cyclical maladaptive patterns (CMP).

Acts of the Self

Jane had been involved in a number of conflictual relationships in which she was verbally and/or physically abused. For example, she felt (and had been, on occasion) exploited by female roommates who did not respect her privacy and borrowed her belongings without permission. She described her first relationship with a live-in boyfriend as "okay, he wasn't abusive," but he was not someone she could really talk to. Finally, she became involved with a man who replicated her relationship with her father. She loved him and felt that if she had only behaved differently, he would not have physically hurt her. Jane began to remember the childhood abuse by her father when her boyfriend ended their relationship.

Jane's current relationship with her parents also remains problematic. Jane reported that her mother ignores her needs and does not listen when Jane tries to set limits around their contact. Even now, Jane's mother/parents are unable to put her feelings and needs first, although Jane keeps hoping that "this time would be different." This is the childhood longing to integrate the good/bad object split. However, once again, the parents disappoint Jane and are unable to engage in the type of empathic relationship that would provide a new experience for her.

Expectations of Others' Reactions. The early childhood task of understanding that the same caretaking person may be both gratifying and frustrating was severely compromised for Jane as she had to reconcile the loved object (her father) with his abusive behavior. Additionally, due to her own problems, Jane's mother was emotionally unavailable to her during the important time of infancy and early childhood. In Winnicott's model of psychic development, the capacity to internalize feelings of soothing, pleasure, or comfort in response to the caretaker can be sustained or summoned in the absence of the caregiver with increasing facility as the child matures. Jane, however, was primarily dependent upon an alcoholic, abusive father whom she both feared and needed. It was within this context that Jane developed behaviors that object relational theorists describe as the "building blocks of what will become organized, encoded, experiential, affective, and cognitive data informing one about the nature of human relatedness and what is generally necessary to sustain and maintain emotional connectedness to others" (Levenson & Strupp, 1997, p. 86).

Acts of Others toward the Self. Jane's expectations of others' behavior is based on her past history of childhood abuse and relational style of accommodation to that abuse experience. Jane expects that others will get angry with her if she is unaccommodating. This is illustrated in the process recording in this chapter. In accommodating others, Jane replicates her original relationship with her abusive father, wherein she compromised her own integrity for her father's intermittent affection and/or to avoid cruel punishment.

Acts of the Self toward the Self. Jane has internalized the bad self-object, causing problems in her self-concept and disturbances in her adult interpersonal relationships. Although she is somewhat aware of what she does, or what she does not wish to do, Jane ignores her feelings or thoughts and acts in a manner that is contrary because she experiences her own needs as secondary. Jane's behavior also indicates the absence of a protective presence, or internalized "good enough" caregiver, that foresees possible hazardous consequences of certain behaviors. Jane has developed a relational style based on accommodation to others. Her self-esteem is damaged because she has internalized blame for the abuse and, in so doing, carries the introject of the bad object within.

(continued)

Case Example: Object Relational Therapy   Continued

Goals of Treatment

The two goals of treatment were to give Jane a new understanding of her interpersonal problems and to provide her with a new relational experience (the therapist). The therapist needed to help Jane to cognitively understand what happened in her life and how it contributed to her interpersonal style of relating. She needed to provide a new relational experience for Jane by sharing her understanding of Jane's struggles and by inviting her to talk about what she may be feeling in therapy. Within this new relational dyad, Jane would have the opportunity to develop a different understanding of herself, of the therapist, and of their interaction. Thus Jane's internalized bad object would be replaced with an internalized good object (i.e., the therapist). Through this process, Jane would relive early memories in a safe, supportive presence, mourn the childhood she never had and can never reclaim, and experience mastery over her conflicts.

The therapist who works with survivors of childhood abuse may initially respond more to the client's damaged relational style than to the trauma itself. Therapy would be an affective learning process in which the therapist would try to alter Jane's internalized working model of a relationship by witnessing, with "interpersonal empathy" (Strupp & Binder, 1984, p. 87), what Jane has endured.

Treatment

Working with Jane's Accommodation to Childhood Abuse Experience.   In the beginning phase of treatment with Jane, the therapist focused on trying to help Jane to see the ways in which she accommodated her father's abuse. The following dialog from an early session demonstrates this.

Clinician: How are you doing today, Jane?

Jane: Well, last night I went out to a bar with two other women and all they wanted to do was to pick up guys. I wanted to hang out with them and relax, so the only way I could get through the night was to drink. We met this one guy who was kind of good looking and he was attracted to me. I wasn't really interested, but he was buying all of us drinks and so it became my job to flirt with him so we could drink for free.

Clinician: What happened after that?

Jane: I left the bar with the guy and my friends stayed. I just wanted to go home and go to bed. I didn't want to sleep with him but I knew that if he wanted to sleep with me, then I would. I always feel that if a guy buys me drinks and spends the night talking to me that somehow I owe him. The guy walked me to my car and started kissing and touching me. I didn't want to make him mad, so I let him.

Clinician: It seems as though you were frightened and immediately thought of a way to give him what he wanted even though you didn't feel good about it.

Jane: Right, otherwise, he might get mad and hurt me.

Clinician: It's understandable that you would be afraid under those circumstances.

Working with Jane's Internalized Self-Blame.   The good father, needed for appropriate affection and attention, was kept in Jane's consciousness as long as she assumed responsibility for his abusive behavior. Jane was able to protect herself from the "bad father" who behaved so cruelly by shifting the blame to herself. Her father's erratic behavior was difficult to psychically integrate within Jane's childhood mind, for how does one reconcile feelings of love with those of fear? The therapist focuses on the multifaceted nature of Jane's internalized self-blame in order to help her to give up responsibility for her own abuse. In the following passage, the therapist works with Jane to shift responsibility for her abuse experience from herself to her father.

Jane: At home, when I think I hear my father's voice, I get very scared.
Clinician: What do you do when you get scared?
Jane: I lock all the doors and hide in my closet on the floor.
Clinician: Does that make you feel better?
Jane: Yes.
Clinician: I'm glad it helps you Jane. Did you hide from your father in the closet when you were a little girl?
Jane: (quietly) Yes . . . I hid in the closet for a long time.
Clinician: Tell me about that little girl hiding in the closet.
Jane: I could hear him cursing, yelling, and calling my name. I knew he was drunk and that I had better stay out of his way. I kept trying to figure out what I did wrong. I was getting tired in the closet. I kept trying to figure out when it would be safe to come out. I listened and listened so I could hear if my father stopped yelling—then he was usually nicer to me—maybe he would even be sleeping.
Clinician: You protected yourself very well during those times, Jane—and in the only way a little girl could. But it wasn't right that you had to have such a tough job; you were a child.
Jane: But why did he act that way? I tried really hard not to upset him. . . . Sometimes it worked and he was nice.
Clinician: As a child you felt that your behavior was causing your father to be so angry and hurtful. Many children who are abused feel that way. But it wasn't your fault, Jane. Your father had some serious problems. . . . One of his problems was drinking. It was alcohol, not you, that caused many of his angry moods.
Jane: Sometimes I feel that way and other times I still feel that if I had been a different child, he wouldn't have hurt me so much.
Clinician: You wanted him to love you and not to hurt you. And that's so understandable. He was your father.

Jane hides in the closet and takes on the burden of monitoring her father's behavior. Here, we see Jane assuming responsibility in order to cope with her fears. The therapist works with Jane to help her to understand that this was a survival skill that she needed when she was a child. She then gently but directly addresses the self-blame that Jane has internalized. Here again, the therapist dually focuses on the cognitive and affective levels, providing new information for Jane in a way that is both understanding and respectful of her coping mechanisms. It is noteworthy that Jane describes hiding in a closet in response to current fear. The feelings associated with the

(continued)

Case Example: Object Relational Therapy   Continued

time of the abuse are summoning old coping strategies. Because Jane has not internalized self-soothing, her fears overwhelm her in adulthood. The therapist is presented with the challenge of providing a soothing presence through direct eye contact, softly spoken words, and focused empathy while Jane speaks of potentially shaming matters.

Working to Help Jane to Gain Mastery over Her Abuse Experience.   In the following excerpt from the middle phase of treatment, the therapist makes a clinical error. She moves too quickly in trying to help Jane to gain mastery. The cognitive blame that becomes associated with the internalized bad object causes guilt and emotional paralysis. Jane's internal psychic structure is not mature enough to envision a confrontation with the powerful, internalized bad object.

Clinician: Did you ever tell your father how afraid you were of him?
Jane: No, never. I couldn't do that.
Clinician: Do you think you could pretend in my office to tell your father why you are afraid of him?
Jane: No, I couldn't.
Clinician: I could help you. I would be right here and we could do it together.
Jane: I'm sorry, I can't. . . . I'm too scared.

The therapist is well intentioned in her desire to help Jane gain mastery over her internal terrors; however, she urges Jane to take action beyond her ability. This may not be helpful to someone who carries the abuser within. The introject of self-blame is too powerful. James (1989, p. 22) writes, "this self blame is embedded in the child's cognitive understanding and in his affective, sensory and muscle memory. . . . the cornerstone of treatment is to help the child understand, mind, heart and soul, that it is not his fault." The therapist must address the legacy of self-blame and shame and help Jane to gain mastery. In the following excerpt, the therapist gives Jane some distance from the internalized bad object:

Clinician: Talking about your father is very difficult and very scary. I can see that. Let's try to understand what this is about.
Jane: I feel he's here in the room with us when I talk about him.
Clinician: In what way is he here in the room?
Jane: I don't know—I can feel his presence somehow.
Clinician: Do you ever feel his presence when you aren't talking about him?
Jane: (softly) . . . Yes, lots of times, especially when I'm alone.
Clinician: What happens when you're alone, Jane?
Jane: I remember the things he said and did to me. . . . Why did he do those things?
Clinician: When you ask that question, it makes me wonder if you are once again feeling that you caused his abusive behavior.
Jane: But why else would he do those things?
Clinician: I think he did those things because he had many problems and was drinking heavily. He needed to feel powerful in ways that were very, very wrong, Jane. I know for sure that nothing you did caused your father to be mean to you.

The therapist, acting like a "good enough" surrogate mother, recognizes Jane's fears and offers her a way to talk about them. This will make it less frightening for Jane to relinquish her earlier style of survival by accommodation.

Working with Jane's Abuse Experience. In the next vignette, the therapist focuses directly on Jane's abuse by her father. Only after issues of self-blame have been addressed can Jane work through the trauma of the actual abuse experience.

Clinician: We've talked a lot about the ways you tried to figure and control your father's behavior. We have also worked on ways you could feel less frightened when you remember your father. You now seem able to understand what you couldn't possibly understand as a child—you were not to blame for the things your father did.

Jane: Yes, I can really see that sometimes, and then at other times, I lose it and can't really believe it wasn't my fault.

Clinician: Jane, I think that happens because you get very scared. I'd like to try and talk about that with you.

Jane: I'm getting scared now.

Clinician: Tell me about it.

Jane: Well, I remember how mean and big he was.

Clinician: Yes, he was mean and big—a lot bigger than you. Jane, what would have happened to you as a little girl if you hadn't felt you could control your father's behavior?

Jane: (very softly crying) It's too scary. . . . It was too scary . . . because then he might have really hurt me and he might even have killed me.

Clinician: Yes, and you see now why you couldn't face that as a little girl . . . but you can look at it as an adult because your father doesn't have that same power over you. No one does.

Working with the Therapeutic Relationship

Object relations theory helps us to understand that if the client cannot part with her bad psychic objects because of guilt and fear, the therapist must become the good object whose care helps the client find her own true self. The therapist must be a sufficiently real person to give Jane the chance to rid herself of the internal bad object, freeing her to become a real person. In the following dialog, the therapist talks to Jane about how she is feeling about her—the therapist—and their relationship.

Jane: Before I started therapy, I didn't always feel so afraid of my father.

Clinician: Do you think that something is happening here in therapy that is making you afraid?

Jane: I feel like you are making me talk about things that are too hard for me to discuss.

Clinician: So, in some ways you're feeling that I am not putting your needs first.

Jane: That's right . . . just like everyone else.

Clinician: I can see how you would be feeling that way, Jane. We are talking about painful things and I say this will be helpful but right now it hurts.

Jane: That's right . . . it hurts a lot to talk about the past.

(continued)

Case Example: Object Relational Therapy   Continued

Clinician: You know . . . maybe when we talk about the past and it hurts . . . maybe you get confused about whether I am really helping you—or hurting you—just as you were confused as a child over what kind of a father you had—was he a loving dad or a hurtful one?

Jane: That's right (moves beyond the therapeutic impasse), there were times when he would bring me candy and be really nice to me. And then when he was drinking he got really mean.

Clinician: And so, sometimes it may be hard for you to accept my help, even though you may want to.

Jane: Yes, even though I really want to.

Clinician: I believe that happens, Jane, when you get frightened. Your trust in other people was betrayed a lot when you were a child. It will take a while to rebuild that trust.

Jane forgets that it was her escalating fears of her father that brought her to therapy. Instead, in the moment, she experiences the therapist as causing her this pain of remembering. Fairbairn understood this to happen because the patient does not want to be reminded of the pain experienced with a bad object. He also cautioned that there is shame associated with the internalized bad object. We may also be witnessing the projection of the internalized bad object onto the therapist as Jane attempts to escape its force. The therapist must also consider that Jane's mistrust of her occurs after they have experienced a good relationship, and after Jane has been relieved of some internal self-blame. This is a poignant illustration of the dilemma Jane faces—she fears trusting the therapist as a good object even though she yearns for this connection.

Evaluation of Practice

Time-limited dynamic psychotherapy provided an important framework that enabled Jane to look at her experience of childhood abuse through adult eyes within the context of a nurturing relationship. In so doing, Jane was able to understand that she was not responsible for her father's actions. Jane began to attend Al-Anon meetings where she became further educated about alcoholism and its effects on family members. She was also able to let her parents know that she was attending these meetings in spite of the fact that they continued to deny her father's problem with drinking. Jane had difficult moments in therapy when the pain over what she had endured as a child seemed overwhelming. She was sustained during these times by the supportive presence of the therapist who, with ongoing self-reflection and focus, remained a good object. Jane told the therapist how important it was to her that she never got angry at her. The therapist acted differently from her parents, as she engaged Jane in an examination of her conflicts. Therapy helped Jane to make different types of relational choices. Her posttraumatic symptoms decreased. She started to consider new employment possibilities. Jane now recognized that her boyfriend had been very abusive toward her. She speculated about what a nonabusive relationship would be like and knew that she would like to have one. At the end of treatment, Jane and her therapist both felt that she had made a great deal of progress and could now be optimistic about her future.

Time-limited dynamic psychotherapy, specifically the contribution of the therapeutic relationship to psychotherapy outcome, has been empirically tested. A number of studies were conducted using single case design and the development and application of several scales (the Vanderbilt Psychotherapy Alliance Scale, Gomez-Sanchez, 1978; the Vanderbilt Therapeutic Alliance Scale, Hartley & Strupp, 1983; O'Malley, Suh, & Strupp, 1983; Windholz & Silberschatz, 1988) to explore the process of therapy and the therapist–patient relationship. A consistent finding in all of these studies was that the quality of the therapeutic relationship was an important predictor of treatment outcome. Treatment tended to be successful if the patient felt accepted, liked, and understood by the therapist.

Source: Case material supplied by Jennifer Cass Markens and Connie Crain.

Research Perspectives

Research shows that object relations continue to develop from immature dependency to mature respect and love until adolescence, then continue to grow and change through adult life experiences (Carlson & Kjos, 2002). Most useful research to help us think about families from an object relations point of view is done by Westen (1990). Slade's attachment research (1996) is also important to the object relations perspective.

As clinicians, we can use attachment theory to help us conceptualize assessment and treatment. We use it in assessment to evaluate strengths and weaknesses in the client's capacity for relating and also in our methods of engagement. Attachment theory guides us in treatment as we develop the therapeutic relationship by providing a secure base from which to work. As Scharff (1998) states: "We can view our participation in therapy as a dynamic interplay between the therapist's attachment organization and the patient's. As clinicians, we are objects of attachment and detachment, actively interpreting how the patient, in the transference, uses us to replay interactions of internal objects as they come to light in the transference and counter transference" (Carlson & Kjos, 2002, p. 256).

Summary

In summary, object relations theory has made a significant contribution to clinical social work because it provides a conceptual framework for understanding the development of the ego in early, as well as later, subsequent interpersonal relationships. The patient must experience the therapist as a good object in order to feel secure enough to risk giving up the internalized bad object. Object relations theory provides a looking glass into the internal world of clients like Jane, and in so doing, offers the therapist a way to help these individuals look back at that world in a new way. Once this occurs, a mature relationship becomes more of a possibility for them. As Guntrip (1969, p. 3), eloquently wrote, "they can now embark on two way relations between emotional equals, characterized by mutuality, spontaneity, cooperation, appreciation and the preservation of individuality in partnership . . . the relationship is the same both ways . . . each goes on being and becoming because of what the other is being and becoming, in their personal interaction and mutual knowledge."

Learning Assignments

1. Why is object relations considered a *relational* psychoanalytic theory?

2. What is the focus of time-limited dynamic psychotherapy from an object relations framework?

3. Identify a client with whom object relational time-limited dynamic psychotherapy could be applied. Discuss your rationale for choosing this particular theory. Write a treatment plan for this client.

4. In small groups, discuss the cyclical maladaptive pattern (CPM) schema. Apply these four concepts to your assessment of a client with whom you are working.

5. Working in pairs, (1) role-play an intervention(s) you would make in attempting to help a client gain mastery over an *internalized bad object;* and (2) role-play how you would work with a patient who demonstrates *internalized self-blame.* Demonstrate your work to the class.

References

Bacal, H., & Newman, K. (1990). *Theories of object relations: Bridges to self psychology.* New York: Columbia University Press.

Carlson, J., & Kjos, D. (2002). *Theories and strategies of family therapy.* Boston: Allyn and Bacon.

DeLaCour, E. (1996). The interpersonal school and its influence on current relational theories. In J. Berzoff, L. Melano Flanagan, & P. Hertz, *Inside out and outside in: Psychodynamic clinical theory and practice in contemporary multicultural contexts* (pp. 199–221). Northvale, NJ: Jason Aronson.

DeYoung, M., & Lowry, J. A. (1992). Traumatic bonding: Clinical implications in incest. *Child Welfare, 71,* 165.

Dutton, D., & Painter, S. L. (1981). Traumatic bonding. *Victimology, An International Journal, 6*(1-4), 139–155.

Fairbairn, W. R. D. (1952). *Psychoanalytic studies of the personality.* New York: Basic Books.

Freud, S. (1953). Three essays on the theory of sexuality. In J. Strachey (Ed.), *The standard edition of the complete psychological works of Sigmund Freud* (Vol. 7, pp. 125–245). London: Hogarth Press. (Original work published 1905)

Freud, S. (1957). Instincts and their vicissitudes. In J. Strachey (Ed.), *The standard edition of the complete psychological works of Sigmund Freud* (Vol. 14, pp. 117–140). (Original work published 1915)

Gainor, K. A. (1992). Internalized oppression as a barrier to effective group work with Black women. *The Journal for Specialists in Group Work, 17*(4), 235–242.

Goldstein, E. (1995). *Ego psychology and social work practice* (2nd ed.). New York: The Free Press.

Gomez-Sanchez, B. (1978). Effective ingredients in psychotherapy: Prediction of outcome from process variables. *Journal of Consulting and Clinical Psychology, 46,* 1023–1035.

Greenberg, J., & Mitchell, S. (1983). *Object relations in psychoanalytic theory.* Cambridge, MA: Harvard University Press.

Guntrip, H. (1969). *Schizoid phenomenon, object relations and the self.* New York: International Universities Press.

Guntrip, H. (1971). *Psychoanalytic theory, therapy and the self.* New York: Basic Books.

Hartley, D. E., & Strupp, H. H. (1983). The therapeutic alliance: Its relationship to outcome in brief psychotherapy. In J. Masling (Ed.), *Empirical studies of psychoanalytic theories, 1,* 1–37. Hillsdale, NJ: Analytic Press.

James, B. (1989). *Treating traumatized children.* Boston: Lexington Books/Macmillan.

James, B. (1994). *Handbook for treatment of attachment-trauma problems in children.* New York: The Free Press.

Klein, M. (1964). *Contributions to psychoanalysis, 1921–1945.* New York: McGraw-Hill.

Levenson, H., & Strupp, H. S. (1997). Cyclical maladaptive patterns: Case formulation in time-limited dynamic psychotherapy. In T. D. Eells, *Handbook of psychotherapy case formulation.* New York: Guilford.

O'Malley, S. S., Suh, C. S., & Strupp, H. H. (1983). The Vanderbilt Psychotherapy Process Scale: A report on the scale development and a process-outcome study. *Journal of Consulting and Clinical Psychology, 51,* 581–586.

Pheterson, G. (1986). Alliances between women: Overcoming internalized oppression and internalized domination. *Signs, 12,* 146–160.

Pine, F. (1990). *Drive, ego, object and self: A synthesis for clinical work.* New York: Basic Books.

Scharff, J. S. (1998, May 2). Discussion of Arietta Slade's paper, "Attachment theory and research: Implications for the theory and practice of individual psychotherapy." Conference on the Clinical Implications of Attachment Theory and Research, sponsored by The Center of Adult Development and the International Institute of Object Relations Therapy, Bethesda, MD.

Segal, H. (1974). *Introduction to the work of Melanie Klein.* New York: Basic Books.

Slade, A. (1996). Attachment theory and research: Implications for the theory and practice of individual psychotherapy. Unpublished manuscript. In preparation for J. Cassiday and P. R. Shaver (Eds.) (1999), *Handbook of attachment theory and research.* New York: Guilford.

Strupp, H. H., & Binder, J. L. (1984). *Psychotherapy in a new key: A guide to time-limited dynamic psychotherapy.* New York: Basic Books.

Sullivan, H. S. (1953). *The interpersonal theory of psychiatry.* New York: Norton.

Westen, D. W. (1990). Towards a revised theory of borderline object relations: Contributions of empirical research. *International Journal of Psycho-Analysis, 71,* 661–693.

Windholz, M. J., & Silberschatz, G. (1988). Vanderbilt Psychotherapy Process Scale: A replication with adult outpatients. *Journal of Consulting and Clinical Psychology, 56,* 56–60.

Winnicott, D. W. (1965). *The maturational process and the facilitating environment.* New York: International Universities Press.

7

Self Psychology
A Relational Psychodynamic Model

Self psychological theory is particularly applicable to social work practice because many of our vulnerable client populations have suffered injury to their self-esteem through traumatic life experiences. The worker's conscious use of self in the present to provide empathic and growth-producing new experiences for clients, and a commitment to avoiding the repetition of past injuries that have left clients feeling emotionally injured (Elson, 1986), clearly resonates with social work values. This chapter includes a discussion of self psychology as a relational theory and its application to brief therapy. Case examples illustrate the major principles and techniques.

Self Psychology as a Theoretical Framework

In self psychological theory, developed by Heinz Kohut (1971, 1977), a person's sense of self (and self-esteem) are described as dependent upon the quality of relationships with parental figures who serve as selfobjects. A selfobject is a person who is experienced intrapsychically as providing an enduring sense of availability to the infant, which fosters the developing self. Kohut introduced three specific selfobject relationships as notably important to achieving a healthy self: the mirroring, idealizing, and alter ego selfobject relationships. The mirroring selfobject recognizes the child's unique capabilities and talents. An idealizing selfobject links the child with the admired caretakers. The twinship (also called alter ego or partnering selfobject) experience provides a sense of sameness with the selfobject that is essential to psychic growth, attainment of skills, and sense of competence (Wolf, 1988).

The selfobjects in the young child's life perform the adaptive functions of soothing and tension-regulation (Hilke, 1998). Through a process Kohut called transmuting internalization, the individual is gradually able to perform these psychological functions himself, even in the absence of the original selfobjects. When the child does not have important selfobject experiences, internalization of psychic structures cannot occur. Shame and humiliation result from the helplessness experienced as a result of ongoing selfobject failure (Siegel, 1996). Conflicts arise when the individual fears that his own expression of needs will diminish whatever selfobject experiences are available. The individual, anxious for the support of the selfobject, may falsely comply with the needs of the other at the expense of the development of a true self. A merger bond with the caretaker is created that is actually an accommodation to the needs of the self. Failure to accommodate to this position leaves the individual feeling isolated and depressed with no selfobject support for one's true self (Bacal & Newman, 1990; Siegel, 1996; St. Clair, 2000). This results in early, appropriate narcissistic needs remaining unnourished. The child (and later, the adult) is on a continual search for selfobject experiences that will provide what is lacking. As the self becomes strengthened through selfobject responsiveness (most notably in the therapeutic relationship), it becomes less shameful of these selfobject needs, and more capable of giving without feeling anxiety about the needs of another. Self psychology defines maturity as the ability to evoke and engage in mutually enriching selfobject relationships with others throughout the life span (Wolf, 1988). An emotionally healthy individual has the ability to choose selfobjects based on adult developmental levels, instead of early, narcissistic needs.

Empathy

Kohut felt that healthy psychological development grew out of and was dependent on a basic attunement between the self and its selfobjects. This repeated attunement gradually builds the internal psychic structures that enable the individual to move from early, narcissistic or self-referenced developmental needs to attachments based on empathic connections appropriate to life cycle stages.

In his progressive and hallmark paper, "Introspection, Empathy and Psychoanalysis: An Examination of the Relationship between Mode of Observation and Theory," Kohut (1959) developed an empathic-introspective model of psychological investigation that he considered essential to the psychotherapeutic process. Kohut referred to empathy as "vicarious introspection" and defined it as the ability of the therapist to investigate the inner world of the patient. He considered empathy to be the tool with which the therapist gathers psychological information (Siegel, 1996). In the empathic introspective model, defense and resistance are viewed as normal attempts at self-protection in a person anticipating pain or injury. The therapist assumes there are valid reasons for resisting the therapist or the therapy and tries to find out what the patient fears in life and in the therapeutic relationship. Thus, every aspect of the therapeutic encounter is framed within the context of empathy.

The Role of the Therapist in Self Psychology

Kohut was a pioneer in his time. He didn't subscribe to the Freudian view of the neutrality of the therapist. The classical drive or one-person psychology model addressed transference as arising from forces solely within the patient. The patient's experiences of the therapist were then felt to be distortions based on projections that the therapist interpreted (Bacal & Newman, 1990; Greenberg & Mitchell, 1983). Self psychology shifted this view to a two-person psychology model in which the patient's feelings are viewed as determined by past experiences, current behaviors, and their relationship with the therapist in the present. Kohut (1959) suggested that an exclusive focus on the patient's experience may not always be empathic or helpful and that the therapist needed to share her experience of the patient with the patient.

According to Kohut, patients come to therapy seeking admiration, guidance, and the opportunity to merge with the calmness and competence of an idealized figure through whom their own worth and capability can take form. Through the process of transmuting internalization, the patient gradually gains capacities that were not achieved earlier in life. The major capacities are the ability to self-soothe, self-comfort, and self-empathize. These capacities are initially provided by the therapist. Elson (1986, p. 49) talks about this therapeutic process as the "healing function to be played in the present by the therapist as a new selfobject." Within the environment of the therapy, a compensatory psychic structure emerges in the patient. This new structure enables the person to seek and find more mature self-object relationships in life.

Kohut noted that there would be times when the therapist would not be able to provide all that the patient required in the way of selfobject needs—because perfect empathic attunement was not possible. Kohut felt that no great harm would come to the patient as long as the therapist recognized and acknowledged his mistake and communicated, without judgment or criticism, an understanding of the impact of this empathic failure on the patient (Siegel, 1996). These minor experiences of the therapist's empathic failures, which he called "optimal frustration" actually contribute to the building of intrapsychic structure. The patient learns to tolerate frustration and is helped to develop internal capabilities in much the same way as young children are helped by parents who do not gratify every need. With these new intrapsychic structures in place, the individual can move from the earlier childhood need for idealizing, mirroring, and twinship selfobject experiences to more mature, emotionally healthy relationships throughout life. The individual can also choose emotionally sustaining selfobjects and be able to provide such experiences for others.

Self Psychology and Brief Treatment

Self psychology is quite applicable to brief treatment. Its proponents (see, for example, Seruya, 1997; Balint, Ornstein, & Balint, 1972; Gardner, 1999; Ornstein & Ornstein, 1972; Goldberg, 1973; & Lazarus, 1982, 1988) feel that patients seek treatment because of a loss of selfobject experiences that then weaken the sense of self. The goal of treatment from a self psychological perspective is to enhance the patient's self-esteem and restore him or her to the level of functioning prior to the loss. Through empathic investigation, the therapist provides the mirroring, idealizing, and twinship functions introduced by Kohut (1959, 1971, 1977) that remain central to the development of the self. Understanding the patient's subjective experience enables the therapist to offer the needed selfobject responsiveness, which, in turn, restores self-cohesion and decreases symptomatology. The therapist helps the patient to appreciate the legitimacy of his needs and feelings, promoting awareness, understanding, and self-acceptance. The relationship with the therapist as a selfobject serves as a bridge to reestablishing a supportive selfobject environment outside the treatment arena (Lazarus, 1982, 1988; Gardner, 1999).

Case Example: Brief Treatment of an Individual from a Self Psychological Perspective

This case illustrates how brief treatment based on self psychology helped an aging mother accept her son's gender change. The therapist's nonjudgmental, empathic approach contributed to the mother's ability to appreciate that although her son's outward appearance was not the same, her daughter remained her child.

Client Information

Mrs. W., a 68-year-old white Catholic woman, came to see me in my private office in a small northeastern city after attending a workshop I had given on grieving and loss in the elderly. Mrs. W. was widowed from an alcoholic husband. She had two grown sons, Jonathan and Lawrence. Her eldest, Jonathan, age 35, was undergoing transgender surgery, and Mrs. W. was sad and afraid. She described Jonathan as bright and somewhat shy as a child. She felt he was always different from the other children, although she couldn't exactly comment on how or why. When Jonathan was 14, she began to discover articles of her clothing missing and on occasion found nylon stockings and undergarments hidden in various locations. She said that somehow she "instinctively knew it was him and not his brother Lawrence." When she approached Jonathan, he confided that he felt "drawn to her clothing" and that he "dressed up when he was alone." Mrs. W. told him that his behavior was not "normal" and that he should not continue it or she would tell his father. She never did share this with her husband as she "feared his reaction" and never found additional clothing missing or hidden. She decided to consider what had occurred as only a "stage." Jonathan left home to marry by age 22. He and his wife had two children. Jonathan's marriage ended in divorce after six years. Neither he nor his family have contact with his children. Mrs. W.'s younger son, age 30, has been married for ten years and is the father of three children. Several years following his divorce, Jonathan confided to Mrs. W. and his brother and sister-in-law that he was "terribly unhappy living as a man" and that he was thinking of pursuing sex reassignment surgery. He had been talking about his gender dysphoria with a psychiatrist for a number of years and wanted his family's support and understanding. Although not surprised that he "was inclined to be feminine," Mrs. W. said she suspected he was gay—"something I could accept more easily." She found the idea of her son having surgery to become a female "shocking" and

(continued)

Case Example   **Continued**

became depressed and withdrawn. Neither she nor her other son rejected Jonathan, but they were not able to offer any emotional support to him. Jonathan had the surgery shortly after telling his family and changed his name to Leslie. The first time Mrs. W. saw her new daughter was very difficult for her; she felt that she couldn't call Jonathan "Leslie" and that, although Jonathan was now a woman, he was still her "son." It was during this intense period of confusion, when the relationship with Jonathan had become very strained, that Mrs. W. decided to seek help.

Clinical Assessment

Initially, Mrs. W. expressed feelings of shame, anxiety, and sadness, which had been present since her son had begun "dressing like a woman in public." Because of the stigma associated with transgenderism (Emerson & Rosenfeld, 1996; Herdt, 1994), Mrs. W. felt isolated and unable to confide in her friends and family. She feared their judgment of her family, and she judged herself to be a bad mother. She was also worried about continuing to include Jonathan in family gatherings. She was concerned about the reaction of her three young grandchildren when they learned that their Uncle Jonathan was now their Aunt Leslie. It was clear that Mrs. W.'s own self-esteem was compromised by her son's sex reassignment surgery and that she blamed herself. She talked quite a bit about "whether she should have left his father" because Jonathan felt he "never acted like a real father." She wondered if things would have been different if "his father had taken him fishing or to ball games like other fathers." She thought she had not protected Jonathan enough from his father's verbal abuse and that somehow this had damaged his sense of self-esteem and identity. Mrs. W.'s strong sense of responsibility and shame led her to be secretive about her son's sex change, diminishing her social supports at a time when they were most needed. Mrs. W. was experiencing selfobject failure and loss in her role as a parent. This was heightened because of her previous experience of selfobject failure in her marriage to an alcoholic husband wherein she felt she compromised her self-esteem as a wife. Now she felt inadequate as a parent. It was important for me to provide idealizing, mirroring, and twinship selfobject experiences in the therapeutic encounter in order to restore Mrs. W.'s sense of worth. My goals for treatment were to decrease her depression, enhance self-esteem, help her to grieve the loss of the relationship with her child as she knew him, and enable her to build a new relationship with her child as a daughter.

Treatment from a Self Psychological Framework

Beginning Phase of Treatment.   My initial focus was to provide an accepting and validating place for Mrs. W. to talk about her son and her grief over what had happened—to be the mirroring selfobject that she lacked. This would be the first step in the journey to help Mrs. W. establish a relationship with her new daughter and to re-establish relationships with caring friends and family where possible. I used empathic inquiry to explore Mrs. W.'s thoughts and feelings about transgenderism. I validated Mrs. W.'s feelings of secrecy and shame by acknowledging the stigma and lack of knowledge associated with transgenderism in our society. I mirrored an understanding of Mrs. W.'s feelings that she may be "the cause" while providing reassurance that she was not to blame. Finally, I offered a twinship experience—the human understanding and connectedness so important during this time of shame and emotional isolation—by telling Mrs. W. that I would help her learn more about transgenderism. The following dialog is from our initial meeting:

Therapist: What brings you to counseling at this time?

Mrs. W.: It's really very hard for me to talk about this. I don't even know how to say it.

Therapist: (listening, nodding encouragingly) . . . What's making it so hard to discuss?

Mrs. W.: (sighs) Well, my son had a sex change operation and now he wants me to call him Leslie. I can't bring myself to do it . . . to me he will always be my son, Jonathan. Do you think I'm wrong?

Therapist: I feel sure it isn't a question of right or wrong but more a struggle you're having over what has happened. . . . Let's try together to sort out some of your feelings or concerns.

Mrs. W.: Well, is this somehow my fault? I don't understand what has caused this to happen. He says he always wanted to be a woman and that he couldn't live as a man any longer. . . . Is this normal?

Therapist: It seems as though you don't have a lot of information about what is involved in a person's decision to pursue sex reassignment. I'm not an expert on the topic but I can certainly assure you it is not something that parents cause to happen although I can see how that is worrying you. I can give you some names of organizations to contact for more information. I would even be glad to get the information for you. For now, I'm concerned about the fact that you seem to believe you did something to cause Jonathan's decision to become a female.

Mrs. W.: Well, mothers get blamed for everything and I can't help but feel like it's all a reflection of me and our family.

Therapist: You seem to be ashamed of what your son did . . . again, I think it will be important to learn more about transsexualism. That might help you appreciate the fact that you were not the cause. . . . Would that help with the shame?

Mrs. W.: I don't know . . . maybe a little . . . but I'm so afraid to talk to anyone about this.

Therapist: What is your fear?

Mrs. W.: That people will be disgusted or horrified.

Therapist: Those are powerful feelings and it's understandable that you haven't been able to reach out to anyone with those fears. I'm glad you decided to come in today to get some help even though it was very hard to do. Hopefully, together we can help you with your feelings.

This excerpt demonstrates how I, as a mirroring selfobject, empathize without judgment with Mrs. W.'s feelings as well as provide educational information. I also forge a twinship selfobject experience for Mrs. W. who, at this juncture, feels alone with her shame. I do this by talking in terms of "we" rather than "you" as I present myself as a companion to Mrs. W. on this new journey.

(continued)

Case Example   Continued

Middle Phase of Treatment.   In this challenging phase of treatment, I struggled to keep the primacy of Mrs. W.'s feelings in sharp relief while showing concern for her son and their relationship. I walk a clinical tightrope—at moments I empathically fall short of Mrs. W.'s desire for unconditional support. Mrs. W. clearly needed the opportunity to grieve the loss of her son, Jonathan, while moving toward acceptance of her daughter, Leslie. She refers to Leslie as "my son" or "Jonathan" or "he" when speaking to me. This causes me some discomfort because Mrs. W. shared that Leslie had asked her mother to "forget Jonathan" and to "call her Leslie." Mrs. W. confided that, although she knew that Leslie had suffered before the surgery and really craved acceptance, she felt torn nonetheless. She would call her son "Leslie" when they were together but she could not bring herself to do that with anyone else. Mrs. W.'s ongoing sense of shame and fear of social rejection were primary concerns. Although I initially turned my attention to her son's needs for an accepting parent, self psychological theory helped me to understand that Mrs. W. was not able to be the selfobject her son wanted at this time. I needed to reframe my response and focus once again on Mrs. W. (providing the appropriate mirroring selfobject experience). I let Mrs. W. know I appreciated her feelings and shared my own feeling of "wanting to be respectful of her son's decision as did Mrs. W. but also understanding that Mrs. W. needed help and time to feel comfortable moving forward." In this way, I joined with Mrs. W. in the twinship experience that would help her to build a relationship with Leslie. This is conceptualized as "optimal frustration" (Kohut, 1971, 1977) or "optimal responsiveness" (Bacal, 1985). In optimal frustration/responsiveness, the therapist is empathically attuned enough to provide certain psychological functions but is momentarily unattuned as well. At this point in the treatment, I had to review my own values, particularly as I too have been influenced by a larger society that regards transgenderism as unnatural. I wanted to be sure that my decision to refer to Leslie as a "he" was a self psychological intervention to help Mrs. W. in her initial stage of grieving and not a collusion with society's devaluation of transgenderism.

Mrs. W.:   I think what makes this all so difficult is the reaction that you get from other people.

Therapist: What are your concerns?

Mrs. W.:   Well, they wouldn't understand. They might laugh, feel sorry for me, or wonder what kind of a family we have.

Therapist: In many ways, you are right to be concerned. Transsexualism is not very well understood and people get uncomfortable with what they don't understand. What would someone's laughing or not understanding mean to you?

Mrs. W.:   (crying) It would hurt because he is still my son and I raised him the best way that I could. I also feel sorry for him because he hasn't had an easy life.

Therapist: You seem to really appreciate some of the difficulties your son has faced and what may have contributed to his decision to have the surgery. Have you shared these feelings with him?

Mrs. W.:   Not really . . . it's just all been so hard for me and I'm afraid I might also say the wrong things.

Therapist: Well, you have a lot of feelings but a good place to start may be to let your son know that you are trying to understand him and his life better.

Mrs. W.:   But I still worry about the other people. . . . If I told someone and they laughed it would just about kill me.

Therapist: What would be a helpful response from people if you were to share this with them?

Mrs. W.:   I guess just to listen and be supportive without judging him, our family, or me.

Therapist: That makes a lot of sense to me. When you've sorted out your own feelings enough to take a risk sharing with others, it may make you feel less burdened. Right now, you are carrying a "secret" that keeps you in isolation.

Mrs. W.:   Do you think I should be telling people?

Therapist: When you are ready I think it may be helpful to no longer feel you need to keep this a secret. But again, we need to be realistic about who you should initially share with and what kinds of reactions people may have.

Mrs. W.:   I did get the information we spoke about. I guess I myself never realized this type of thing existed . . . it makes me feel as though it's not only my son or my family.

End Phase of Treatment.   With my encouragement, Mrs. W. moved from her initial period of adjustment and showed an increased willingness to refer to Jonathan as "Leslie." She was also very anxious that Leslie be accepted by the family and took a leadership role by providing information to her son and his wife about transgenderism. With my assistance, she told them what to tell her grandchildren. Mrs. W. was no longer concerned about Jonathan's sex change as a reflection of her parenting. She was even able to confide in one of her sisters about Leslie. At this turning point Mrs. W. had taken a chance, reached for a selfobject outside the therapeutic relationship, and found support. Mrs. W. gave information on transgenderism to her sister, offering herself as a selfobject much as I had provided this experience for her. She decided not to share with other family members whom she felt would be critical and hurtful. This was another sign of enhanced self-esteem as Mrs. W. made selfobject choices that were appropriate for her at the time.

Mrs. W.:   Well, we all got together at my other son's house last week and this was the first time Jonathan . . . Leslie . . . came over.

Therapist: How did things go?

Mrs. W.:   It was okay . . . it seemed strange at first partially because to me he still sounds like Jonathan. And I could see the older children were confused and uncomfortable; the little girl was totally loving because she doesn't really know what is happening; she was hugging and kissing Jonathan. He was great with her too.

Therapist: Perhaps we can all learn from how your youngest granddaughter was dealing with the situation, by simply relating to the person around her. This little girl actually may help pave the way for others in your family.

Mrs. W.:   I hope so because it would kill my son . . . I mean, my daughter . . . if the kids didn't want anything to do with her. I guess we all have to try hard or we'll fall apart as a family over this.

Therapist: I don't think you are going to fall apart. We'll continue to work together with other members of the family to make sure that doesn't happen.

(continued)

Case Example **Continued**

In this final exchange, I again used the language of twinship to provide a merger selfobject that helped support Mrs. W. as she wondered if her family would ever reunite.

Evaluation of Practice

According to self psychological theory, the essence of cure resides in the patient's ability to identify and seek out appropriate selfobjects in her surroundings and to be emotionally sustained by them. Like its theoretical predecessor, object relations theory, self psychology places the therapeutic relationship at the center of treatment. Therapy provides the corrective emotional experience of being understood in an empathic manner and nontraumatically frustrated in a way that promotes a solid sense of self-identity and self-esteem. Kohut felt that the internal world can and should only be studied through the instrument of the therapist's empathy. In other words, the therapist uses empathy to collect data, immerse himself in the patient's experience, and reflect upon the meaning of that experience (Siegel, 1996). Treatment conducted from a self psychological perspective may therefore lend itself to heuristic research and qualitative methodology, where the question of validity is one of meaning. In such studies the researcher shares her understanding of the participants' experiences with them and seeks their verification. In self psychology, the therapist must be able to understand the patient's subjective experience, share that understanding with the patient, and be willing to listen and change therapeutic directions if the patient does not feel his experience is fully appreciated. Kohut wrote: "If there is one thing I have learned during my life as an analyst, it is the lesson that what my patients tell me is likely to be true—that many times when I believed that I was right and my patients were wrong, it turned out, though often only after a prolonged search, that my rightness was superficial whereas their rightness was profound" (Kohut, 1984, p. 94, cited in Siegel, 1996).

Although I did not conduct a formal research study, several important outcomes of Mrs. W.'s treatment were evident. Mrs. W. learned that transgenderism is misunderstood and devalued in our society and that it is not something that a parent can cause. She was able to tell her sister about her son's operation and then introduce her to her niece Leslie. Mrs. W. began to call Jonathan "Leslie," and facilitated her daughter's acceptance by her brother, sister-in-law, and their children. Mrs. W. was involved in a number of senior groups where she was able to be selective regarding whom she could tell about her daughter and whom it might be best not to tell. This reflected Mrs. W.'s increasing ability to choose appropriate selfobjects that could continue to emotionally sustain her. Finally, at the end of therapy, Mrs. W. was able to empathize with Leslie's experience rather than remain focused solely on her own feelings. In this regard, Mrs. W., after having empathic selfobject experiences with myself and others, was able to be an empathic selfobject for her daughter.

Source: Adapted by permission from Lesser, J.G. (1999). When your son becomes your daughter: A mother's adjustment to a transgender child. *Families in Society: The Journal of Contemporary Human Services, 80*(2), 182–189.

Group Example: Brief Psychotherapy with Women

I have used the group modality and brief treatment from a self psychological perspective in treating a number of women with self-esteem problems. This evolved from my experiencing these women as having a paucity of appropriate selfobject relationships in their lives. The following clinical case example describes a twelve-week group devoted to women in abusive heterosexual relationships.

The Group

This group was composed of eight women ranging in age from 25 to 45 who came from similar socioeconomic and educational backgrounds. Each of the group members had previously been in individual treatment with me because of past and present involvement in abusive relationships. The group goal was to provide an opportunity for women who shared similar problems to work together toward change. The group met on a weekly basis for one and one-half hours for twelve consecutive weeks.

Stages of Group Development and Role of the Therapist

Beginning Stage.   The two major themes that emerged in the beginning stage were trust and shame (Hartling, Rosen, Walker, & Jordan, 2000). The women were understandably concerned with whether they would be accepted by other members of the group. I took an active role at this early stage by addressing and diminishing the group members' anticipation that they would be shamed. "I appreciate everyone's taking a big chance with the unknown and coming here today. I know it wasn't easy. Beginnings can be hard and meeting new people isn't always easy. Now that we all know each other's names, I'd like to ask each of you to try to share any particular concerns you had joining the group. . . . You may find you share some common worries."

The member's responses reflected their feelings of shame and vulnerability:

"I felt very afraid because I was never in a group and I wasn't sure if my problems were real enough."

"I was worried that someone I knew might be here and that would be embarrassing for both of us."

"I was anxious . . . worrying about what I would say and whether I would sound stupid."

"I thought people would probably be here but I worried about whether they could help me."

"I was afraid of what would happen. . . . What if someone got really upset and I couldn't help, or if I got really upset and no one could help me."

I validated the women's feelings and reframed them as self-protective responses.

I then suggested other ways the women could experience themselves and each other:

"It occurs to me that each of you is really talking about the way in which you tried to prepare yourself to enter the group—maybe how to be ready to protect yourself from hurt just in case others didn't understand your feelings." I also introduced the idea that their feelings of fear and shame might also come up in our group.

"Let's talk about how we can help if we think someone is ashamed to talk about a problem in group or worried about what others might say or think. Hopefully, we'll

(continued)

Group Example   Continued

be able to feel comfortable enough to talk about those fears so that you can be help-ful to each other. . . . My job is to try to help you with that." In this way, I established a safe and empathic selfobject environment where the women were able to feel un-derstood by each other. I engaged the members in making connections with new self-objects in the group.

Middle Stage of Group.   In sessions four through nine I focused on helping the members to remain attuned to each other's affective states and continued to validate experiences that might be different from their own. I also helped them to recognize each other's uniqueness, thereby beginning the process of restoring damaged self-esteem. The women became sensitized to potential shame in other members and began to assume the role I had modeled in the initial stage of the group. An example of this occurred when one member responded to an apology by another who felt un-able to leave an abusive male partner:

"Sue, you don't have to apologize for staying with your boyfriend. . . . No one here is judging you. . . . We understand how scary it is to be alone."

One woman consistently provided counsel to others in the group and spoke of her problems as being "in the past." Another woman confronted her by saying, "Why are you in this group if everything in your life is all better now?" The first woman be-came defensive and angry. She said, "If you don't want me here, I'll leave." Before I could intervene, another group member said, "Maybe Jane is ashamed to talk about her problems even here in the group. . . . I still feel that way sometimes." At this, Jane told the group that her boyfriend had been drinking and was verbally abusive to her again. She was ashamed to tell this to the group because she had said in an earlier meeting that she would leave him if he drank again. "I feel like everyone else here is changing but I'm stuck. . . . I'm always stuck. . . . My family says they weren't sur-prised and never expected me to leave." At this point, I addressed the issue of shame again: "We need to help each other in whatever way possible and be mindful of how shame continues to make us feel badly about ourselves. . . . Let's agree right now to challenge shame to leave the group . . . the rest of us can stay."

Using the language of twinship (Elson, 1986; Kohut, 1971, 1977), I provided the context for a common human bond. This was especially important because talking about shame can itself be a shaming experience. I reminded members of the time frame, encouraged them to review what had taken place thus far, and restated goals for the remaining sessions: "We are at the midpoint in our group meetings. Let's take some time to check in and see where everyone is at." I also raised the possibility that members may feel like leaving the group before the actual termination date particu-larly as concerns around separation and loss were raised: "There may be moments when people feel like it would be easier to just not come back. The reason I say this is because endings can be hard."

End Stage of Group.   During sessions nine through twelve I helped the women identify ways to transfer their learning from the group experience to their daily lives: "I'm interested in having us share ways in which members of this group will continue to get support when the group ends. You've all experienced support here and you now know what it feels like and what to look for. . . . That's the first step to finding it."

The members talked about what they would need to look for in relationships and what they needed to avoid:

"I need someone who lets me talk without telling me I don't know what I'm saying."

"I know I'm not crazy now and I want someone to respect me. I need someone who can listen instead of talk."

"I'll never be involved with someone who only wants to control me. That's definitely over."

"I won't take any verbal abuse; it hurts too much; I want a man who talks to me like I'm worth something."

We used role-plays to practice directly expressing feelings, and setting limits on inappropriate behaviors. I actively facilitated these behaviors by playing the abusive partner:

"Right now, I will be your boyfriend. . . . Can you try to tell me exactly how you are feeling?"

As the women become more relaxed with this exercise, I suggested they try to play different roles for each other. The women agreed that they would like to have something in writing when the group ended so they could periodically review the important points they were practicing. I supported this group decision and talked about it as a way "you will be holding onto the group experience concretely as a reminder when you are feeling shaky inside." During this end phase of group, fear and grief were prominent themes. I was concerned about possible retraumatization of earlier injuries to the self due to the withdrawal of the selfobject(s) of the group as the women began to talk about past losses and relationships that left them feeling depleted and rejected. They expressed some anger toward me as they were experiencing the termination of the group as a rejection. They also expressed fears that the end of the group would mean the end of psychosocial support:

"I have had so much loss in my life and this group is really important to me. I feel angry that the group can't just continue. . . . I'm not sure I understand why it can't."

"I feel sad, too, but I also have to say that this time it's different. I feel sad—but not like I'm a terrible person or that I did something wrong. That's the way I usually feel when a relationship ends . . . like it was my fault."

"And this time we're saying it's not our fault (laughing. . . actually maybe we can blame Joan for this one."

"When something upsetting happened during the week, I didn't get as anxious because I knew I was going to come here and tell people about it and they would listen and help me. I wasn't alone."

I made a decision at this time to address the veiled feelings of anger and disappointment behind the termination statements. I gave the women the important message that I have heard their feelings, and in so doing, continued to provide an important selfobject experience: "I think it may be important to talk about some possible disappointment that I am not continuing the group . . . maybe even some anger about that."

(continued)

Group Example   **Continued**

In the twelfth and final session of the group, I gave each member the chance to talk about what the group had contributed to her life:

"This is our last meeting . . . a time for ending but also for new beginnings. How has the group helped with those new beginnings?"

"I will always remember the kindness, especially when I couldn't be kind to myself. . . . I won't let people put me down like I used to."

"I'm not the only one who makes mistakes. . . . I don't have to always feel lousy about everything I do and say."

"I learned that I deserve to have people in my life who really like me and want me to do well."

A followup meeting was scheduled for the next month. Excerpts from this group illustrate some of the confidence the women gained from their experience and some of the struggles they had yet to overcome:

"It is so good to see everyone again. I really missed all of you . . . but I have to say I also feel pretty good about my life right now. My family has backed off—basically because I told them I wasn't going to be treated badly any more."

"My boyfriend tells me that I have changed and I'm not so timid anymore . . . in the beginning I wasn't sure he liked this but now we actually seem to be getting along better."

"I'm still afraid to meet someone or get involved in a relationship . . . that will be the real test of whether I have made any changes."

"Whenever I felt myself slipping into old patterns, I thought of this group and remembered what it was like to really be understood and accepted. I really want that in my life."

The inner strength that members had gained from the group experience sustained them. Confidence replaced shame and doubt.

Countertransference

I was challenged during this group as I struggled to provide an appropriate selfobject environment where the members felt validated by me and each other. I sought consultation from peers who were able to be validating selfobjects for me during these times. I felt relieved when, during the middle stage of the group, the women began to listen and respond to each other in ways similar to how they had initially experienced me. During the termination phase, when the women wanted to continue meeting, I felt guilty. I wondered about the time limit I had imposed and whether this was sound practice or a capitulation to a managed care environment. I realized I was experiencing what Seruya (1997, p. 88) describes as "the loss of the therapy as a selfobject experience that may have provided mastery, growth and professional stability." I shared my feelings with the women: "I'd like to let you know how much you have all helped me in my work as a therapist. You taught me something new about the courage it takes to change and about how capable people are of making their lives better with some help and support. I will take this experience I have had with you to my work with other women. In this way, I will always remember each of you and the special journey we took together. Thank you for giving me the chance to work and to grow along with you."

Source: Adapted from Lesser (2000).

Summary

Heinz Kohut (1959) pioneered the term "empathy" as a clinical concept and an important component of the healing process in psychotherapy. Empathy, in self psychological theory, is more than the therapist feeling for the patient—it is listening in such a way that the therapist hears the patient's story and is able to communicate her understanding of that story and its impact on the patient's life. Kohut saw the therapist's empathy as the scientific tool of psychotherapy. "Empathy is the means by which the psychological observer gathers information about the inner world of human experience. . . . If one wishes to know how to act toward another, one needs to put oneself in the other's shoes" (Siegel, 1996, p. 187). Being understood by another person (the therapist) gives the patient the affirmation so vital for establishing other meaningful relationships. Elson (1986, p. 3) aptly sums this up by saying, "The practitioner has only one tool and that tool is herself." This statement underscores the primacy of the therapeutic relationship in clinical social work practice from a self psychological perspective.

Learning Assignments

1. Write down a brief summary of your understanding of self psychology. Include the concepts of empathy, mirroring, idealizing, and alter ego relationship as well as the role of the therapist as a selfobject.

2. Working in small groups, choose a client. Write a process record of a session in which you attempted to use self psychological theory. Discuss how well you integrated the theory with your practice. Using the feedback from the group, revise the process record, considering interventions that would better integrate the theory with your practice.

3. Do a preplanning exercise for a group you may be developing. Consider the needs of the clients with whom you will be working and whether self psychology would be an appropriate theory to guide your group practice. If so, what would the purpose of the group be? How would you structure the group? What would be your role—as leader? Working with a group of seven or eight students, role-play the first meeting in which you discuss the purpose with the group members and facilitate their introductions and engagement, using the self psychology model.

References

Bacal, H. (1985). Optimal responsiveness and the therapeutic process. In A. Goldberg, (Ed.) *Process in self psychology* (pp. 202–226). New York: Guilford.

Bacal, H., & Newman, K. (1990). *Theories of object relations: Bridges to self psychology.* New York: Columbia University Press.

Balint, M., Ornstein, P. H., & Balint, E. (1972). *Focal psychotherapy: An example of applied psychoanalysis.* London: Tavistock.

Elson, M. (1986). *Self psychology in clinical social work.* New York: Norton.

Emerson, S., & Rosenfeld, C. (1996). Stages of adjustment in family members of transgender individuals. *Journal of Family Psychotherapy, 7*(3), 1–12.

Gardner, J. R. (1999). Using self psychology in brief psychotherapy. *Psychoanalytic Social Work, 6*(3/4), 43–85.

Goldberg, (1973). A psychotherapy of narcissistic injuries. *Archives of General Psychiatry, 28,* 722–726.

Greenberg, J., & Mitchell, S. (1983). *Object relations in psychoanalytic theory.* Cambridge, MA: Harvard University Press.

Hartling, L., Rosen, W., Walker, M., & Jordan, J. (2000). *Shame and humiliation: From isolation to relational transformation.* Work in Progress (88). Wellesley, MA: Stone Center Working Paper Series.

Herdt, G. (1994). *Third sex, third gender: Beyond sexual dimorphism in culture and history.* New York: Zone Books.

Hilke, I. (1998). The playing through of selfobject transferences of a nine-year-old boy. In A. Goldberg (Ed.), *Progress in Self Psychology, 14,* 71–84.

Kohut, H. (1959/1978). Introspection, empathy and psychoanalysis: An examination of the relationship between mode of observation and theory. In P. Ornstein (Ed.), *The search for the self* (Vol. 1, pp. 205–232). New York: International Universities Press.

Kohut, H. (1971). *The analysis of the self.* New York: International Universities Press.

Kohut, H. (1977). *The restoration of the self.* New York: International Universities Press.

Kohut, H. (1978). Introspection, empathy and psychoanalysis: An examination of the relationship between mode of observation and theory. In P. Ornstein (Ed.), *The search for the self* (Vol. 1, pp. 205–232). New York: International Universities Press. (Original work published 1959)

Kohut, H. (1984). *How does analysis cure?* Chicago and London: University of Chicago Press.

Lazarus, L. (1982). Brief psychotherapy of narcissistic disturbances. *Psychotherapy: Theory, Research and Practice, 19*(2), 228–236.

Lazarus, L. (1988). Self psychology: Its application to brief psychotherapy with the elderly. *Journal of Geriatric Psychiatry, 21,* 109–125.

Lesser, J. G. (2000, July). The group as selfobject: Brief psychotherapy with women. *International Journal of Group Psychotherapy, 50*(5), 363–380.

Ornstein, P. H., & Ornstein, A. (1972). Focal psychotherapy: Its potential impact on psychotherapeutic practice in medicine. *Journal of Psychiatry in Medicine, 3,* 11–325.

Seruya, B. (1997). *Empathic brief psychotherapy.* Northvale, NJ: Jason Aronson.

Siegel, A. (1996). *Heinz Kohut and the psychology of the self.* London and New York: Routledge.

St. Clair, M. (2000). *Object relations and self psychology* (3rd ed.). Pacific Grove, CA: Brooks/Cole.

Wolf, E. S. (1988). *Treating the self: Elements of clinical self psychology.* New York: Guilford.

8

The Psychology of Women

In this chapter we will discuss three major contributors to the theory of women's development—Nancy Chodorow, Carol Gilligan, and the scholars from the Stone Center at Wellesley University. The work of this last group of women, known as the self-in-relation theory, will be presented in some detail, and dialog from a women's group will help to illustrate the theoretical constructs.

Historical Perspective

Traditional western psychological theories of development have stressed separation, individuation, and autonomy as key. Jordan (1997b) speaks of the American cultural imperative to wean the helpless and dependent infant to greater self-sufficiency. She notes the derivative psychoanalytic theories (see, for example, Mahler, Pine, & Bergman, 1975) that view the individual as growing from an undifferentiated stage, then embedding in a symbiotic phase, and ultimately entering a separate individuated state. In Erikson's schema of ego identity (1963), autonomy is established before intimacy, once identity is consolidated. An increasing capacity to use abstract logic and a movement toward self-sufficiency have also been characteristic of Western developmental theories.

A psychoanalytic sociologist, Chodorow (1978), re-examined object relations theory and found that it failed to acknowledge the importance of the early and longer-lasting bond between the girl and her mother—a bond that leads to a different experience of identity than what the boy experiences with his mother. She emphasized that the early years, with the relationship with mother as the primary caretaker, form the core of the self. Chodorow noted that mothers don't experience female infants as separate in the same way as a son, as daughters are extensions of themselves. Girls continue to have ongoing preoccupation with relationships and are prepared to reproduce mothering. Boys are an opposite, allowing them to be more differentiated. Boys are prepared for the world of work and the nonrelational sphere. Women produce men with nurturing needs repressed and curtailed and daughters with mothering capacities. This prepares us for our social roles. Chodorow theorized that it is these social roles and patriarchal norms that are internalized and that they are perpetuated and repeated in the next generation.

Influenced by Freud (1955), Chodorow acknowledged the theory of the Oedipus complex, and the concept of penis envy. However, she believed that the penis was envied because it is associated with independence and freedom to separate—a freedom that girls did not have. Thus, girls emerged from the oedipal period with a less differentiated sense of self and ego boundaries than boys, but, because of their identification with mother, they had more of a basis of empathy. Boys, she wrote, repress the oedipal conflict and also repress their strong tie to mother because she is powerful and omnipotent in infancy. The love is too overwhelming and threatening to the ego, and the mother/son love arouses jealousy in the father.

Adolescence is more difficult for girls than for boys, as girls are more entangled in family relationships. Mothers tend to feel ambivalent about their daughter's separation, making it hard for girls to break away. Daughters, being more attached, handle their mothers' ambivalence by being very critical of their mothers, alternating between dependence and rejection. The father contributes to this by feminizing his daughter and encouraging traits like passivity and dependence on men. Chodorow believed that the way to change this highly entrenched system was by having both mother and father parent, so that their child would internalize both roles as nurturing, and grow to become a nurturer regardless of his or her sex.

Gilligan (1982) derived her ideas about female development from her awareness that existing theories of moral development (Kohlberg, 1984) did not apply to women, and, in fact, were used in such a way as to make women appear defective. She noted that women's moral development had a separate trajectory than that of males, who, according to Kohlberg, were at a higher level than females because they made moral decisions according to rational thought, internalized ethical principles, and by what was right. Gilligan noted that women tended to view morality in terms of personal situations instead of societal situations and that they often had trouble moving from a very personalized interpretation of morality to a focus on law and order. Their moral development is often based on their personal interest and commitment to the good of others close to them. Goodness, kindness, and self-sacrifice are emphasized.

In Gilligan's research she found that women tend to view morality in terms of selfishness and responsibility, as an obligation to exercise care and avoid hurt. People who care for each other are the most responsible, whereas those who hurt someone else are selfish and immoral. While men think in terms of justice and fairness, women think more about specific people. Gilligan noted that women were seen as lacking in moral development only when compared with data gathered on all-male samples collected by Kohlberg. In examining the female experience of morality, she demonstrated how much it is organized around issues of responsibility for other people within the context of investment in relationships. In the same way, current developmental theory has stressed the process of separation and individuation, and the achievement of independence and autonomy as the hallmarks of maturity. This model, however, seems more applicable to male than female development in our culture, and, in point of fact, the emphasis on separation has had negative influences on men; most specifically as it affects men's ability to develop their relational styles. When we apply the model to women, they are seen as relatively immature and dependent, since the model overlooks the power and significance of human relationships for women and ignores important differences in the developmental paths followed by men and women (Stiver, 1991).

Self-in-Relation Theory

The Stone Center writings (see, for example, Jordan, Kaplan, Miller, Stiver, & Surrey, 1991, 1998; Miller, 2002, 2003; Eldridge, Surrey, Rosen, & Miller, 2003) present a feminist psychodynamic model of female developmental theory known as the self-in-relation. This model challenges earlier separation–individuation in favor of a perspective that stresses relationship differentiation. They, as Chodorow and Gilligan before them, note that female infants do not separate but, instead, develop a self-in-relation to others (Miller, 1987). Within this theoretical framework, problems in development occur, not because of a failure to separate, but due to difficulties women have in remaining relationally connected while trying to assert a differentiated sense of self (Enns, 1991). Self-in-relation theory suggests that women are oppressed by the patriarchal social structure—where their relational bonds are devalued and labeled as dependent.

Mutual Empathy

Self-in-relation theory postulates that a girl's most basic sense of self is formed in identification with her primary caretaker. Through the process of mutual identification, she learns to be the mother (i.e., caretaker of others). Relational maturity involves moving from this original dyadic relationship to more varied patterns of relational development. Jordan (1991) and Jordan, Surrey, and Kaplan (1983), writing specifically on the development of empathy in women, introduce the mother-daughter dyad as the prototype for understanding the origins of the capacity for developing empathy. This model sees the self as organized and developed through practice in relationships where the goal is increasing development of mutually empathic relationships. The emphasis is on women's desire to understand the other in relationships, as well as their desire to be understood by them. This is a reframing of the concept of empathy from its introduction in self psychological theory (Kohut, 1959/1978, 1971, 1977) where empathy was unidirectional (i.e., from caretaker to child). Empathy is now a mutual, interactive process and is the basis for creating and being in a growth-enhancing relationship. This key relational concept of mutual empathy appears extensively in the Stone Center writings (see, for example, Jordan, 1991, 1993, 1994, 1997a; Kaplan, 1986; Jordan, Surrey, & Kaplan, 1983; Miller & Stiver, 1995; Stiver, 1991, 1992; Surrey, 1991,

1997). Mutual empathy suggests a way of being present or joining together in which each person is emotionally available, attentive, and responsive to the other(s) in the relationship (Surrey, Kaplan, & Jordan, 1990).

Self-in-relation theory also addresses the quality of empathy in those who seek the help of therapists, emphasizing that while it is important to be understood (i.e., that the patient feels understood by the therapist), it is also important to understand others (i.e., that through the experience of being understood something changes in the patient and she is able to understand both herself and others). The movement toward mutuality in a relationship is central to healing and empowerment. Self-in-relation theorists regard the capacity to participate in the creation of a mutual and empowering relationship with another person to be vital to the development of self-esteem in women. Individuals often create self-effacing identities when they do not have the possibility of mutual engagement with their primary caretakers and family members. Once one begins to feel unworthy, it becomes more difficult to move toward other kinds of relationships; the original relational image becomes internalized in a way that remains oppressive and disempowering.

Relationship Authenticity

Another important theoretical construct that follows from mutual empathy is that of relationship authenticity, defined by Surrey (1991, 1997) as the ongoing challenge to feel emotionally real, connected, vital, clear, and purposeful in a relationship. It describes the ongoing and mutual need in a relationship to be seen and recognized for who one really is. Relationship authenticity, like mutual empathy, refers to a process, rather than a static state. A relationship, of necessity, must change to meet the growth of each person within it (Rosen, 1997). In dealing with a sense of lack of personal authenticity, people mention striving to speak the truth or to find their voice. Carol Gilligan's book, *In a Different Voice,* brings this into clear focus (1982). Being able to say what you see, think, feel, and need is of the utmost importance. Both the voice as reality and the voice as metaphor are to be taken seriously. Voice, like the notion of real self, rather than being something that emerges fully formed from within, is contextual. Thus, the audience to whom we speak greatly affects the way we speak and the content of what we say (Jordan, 1997a, p. 142). In real dialog both speaker and listener create a liveliness together and come into a truth together. Dialog involves both initiative and responsiveness—two active and receptive individuals.

Relationship Differentiation

The third important concept of self-in-relation theory is relationship-differentiation (Jordan, 1997a). This is a process of increasing levels of complexity and choice within the context of human relationships. Self-in-relation theory facilitates a process of growth within a relationship where the individuals involved are challenged to maintain connection with each other. Connection, rather than separation, becomes the core feature of human development. It is not through separation but through this expanded relational experience that individual development occurs. This ability to change in a relationship depends on the capacity and the willingness of each person to change and grow. The word *relationship* in this context is defined intersubjectively (i.e., the ongoing, intrinsic inner awareness and responsiveness to the continuous existence of the other or others and the expectation of mutuality in this regard (Jordan, 1997a, p. 61). Identity and relationship develop congruently within the context of self-in-relation theory and move from one of caretaking to one of caring and empowering. This involves development with both external relationships and with the inner sense of relationship. This latter is the internalized sense of empathy that women develop toward themselves and others.

Self-Empathy

Self-empathy requires a new way of relating in which one's internalized self representations must undergo a change so that the empathy women bring to their relationships with others may also be directed toward the self. Women have difficulties developing self-empathy. The reasons for this include the strong pull of empathy for the other; the social conditioning of females to attend to others first; and the subsequent guilt around giving attention to themselves. This contributes to the difficulties some women have in separating from destructive relationships. In other words, whatever the expense to herself, it becomes difficult for a woman to hurt another person. She cannot tolerate separating from the person because it becomes equated with abandoning the other, and women often feel responsible for the other person's feelings (Jordan, Surrey, & Kaplan, 1983). The goal of self-in-relation therapy is to help people understand and experience their relational images differently and, consequently, open up the possibilities of engagement in new types of relationships. The process of therapy and actual engagement in a relationship with a therapist promotes the building of a mutually empathic bond. Within this bond, the patient is helped to give up those internalized relational images that have left her feeling disconnected and in pain (Miller & Stiver, 1995). Empowering the empathy of another person facilitates the development of self-empathy as the individual is joined in a process of empathic witnessing and acceptance, with a resulting decrease of harsh self judgments (Surrey, Kaplan, & Jordan, 1990, p. 13).

The Therapeutic Relationship

Empathy in therapy is essential for the patient's emotional growth and development. It is a quality that is learned within the context of the therapeutic relationship that further develops over the course of time as new relational experiences are internalized. In fact, the growth of mutuality and enlarged connection in the therapy relationship are at the core of self-in-relation theory and practice. Mutu-

ality evolves from empathy, relationship authenticity, and relationship differentiation, and involves openness to change and healing on both sides. Therapy requires mutual trust, respect, and growth. While the therapist exercises certain
kinds of authority and the client moves into a place of vulnerability, the attitude
is one of empowerment rather than one of having power over (Jordan, 1997b, p.
143). The therapy relationship should never include an attitude of superiority;
both members of the interaction must be open to influence by the other and willing to risk the change and uncertainty that accompanies growth.

Some clinicians have expressed concern about the meaning of mutuality in
therapy. Surrey (1997) clarifies that it does not mean disclosing anything and
everything with no sense of purpose, impact, timing, or responsivity. An ethic of
mutuality does not mandate disclosing facts or answering questions. Decisions
about disclosure depend on the situation and the personal and relational aspects
of the therapy at any given time. Jordan (1991), writing on the important connection between empathy and self-boundaries, notes,

> Empathy always involves surrendering to feelings and active cognitive structur-
> ing; in order for empathy to occur, self boundaries must be flexible . . . this in-
> volves temporary identification with the other's state during which one is aware
> that the source of the affect is in the other. In the final resolution period the af-
> fect subsides and one's self feels more separate; therapeutically, the final step in-
> volves making use of this experience to help the patient understand his/her inner
> world better. (p. 3)

It seems important in discussing a feminist model of practice to consider
whether the gender of the therapist is significant in the treatment dyad. Kaplan
(1984, p. 3) cautions that "female therapists working with women bring to their
role some sense of their core self . . . as a relational being, and also some internalized experience of being in a subordinate position . . . male therapists bring to
their role some sense of a core self as a separate, autonomous being, and an internalized experience of being in a dominant position." Although we feel that it may
be important for some women to work with female therapists, we also think the
opportunity to have an authentic and empathic therapeutic relationship with a
man could be very healing. The challenge for men would be to avoid the possibility that they might empathize not with the patient, but with the man she may be
talking about, particularly if the male therapist feels identified with him (Kaplan,
1984).

Traditional emphasis in the field has been on the neutrality of the therapist
and the negative impact of therapist involvement. The relational psychoanalytic
models of psychotherapy moved away from the neutrality construct (see Chapters
6 and 7 on object relations and on self psychology for further discussion), high-
lighting the interpersonal and intersubjective nature of the therapeutic relationship. Self-in-relation theorists reframe these concepts as relational reciprocity.
Surrey suggests it is more likely that therapist abuse comes from a lack of authenticity, openness, and responsiveness, and defines this as *relational abuse*. Jordan
and colleagues (Jordan, Miller, Jordan, Kaplan, Stiver, & Surrey, 1990) discussed

the negative impact of emotional neutrality and nonresponsiveness in therapy with sexually abused patients and incest survivors. Writing on the development of transference, Stiver (1997) notes that a lack of neutrality does not seem to ward it off. Historically, we are taught that the therapist's neutrality and nongratification of the client are supposed to facilitate the negative transference, allowing for the release of angry feelings toward significant early figures (mostly mothers) and their projection onto the therapist. However, Stiver (1997, p. 38) makes an excellent point that "These angry outbursts toward the therapist may be more an artifact of this therapy model itself, rather than an expression of negative transference." The therapist's withholding and nongratifiying stance and the consequent lack of responsiveness may be enormously frustrating and alienating for the client, who responds with anger, despair, and other negative reactions.

Self-in-Relation Theory and Women's Groups

Several authors promote groups as the context within which to focus on their unique experiences as women (Bernardez, 1978; Fedele & Harrington, 1990; Goodman & Allan, 1995; McWilliams & Stein, 1987). Due to the frequent devaluation of women's need for connection to others in the larger society, groups provide an important place for women to validate each other's development. Women feel disconnected when they are in relationships that are not responsive to their needs or when they feel they have no impact. This contributes to low self-esteem. Groups provide comradery. Women in groups can experience themselves having an effect on each other's lives, and that is empowering. From a relational perspective, power emerges from and enhances connection (Fedele & Harrington, 1990). In groups, women can also develop awareness of the cultural standards of their gender group and can support each other in challenging these norms.

Schiller (1995) stresses the importance of connection for a woman's sense of self and the ways in which this need influences how women approach conflict. She offers a stage model particular to women's groups based on self-in-relation theory. Stage one of the relational model, preaffiliation is fairly typical of other group therapy models. Stage two, establishing a relational base with peers, is in contrast to moving into a phase of power and control more common in groups. This is a time when the women discover shared experiences and seek approval and connection from the members and the group leader. This sense of connectedness to others in the group is what contributes to a sense of safety. Safety is a prerequisite for women to be able to share with each other. Stage three, mutuality and interpersonal empathy, is an extension of stage two, when the women are able to develop trust as they share and begin to respect differences. The role of the therapist is crucial at this juncture as she remains focused on the relational context within which the sharing takes place. The therapist does this by helping the women find ways to understand each other even when they may differ. Jordan (1991), refers to this as a type of empathic attunement marked by intimacy and mutual intersubjectivity. Stage four, challenge and change, is when the women more directly begin to question themselves, each other, and the leader. They are able to risk the direct expression of anger and disappointment because they feel secure in the connections that have been established. Stage five, termination, is in keeping with standard practice of endings with groups.

Group Example: Women's Support Group—New Connections

Introduction

Self-in-relation theory was used as a framework for an eight-week group for white, heterosexual women in their fifties and sixties who came from working-class backgrounds. They were raised in traditional female gender roles to be caretakers of husbands, children, and aging family members. Most had not worked until after their children were grown and then found employment in factory and service jobs. Their husbands, the primary breadwinners, were skilled and unskilled blue collar workers. The women had been referred by their primary care physicians after frequent visits and various somatic symptoms.

Self-in-relation theory posits four elements that contribute to depression in women, each of which was quite evident during the individual screening interviews I conducted: experience of loss, inhibition of anger, inhibition of assertion, and low self-esteem (Kaplan, 1986). The women were disappointed in their relationships with significant people in their lives, most notably husbands or adult children. They were unable to express their anger and disappointment because they felt the relational bond would then be broken. They consequently doubted their own relational worth and were left feeling ineffectual in their roles as wives and mothers. The absence of intimacy was experienced as a failure of the self as well as failure of love from another. I felt that a group would provide a chance for these women to see that they were not alone in their experiences. Through sharing personal and family histories, they might begin to understand how they had decided that taking care of themselves meant that they were selfish. The group would hopefully provide a safe place to begin to talk about how they would feel about being in a role other than that of caregiver.

Role of the Therapist

Enns (1991), writing on the importance of social intimacy to identity development, suggests that the experience of connecting with a counselor and with other women may be the most important corrective experience for women who have not had the chance to take part in mutually affirming relationships. Fedele (1994) highlights three essential relational paradoxes that the therapist needs to work with in women's groups in order to facilitate this process. I will discuss and illustrate how I worked with these paradoxes with this group of women.

The *first paradox* is the ongoing dialectic between the desire for gratifying connections and the need to maintain strategies to stay out of connection for fear that one's feelings will not be understood. This was most evident in the first stage of the group, as illustrated in dialog from the initial meeting.

Seven women agreed to participate in the group, and they all attended the first meeting. I greeted them in the waiting room, where I immediately noticed that each woman sat alone, either reading a magazine or staring straight ahead. I said:

"Hello everyone . . . . I think you're all here for the women's group. . . . Why don't we go inside and get acquainted?"

The women acknowledged me but continued to avoid looking at each other. As they filed past, I extended my hand and personally greeted each one in a similar manner: "Hello, Anne, I'm glad you're here, nice to see you tonight, June . . ."

I felt this meeting was very important because if the women felt connected and safe, they would look forward to returning. I introduced myself as the group leader, saying:

"I've had the opportunity to meet each of you. I'm very happy we are all here tonight. I put this group together as a place for women to have a chance to talk about their lives, their concerns, and their relationships with important people in their lives. I decided to do this because it is sometimes difficult for women to talk about their disappointments in people they care about—either to the individuals themselves or to other people. Sometimes women have trouble letting others know they are angry. Instead, women tend to blame themselves and keep their feelings inside. But this can lead to sadness, poor health, and lots of other problems. I hope this group can be a place where each of you will feel comfortable sharing your feelings and finding your voices over the next eight weeks. Now, I'd like to ask each of you to introduce yourself. Please tell us your name, something about your life, and what made you decide to come to this group. Let's begin on my right and go around in a circle—remember it may feel a little uncomfortable at first but it will get easier."

I gave a rather long introduction to the group before asking the women to speak. This set the tone for the group, establishing the common relational ground that will enable the women to feel safe sharing. And so it begins with June:

"I feel a little foolish being here because my life is supposed to be going well right now . . . I just retired. I was always able to handle things in the past. I adopted and raised three children. My husband had a drinking problem . . . I was always able to handle things but now I'm falling apart . . . I'm depressed and anxious all the time. Everyone is sick of listening to me. I need a place to talk."

I look directly at June and say, "Well you came to the right place." Then, I look at each of the women in the room and ask, "Isn't that right, ladies?" For the first time, the women smile and begin to look at each other.

Debra says, "You sure did . . . let me tell you what happened to me. After thirty-five years of marriage, my husband decides to leave me for another woman—a young one, of course. He cheated on me all our married life, and I always took him back . . . I thought that was what I was supposed to do . . . but this time when he wanted to come back, I said no and I got a divorce. I know I did the right thing but I feel lousy."

Silence. I interject, "Well, maybe some of these other women will help you figure that out, Debra. I'm glad you decided to come to the group. Let's hear from Mary . . ."

Mary shares that her husband won't support her in trying to set some limits with an adult daughter who recently returned home to live, without a job and with a young child. Lucy is afraid to even speak to her husband of twenty-five years because

(continued)

she wants to avoid confrontation at all costs, despite the fact that he leaves her alone most of the time. She is perhaps the most traditional of the women, raised in a very religious home to believe that the man is the head of the household. Abby married late in life and is taking care of an aging parent with dementia. Her brother does not help, and she suffers from caregiver stress. Donna has been married for twenty years and simply says, "My husband won't talk to me; whenever I try to tell him something he just rolls his eyes and walks away." And Anne is married to a man who abuses alcohol on a daily basis. She continues to cook his meals and take his verbal abuse when he is intoxicated because she doesn't know what else to do or where else to go.

As I listened to the women tell their stories, I considered the ways in which they would be able to connect with each other. I saw so clearly how much they wanted to belong and to be understood. I could also see how frightened they were of being judged. I said, "What really strikes me as I listen to each of you is how much you have in common—maybe we can talk more about that. I'll begin by saying that it's clear how very hard each of you has tried to take care of so many people and situations in your lives. A couple of the women smile. Two of them start to tear and there is silence in the room. This time, however, it feels like a silence of connection, not disconnection, because I have struck a cord that resonates with the caretaker role each knows so very well. And so, the tone is set for validation of the women's experiences, development of self-empathy, and mutuality—three of the four most curative factors in women's groups. The fourth factor, empowerment to act in relationships, will hopefully come at a later stage of the group (Fedele & Harrington, 1990).

The *second paradox* is between similarity and diversity. This takes place in the middle phase of group, during stages two and three of Schiller's model. The women have discovered shared experiences and have made a connection with peers.

I continue to focus on creating a safe context so that there will be mutuality and shared empathy. If the women feel connected, they will be able to develop trust. This is illustrated by the following dialog from the fifth group meeting:

Mary is crying and talking about how disappointed she is in her daughter, who returned home for the second time with her 7-year-old child. "She doesn't respect me at all. She comes and goes as she pleases and even though she sees how hard I work, she doesn't pay any rent or give money for food. She wants me to babysit and if I don't, she takes my granddaughter with her. I don't like that either because I don't know who her friends are or where she is going."

June responds tentatively, "I know what you're going through. I had a lot of problems with my daughter; she got involved with drugs. . . . I hate to say this but maybe your daughter is taking drugs."

Mary quickly interjects, "No, I don't think she's taking drugs."

June replies, "It was hard for me to accept and maybe your daughter isn't . . . I hope not . . . but whatever . . . I finally just got tough and said she couldn't live at home any more. . . . It was the hardest thing I ever did."

Mary: (crying softly) "I don't know if I can do that. . . . How did you find the strength?"

I feel somewhat anxious during this exchange because Mary and June are sharing different experiences and expressing different emotions. I am worried about whether they can talk about their differences and remain connected. As I grapple with this, I realize that I am moving away from the group process and experiencing what Miller and Stiver (1995) suggest are the therapist's own paradoxical struggles for connection and disconnection that emerge throughout the group's development. As a woman, I also have found it difficult at times to remember I can express difference and remain connected to others. And so I say, "You know, there are ways in which your situations with your children differ but what's so important is that you share in your struggles as mothers—not always knowing what to do and feeling the pain and loneliness this brings. I can see that June hears Mary's pain and is trying to find a way to help her. And Mary may not do things exactly as June did, but she now knows that she is not alone in her disappointment and may find comfort in knowing that another mother found a way out that was right for her. Can anyone else share any moments of difficulty as mothers to their adult children?"

The *final paradox*, conflict in connection, involves the ways in which the leader sets the tone for group members to discuss feelings of anger without judgment. In this way, the group provides the opportunity for the women to experience disconnection within a context of connection, making reconnection a possibility. In the following excerpt from the sixth group meeting, the therapist identifies the strong emotions being expressed in a calm, accepting, and nonjudgmental manner—modeling authenticity and connection in the midst of tension.

Lucy is the quietest member of the group. For the first three meetings, she only said that she was married and had three grown children. When the other women spoke, she tentatively asked questions or tried to make supportive comments. Now, she tells her story:

"I don't know what to do any more. . . . My husband doesn't listen to me at all. . . . Our house has been under construction for about five years because he won't finish the work, and he won't let me get anyone else to do it either. I can't have anyone over, even my children don't want to come over any more."

Debra, recently divorced after a long marriage, immediately says, "I don't think you should take that. Why do you stay with him? You need to leave."

Abby says, "Maybe if you show him you're not going to take it any more, he'll get the message."

Lucy says, looking somewhat shaken, "I can't get divorced. . . . He's my husband. . . . Besides, where would I go? I don't have any money of my own."

I say, "Some of you are angry at what Lucy is going through with her husband . . . and that's okay, as women we should be angry when we see other women getting hurt."

Carol, married to an alcoholic, takes Lucy's hand, and says, "I know how you feel, Lucy, because I feel the same way. . . . I feel too old and afraid to start over . . . at least I know what I've got with Joe."

Abby responds, "I didn't mean to sound harsh; it's just that after a while you have to take some action."

I say, "I can see this is a tough subject and brings up strong emotions. Let's try to understand what this is about. . . . Lucy is expressing some feelings of help-

(continued)

Group Example   Continued

lessness in her life. Have any of you ever felt you were helpless to change a situation?"

Debra (who had initially been quite angry when confronting Lucy) was the first to speak: "I felt helpless for years but finally I had had enough . . . . I took abuse for a long time . . . it was hard for me to get a divorce. . . . I was raised to believe that marriage was forever. . . . A long time ago I even went to a priest and told him what my husband was doing and he said I should pray but marriage was forever. I know they don't talk that way now, but I went through hell. I don't think you have to stay (crying now). I just don't want to see you or anyone else go through what I did for such a long time. I had to get tough. . . . I have to be tough or I'll fall apart."

June says, "I know what you mean; my husband drank for twenty years. When I look back I don't know how I took it—but I had three children. . . . Today women don't take these kind of things . . . but Lucy is from our generation."

Donna says, "My husband isn't abusive and I know he loves me in his own way, but he doesn't listen to me. I also wouldn't leave. We've been together a long time. . . . We raised children together. But he didn't cheat on me. . . . I can understand why Debra left, but I can also understand why Lucy stays."

Throughout the remaining sessions the women began to grow in connection to one another. Termination took place after eight weeks, as was our contract, although no one, including me, really wanted the group to end. And so we agreed to continue to meet in the same format once a month for the next four months, to provide further relational development and support. At the point that I left the group, most of the women had become empowered to act on their own without my leadership. Abby had instituted respite care for her aging mother and told her brother that he had to share in the responsibilities of caregiving. Mary had confronted her daughter about the need to get a job, adding that she might have to leave the household if she did not comply. Anne had started to attend Al-Anon to get additional help with her marriage to an alcoholic husband. June began volunteering at a local library, which brought new connections into her life to replace those relationships she had lost through retirement. And Lucy, the most traditional and timid of the group, began to assert herself with her husband, and he, in turn, started to listen.

At the last meeting, the women decided to meet on their own every few months for continued validation and support. They get together at restaurants, or meet at each others' homes. Recent feedback from some of the women in the group revealed that this continued social intimacy has not only provided connection, but has also been instrumental in furthering the development of their personal identities.

Summary

Self-in-relation theory revolutionized traditional western models of psychotherapy that view the notion of separation and individuation as the hallmarks of emotional stability. Daring to consider that males and females may be different—psychologically as well as physically—feminist theory conceptualizes women's need for relational connection—a need that often brings them into mental health offices. This model embraces vulnerability and reduces shame and isolation associated with a notion of failed autonomy (Jordan, 2003). Self-in-relation theory introduces the important concepts of "mutual empathy" and "self-empathy" and emphasizes that it is vital to the well-being of women that they are understood, able to understand others, and able to understand themselves. In feminist theory, the experience of being understood by the therapist allows the patient to grow in her understanding of others, as well as of herself. It is the movement toward mutuality in a relationship—relationship authenticity—that self-in-relation theorists consider to be the hallmark of health.

Learning Assignments

1. Working in groups, develop a group for battered women. Discuss why you would choose self-in-relation theory as a conceptual framework for organizing and leading this group.

2. How would you orient and prepare a potential group member for this group? Role-play a screening interview in which you discuss the purpose of the group within a self-in-relation model.

3. What would be your role as the leader of this group in the beginning, middle, and end phases?

4. Role-play a group session in the beginning, middle, or end phase of the group that demonstrates how you use self-in-relation theory to facilitate group dialog.

References

Bernardez, T. (1978). Women's groups: A feminist perspective on the treatment of women. In H. H. Grayson & C. Loew (Eds.), *Changing approaches in psychotherapies.* New York: Spectrum.

Chodorow, N. (1978). *The reproduction of mothering: Psychoanalysis and the sociology of gender.* Berkeley: University of California Press.

Eldridge, R., Surrey, J., Rosen, W., & Miller, J. B. (2003). What changes in therapy? Who changes? *Work in Progress.* Wellesley, MA: Stone Center Working Paper Series.

Enns, C. Z. (1991). The "new" relationship models of women's identity: A review and critique for counselors. *Journal of Counseling & Development, 69,* 209–216.

Erikson, E. (1963). *Childhood and society* (2nd ed.). New York: Norton.

Fedele, N. (1994). Relationships in groups: Connection, resonance, and paradox. *Work in Progress, 60.* Wellesley, MA: Stone Center Working Paper Series.

Fedele, N., & Harrington, E. (1990). Women's groups: How connections heal. *Work in Progress, 47.* Wellesley, MA: Stone Center Working Paper Series.

Freud, S. (1955). Beyond the pleasure principle. In J. Strachey (Ed. & Trans.), *The standard edition* of the complete psychological works of Sigmund Freud (Vol. 18, pp. 3–64). London: Hogarth Press. (Original work published 1920)

Gilligan, C. (1982). *In a different voice.* Cambridge, MA: Harvard University Press.

Goodman, M. S., & Fallon, B. C. (1995). *Pattern changing for abused women: An education program.* Thousand Oaks, CA: Sage.

Jordan, J. V. (1991). Empathy, mutuality and therapeutic change: Clinical implications of a relational model. In J. V. Jordan, A. G. Kaplan, J. B. Miller, I. P. Stiver, & J. L. Surrey, *Women's growth in connection, Writings from the Stone Center* (pp. 283–290). New York: Guilford.

Jordan, J. V. (1993). Challenges to connection. *Work in Progress, 60.* Wellesley, MA: Stone Center Working Paper Series.

Jordan, J. V. (1994) A relational perspective on self esteem. *Work in Progress, 70.* Wellesley, MA: Stone Center Working Paper Series.

Jordan, J. V. (Ed.). (1997a). Relational development: Therapeutic implications of empathy and shame. *Women's growth in diversity.* New York: Guilford.

Jordan, J. V. (Ed.). (1997b). A relational perspective for understanding women's development. *Women's growth in diversity.* New York: Guilford.

Jordan, J. V. (2003). Valuing vulnerability: New definitions of connection. *Work in Progress, 102.* Wellesley, MA: Stone Center Working Paper Series.

Jordan, J. V., Kaplan, A. G., Miller, J. B., Stiver, I. P., & Surrey, J. L. (1991). *Women's growth in connection, Writings from the Stone Center.* New York: Guilford.

Jordan, J. V., Miller, J. B., Jordan, J. V., Kaplan, A. K., Stiver, I. P., & Surrey, J. L. (1990, December 6). Wellesley, MA: Stone Center Colloquium.

Jordan, J. V., Surrey, J., & Kaplan, A. (1983). Women and empathy. *Work in Progress, 2.* Wellesley, MA: Stone Center Working Paper Series.

Kaplan, A. G. (1984). Female or male psychotherapists for women: New formulations. *Work in Progress, 5.* Wellesley, MA: Stone Center Working Paper Series.

Kaplan, A. G. (1986). The "self-in-relation": Implications for depression in women. *Psychotherapy: Theory, Research and Practice, 23,* 234–242.

Kohlberg, L. (1984). *The psychology of moral development: The nature and validity of moral stages.* San Francisco, CA: Harper and Row.

Kohut, H. (1971). *Analysis of the self.* New York: International Universities Press.

Kohut, H. (1977). *The restoration of the self.* New York: International Universities Press.

Kohut, H. (1978). Introspection, empathy and psychoanalysis: An examination of the relationship between mode of observation and theory. In P. Ornstein (Ed.), *The search for the self* (Vol. 1, pp. 205–232). New York: International Universities Press. (Original work published 1959)

Mahler, M. S., Pine, F., & Bergman, A. (1975). *The psychological birth of the human infant: Symbiosis and individuation.* New York: Basic Books.

McWilliams, N., & Stein, J. (1987). Women's groups led by women: The management of devaluing transferences. *International Journal of Group Psychotherapy, 37*(2), 139–162.

Miller, J. B. (2002). How change happens: Controlling images, mutuality, and power. *Work in Progress, 96.* Wellesley, MA: Stone Center Working Paper Series.

Miller, J. B. (2003). Telling the truth about power. *Work in Progress.* Wellesley, MA: Stone Center Working Paper Series.

Miller, J. B., & Stiver, I. (1995). Relational images and their meanings in psychotherapy. *Work in Progress, 74.* Wellesley, MA: Stone Center Working Paper Series.

Miller, J. G. (1987). *Toward a new psychology of women* (2nd ed.). Boston: Beacon Press.

Rosen, W. (1997). On the integration of sexuality: Lesbians and their mothers. In J. V. Jordan, A. G. Kaplan, J. B. Miller, I. P. Stiver, & J. L. Surrey, *Women's growth in connection, Writings from the Stone Center.* New York: Guilford.

Schiller, I. Y. (1995). Stages of development in women's groups: A relational model. In R. Kurland & K. Salmon (Eds.), *Group work practice in a troubled society.* New York: Haworth.

Stiver, I. (1991).The meaning of care: Reframing treatment models. In J. V. Jordan, A. G. Kaplan, J. B. Miller, I. P. Stiver, & J. L. Surrey, *Women's growth in connection, Writings from the Stone Center* (pp. 250–267). New York: Guilford.

Stiver, I. (1992). A relational approach to therapeutic impasses. *Work in Progress, 58.* Wellesley, MA: Stone Center Working Paper Series.

Stiver, I. (1997). Some misconceptions and reconceptions of a relational approach. In J. Jordan (Ed.), *Women's growth in diversity.* New York: Guilford.

Surrey, J. (1991). The 'self-in-relation:' A theory of women's development. In J. V. Jordan, A. G. Kaplan, J. B. Miller, I. P. Stiver, & J. L. Surrey, *Women's growth in connection, Writings from the Stone Center* (pp. 51–67). New York: Guilford.

Surrey, J. L. (1997). What do you mean by mutuality in therapy? In J. V. Jordan, A. G. Kaplan, J. B. Miller, I. P. Stiver, & J. L. Surrey, *Women's growth in connection, Writings from the Stone Center.* New York: Guilford.

Surrey, J., Kaplan, A., & Jordan, J. (1990). Empathy revisited. *Work in Progress, 40.* Wellesley, MA: Stone Center Working Paper Series.

9

11/17/05

Cognitive Theory

A Structural Approach

History and Definition

Cognitive theory began in 1911 when Alfred Adler (1964), who worked closely with Sigmund Freud in Vienna, came to disagree with Freud's structural theory and the concept of conflict between the id and the superego. Adler viewed the personality more as a unified whole, which later became known as the "holistic" approach. Adler concluded that it was inaccurate perceptions, and not underlying unconscious processes, that resulted in a person's inappropriate behavior. Adler's ideas were accepted in Europe and the United States, but for almost twenty years after his death in 1937 there was little interest, as Freudian thought reigned supreme in Western analytic circles. Today, when practice is frequently dominated by brief treatment modalities, there is a renewed interest in cognitive therapy.

Cognitive theory is based on the concept that there is a reciprocal interaction between what we think, how we feel, and how we behave. Our thoughts determine our feelings, which then determine our behavior. Cognitive theorists deal with current realities, not unconscious conflicts. Dreams are not what Freud termed the "royal road to the unconscious," but instead, dreams are viewed as reflections of situations or problems we fail to master in our waking existence (Werner, cited in Turner, 1986). Cognitive practitioners work to change the clients' conscious thought processes so that their perceptions are more accurately grounded in reality. It is a skills-based therapy in which clients acquire new techniques and strategies that foster healthier ways of thinking and communicating.

The Therapeutic Relationship

The relationship between client and therapist in the cognitive realm is based on collaboration. The therapist is not assumed to be an authority who holds all the answers, but a trusted teacher, trainer, and coach who enables the client to actively participate in solving problems and meeting goals. The therapist engenders mutual respect and openness and inspires confidence by being highly professional and exemplifying positive qualities, both of which enable the client to see things more accurately. Beck and Young (1985) point out that part of the process of developing a good collaborative relationship involves working together with the patient to set therapeutic goals, determine priorities, and develop an agenda for each session.

The cognitive therapist gives an adequate rationale for a treatment procedure, as well as elicits regular feedback from the patient to determine if the patient is complying with instructions. Within the therapeutic relationship, self-disclosure by the therapist is permitted, but only when it is within the client's interests to learn how the worker may have experienced and overcome similar problems.

Cognitive therapists seem to be especially skilled at seeing events through the client's perspective (accurate empathy) and are logical thinkers. They would make good trial lawyers, as they can spot the subtle flaws in someone's reasoning and skillfully elicit a different interpretation of the same events. Cognitive therapists are active/directive in their approach, and they can plan strategies and anticipate desired outcomes.

Although cognitive theory has not consistently underscored the therapeutic relationship as an important variable in the change process, the empirical evidence points to the fact that patients perceive the relationship as crucial, even if their therapists do not. Persons and Burns (1985, cited in Safron & Segal, 1996) found that patients' assessments of the quality of the therapeutic relationship were significantly related to mood changes in cognitive therapy.

Client Characteristics

It is as yet unknown what client characteristics respond best to cognitive therapy. Clients with delusions, dementia, or thought disorders would make poor candidates. Clients who are good planners, conscientious about carrying out responsibilities, and well organized are predicted to have more rapid success with cognitive therapy. On the other hand, clients who are excessively angry and rigid in their thinking may not be good candidates for cognitive therapy. Recent findings, especially with depression, indicate that age is not an obstacle, as older adults seem to benefit as much as younger persons (Gallagher-Thompson, Hanley-Peterson, & Thompson, 1990) although mildly to moderately depressed patients are more likely to benefit than more severely depressed patients (Klosko & Sanderson, 1999). Recent literature addresses the effectiveness of cognitive therapy with children and adolescents (Carr, 2000; Friedberg & McClure, 2000; Kendall, 2000; Reinecke, Datillo, & Freeman, 2003) particularly for management of ADHD, ODD, chemical dependence, low self-esteem, eating disorders, and academic skills problems.

A Structured Approach

Cognitive therapy interviews are structured, and each session usually begins with an agenda that the client has set and ends with the provision of feedback and assignment of homework. Some cognitive therapists write summaries of sessions and others make audiotapes for clients to take home with them. Sessions must include a review of the homework to underscore its importance to the therapeutic process. Homework helps clients to practice skills learned in therapy sessions and to generalize them to daily life. If clients fail to complete homework, cognitive therapists do not speak of a client's lack of motivation or resistance; rather, they consider that there are obstacles to progress. Because cognitive therapy requires courage and can be extremely painful and difficult to undertake, therapists need to be extremely supportive when discussing these obstacles. Sometimes there is role rehearsal within the session, to play events or thoughts that might get in the way of the client's completion of assignments. The client should play himself as in the example below:

Worker: Can you think of any reasons why you wouldn't be able to complete the homework?

Client: No. I will do it.

Worker: I know that is your intention, and that's good, but sometimes we don't get to do all that we intend.

Client: I'll do it.

Worker: Let's talk about when you will do it—that might give us some clues to things that could get in the way.

Client: Well, I'll do it when I come home from work, with the kids before they have dinner.

Worker: Will the children require your attention at that time?

Client: Well, they might. I could do it sometimes with them, and other times maybe in the morning or evening.

Worker: It's good to get a routine established for doing the homework. Some people like to do their homework right before bed. This works especially well if you are keeping a log of the events of the day and want to recapture them and write them down during a quiet moment. Homework is really important, because the more that you can do between sessions to practice the skills that we've talked about, the faster you will progress. That's why you need to give it an important place in your life.

Some therapists use prompts between sessions—spontaneous "hello" telephone calls to clients. Often, hearing the therapist's voice serves as a reminder to the client that homework needs to be done.

Cognitive therapists make sure that clients take credit for the changes they make and do not attribute their success to the practitioner. This is important because it reinforces the client's ability to undertake further change without the help of the therapist.

Rational Emotive Therapy

In 1955, Albert Ellis founded Rational Emotive Therapy (RET, or REBT—Rational Emotive Behavioral Therapy, as it is sometimes called). Ellis had an interest in philosophy, in particular the frequently quoted phrase of Epictetus, "People are disturbed not by things but by their view of things." Although he was trained in psychoanalytic methods at the Karen Horney school, he acknowledged his debt to Alfred Adler with his central concept that social interest has a primary role in determining psychological health (Adler, 1964). The concept of rationality is central to understanding RET. The term *rational* means that which aids and abets people in achieving their basic goals and purposes. The term *irrational* means what does not aid and abet people in achieving their basic goals and purposes. Ellis believes that people can rid themselves of most of their emotional or mental unhappiness, ineffectuality, and disturbance if they learn to maximize their rational and minimize their irrational thinking (Ellis, 1962). RET theory posits that people vary in their ability to be disturbed. Ellis noted that some people emerge relatively unscathed psychologically from uncaring or overprotective parents, and others emerge emotionally damaged from more "healthy" childbearing practices.

The ABCs of RET

Ellis is famous for his concept of the ABCs of RET. **A** stands for an activating event or the perception of the event, **B** for the way that perceived event is evaluated, or the person's beliefs, and **C** for the emotional and behavioral consequences that stem from **B** (Ellis, cited in Mahoney & Freenab, 1985). How we feel also affects our beliefs. So there is a constant interaction within the social and material environments. Ellis identifies a number of irrational ideas that are elaborated on by Werner (cited in Turner, 1986, pp. 108–109). These ideas are taught and transmitted by culture, the family, or significant others:

1. It is a dire necessity for an adult to be loved and approved by most of the significant people in his environment.
2. One is not worthwhile unless he is virtually perfect in all respects.
3. Certain people are bad and should be blamed and punished for their badness.
4. It is terrible when things are not the way one would like them to be.
5. Human unhappiness is externally caused and people have little ability to control their sorrows.
6. One should keep dwelling on the possibility of dangerous things happening and be deeply concerned (e.g., being in a car accident).
7. It is better to avoid difficult situations or responsibilities than to face them.
8. One should depend on someone else, for we each need someone stronger on whom to rely.
9. One's past history is an all-important determiner of present behavior, and a significant past event will indefinitely continue to influence us.
10. We should become quite upset over other people's problems or disturbances.

11. There is a correct and perfect solution to human problems, and it is catastrophic if the perfect solution is not found.

RET proposes to help people rid themselves of these irrational beliefs by sub-
stituting rational ones. Ellis would say, for example, that there is no dire necessity for
one to be loved. It would certainly be preferable, but not catastrophic if one weren't.

Frequent Disturbances in Thinking

Ellis, who is known for his irreverence and sense of humor in his work with
clients, also evolved a concept he called "musturbation." This was borrowed from
Karen Horney's ideas on the "tyranny of the shoulds" (Horney, 1950). Humans,
he said, make absolutistic evaluations of the perceived events in their lives,
couched in the form of dogmatic "musts, shoulds, have tos, got tos, and oughts"
that lead to psychological disturbances. Distortions in thinking almost always stem
from the musts. Some of the most frequent disturbances in thinking and their examples, according to Dryden and Ellis (cited in Dobson, 1988) are:

1. All-or-none thinking. "If I fail at an important task, as I must not, I'm a total
failure and completely unlovable."
2. Jumping to conclusions and negative non sequiturs. "Since they have seen
me dismally fail, as I should not have done, they will view me as incompetent."
3. Fortune telling. "Because they are laughing at me for failing, they know that
I should have succeeded, and they will despise me forever."
4. Focusing on the negative. "Because I can't stand things going wrong, as they
must not, I can't see any good that is happening in my life."
5. Disqualifying the positive. "When they compliment me on the good things I
have done, they are only being kind to me and forgetting the foolish things
that I should not have done."
6. Allness and neverness. "Because conditions of living ought to be good and
actually are so bad and so intolerable, they'll always be this way and I'll
never have any happiness."
7. Minimization. "My accomplishments were the result of luck—unimportant.
But my mistakes are unforgivable, and I should never have made them."
8. Emotional reasoning. "Because I have performed so poorly, as I should not
have done, I feel like a total nincompoop, and my strong feeling proves that
I am no damned good."
9. Labeling and overgeneralization. "Because I must not fail at important work
and have done so, I am a complete loser and failure."
10. Personalizing. "Since I am acting far worse than I should act, and they are
laughing, I am sure they are only laughing at me, and that is awful."
11. Phonyism. "When I don't do as well as I ought to do and they still praise and
accept me, I am a real phony and will soon fall on my face."

12. Perfectionism. "I realize that I did fairly well, but I should have done perfectly well on a task like this and am therefore really an incompetent."

RET practitioners hold that clients must be helped to discover the illogicalities just listed, and the unconditional shoulds, oughts, and musts, if change is to take place. The cognitive technique is a Socratic one—disputing irrational beliefs, debating, and looking for evidence. Clients are encouraged to listen to tapes of therapy sessions and dispute their own irrational beliefs. Rational self-statements are written on cards, such as, "I want my boyfriend's love but I don't need it," to be reviewed between sessions. Imagery (having a client close her eyes and visualize) is used to change a negative feared event to a positive one or to see that life goes on after the awful event. This helps a client to recover and continue to pursue his or her original goals or develop new ones. Rewards and penalties are used to encourage clients to undertake uncomfortable assignments. Behavioral techniques include activities to help clients tolerate discomfort while remaining in uncomfortable situations for a long period of time. Anti-procrastination exercises encourage clients to push themselves to start tasks sooner rather than later while tolerating the discomfort of breaking the habit.

RET therapists strive to unconditionally accept their clients as fallible humans who do self-defeating things. They are patient and reassuring when obstacles occur, but not unduly warm, as Ellis believes that a client's self-acceptance should not depend on the therapist's approval. The template in Figure 9.1 (p. 134) provides a model for identifying and disputing irrational beliefs.

Beck's Model of Cognitive Therapy

Beck's model of cognitive therapy also aims at correcting dysfunctional thoughts, and, at a deeper level, at uncovering underlying schemas that frame the client's experience and form the basis for the cognitive distortions. These are similar in breadth to Ellis's irrational beliefs (DeRubeis & Beck, cited in Dobson, 1988). These schemas are not as readily available to the person as are automatic thoughts, but become apparent as the client and therapist identify the themes that run through the client's upsetting instances. Beck, like Ellis, initially operated from a classically Freudian perspective, but following several systematic studies (Beck, 1961; Beck & Hurvich, 1959; Beck & Ward, 1961), he came to reject Freud's concept of the depressive syndrome (melancholia), a model based on the premise that in the depressed client, anger is turned inward toward the self. Instead, Beck believed that, clinically, depression seemed to stem from the depressed person's negative thinking.

In sessions, using Beck's model, the client focuses on the content of his cognitive reaction. By carefully considering this content, the client can arrive at a different view. He is then encouraged to view this belief as a hypothesis—a possibility but not necessarily a fact (Hollon & Kriss, 1983). Reframing a belief as a hypothesis

A (Activating Event)

- Briefly summarize the situation you are disturbed about (what would a camera see?).
- An A can be *internal* or *external*, *real*, or *imagined*.
- An A can be an event in the *past*, *present*, or *future*.

IBs (IRRATIONAL BELIEFS)

To identify IBs, look for:
- DOGMATIC DEMANDS (musts, absolutes, shoulds)
- AWFULIZING (It's awful, terrible, horrible)
- LOW FRUSTRATION TOLERANCE
- SELF/OTHER RATING (I'm/he/she is bad, worthless)

D (DISPUTING IBs)

To dispute, ask yourself:
- Where is holding this belief getting me? Is it *helpful* or *self-defeating*?
- Where is evidence to support the existence of my irrational belief? Is it *consistent with reality*?
- Is my belief logical? Does it follow from my preferences?
- Is it really *awful* (as bad as it could be)?
- Can I really not *stand* it?

C (Consequences)

Major unhealthy negative **emotions**

Major self-defeating **behaviors**

Unhealthy negative emotions include
- Anxiety
- Rage
- Shame/Embarrassment
- Jealousy
- Depression
- Low Frustration Tolerance
- Hurt
- Guilt

RBs (RATIONAL BELIEFS)

To think more rationally, strive for:
- NONDOGMATIC PREFERENCES (wishes, wants, desires)
- EVALUATING BADNESS (It's bad, unfortunate)
- HIGH FRUSTRATION TOLERANCE (I don't like it, but I can stand it)
- NOT GLOBALLY RATING SELF OR OTHERS (I—and others—are fallible human beings)

E (NEW EFFECT)

Healthy negative emotions include
- Disappointment
- Concern
- Annoyance
- Sadness
- Regret
- Frustration

FIGURE 9.1 *REBT Self-Help Form*
Reprinted by permission of The Albert Ellis Institute.

has been called "distancing." This technique helps the client to look at the belief more objectively.

Beck teaches that there are several kinds of errors of thinking that occur more frequently during affective episodes. These errors can be labeled by the therapist to remind the client of maladaptive thought processes that are taking place. Included in the types of cognitive errors are

1. Arbitrary inferences. These refer to the process of drawing a specific conclusion in the absence of supporting evidence, or when the evidence is contrary to the conclusion.
2. Selective abstraction. This consists of focusing on a detail taken out of context and conceptualizing the total experience on the basis of that detail.
3. Overgeneralization. This refers to a pattern of drawing a general rule or conclusion on the basis of one or more isolated incidents and applying it across the board to related and unrelated situations.
4. Magnification and minimization. These are errors in evaluating the magnitude of an event. They are so gross as to constitute a distortion.
5. Personalization. This is the client's tendency to take things personally even when there is no such connection.
6. Dichotomous thinking. This is the client's tendency to place experiences in one of two opposite categories, for example, viewing people as either saints or sinners (DeRubeis & Beck, cited in Dobson, 1988, p. 7).

The client must take an active role in questioning his thoughts, when in the midst of emotional upset or shortly thereafter. Much of the work in Beck's model of cognitive therapy centers around the use of a device called the *Daily Record of Dysfunctional Thoughts* (see Beck, Rush, Shaw, & Emery, 1979), which is reprinted in Figure 9.2 (p. 136).

On this daily record, the client reports situations, thoughts, and emotional reactions, preferably at the time of the event. Using this template, intervention can begin. Intervention consists of coming up with rational responses to these automatic thoughts by examining the inferences made when the client is emotionally upset. The simplest method of uncovering automatic thoughts is for the therapist to ask the client what went through his or her mind in response to a particular event. This questioning gives clients a model for exploration that they can use on their own. Imagery is also used to help the clients picture the situation in detail. Clients can describe the distressing event as they relive it in their minds in the therapist's office. If the upsetting event is an interpersonal one, role-play can be utilized. The therapist plays the role of the other person in the situation, while clients play themselves. This further helps to elicit automatic thoughts. The therapist is careful to note any mood changes that occur during the session, such as tears or anger, and ask the clients what thoughts occur prior to the shift in mood. This helps clients to make the connection between mind and mood, and furthers the teaching of identification of automatic thoughts.

FIGURE 9.2   *Daily Record of Dysfunctional Thoughts*

Date	Situation	Emotion(s)	Automatic Thought(s)	Rational Response	Outcome
	Describe 1. Actual event leading to unpleasant emotion, or 2. Stream of thoughts, daydream of recollection leading to unpleasant emotion.	1. Specify sad/ anxious/ angry, etc. 2. Rate degree of emotion, 1–100%.	1. Write automatic thoughts that precede emotion(s). 2. Rate belief in automatic thoughts, 0–100%.	1. Write rational response to automatic thought(s). 2. Rate belief in rational response, 0–100%.	1. Rerate belief in automatic thought(s). 2. Specify and rate subsequent emotions, 0–100%.

Explanation: When you experience an unpleasant emotion, note the situation that seemed to stimulate the emotion. (If the emotion occurred while you were thinking, daydreaming, etc., please note this.) Then note the automatic thought associated with the emotion. Record the degree to which you believe this thought: 0% = not at all. 100% = completely. In rating degree of emotion: 1 = a trace: 100 = the most intense possible.
Source: DeRubeis R., & Beck, A. (1988). Cognitive therapy. In K. S. Dobson (Ed.), *Handbook of cognitive-behavioral therapies*. New York: Guilford. Reprinted with permission.

Testing of Automatic Thoughts

Testing of automatic thoughts is done by asking clients to list the evidence from their experiences for and against the hypothesis under consideration. It is sometimes necessary to help clients operationalize a word. For example, the recurring automatic thought, "I'm a failure in math," could be narrowed down to being unable to achieve a grade of 'C' after investing an average amount of studying time. Now the client could examine past evidence and test the validity of the hypothesis. This process helps clients to see the all-inclusiveness of their negative self-assessments and the idiosyncratic nature of their thoughts (Young, Beck, & Weinberger, cited in Barlow, 1993).

Beck also addresses the schema, or underlying cognitive structures or core beliefs, that organize the client's experience and form the basis of disturbances in thinking. Schemas originate in childhood, through the experiences of the developing child. They may not be as readily accessible as automatic thoughts, but become clear to the client and therapist as both strive to identify the consistent themes that run through the <u>client's disturbing events.</u> This schema work has been elaborated on by Bricker, Young, and Flanagan (1993), and the fifteen schema that they have identified are

1. **Emotional Deprivation (ED)**
   Expectation that one's desire for a normal degree of emotional support will not be adequately met by others.
   A. *Deprivation of Nurturance:* Absence of attention, affection (physical or emotional), or warmth from others.
   B. *Deprivation of Protection:* Absence of strength, direction, or guidance from others.
   C. *Deprivation of Empathy:* Absence of understanding, listening, self-disclosure, or mutual sharing of feelings from others.

2. **Abandonment/Instability (AB)**
   The perceived instability or unreliability of those available for support and connection. Involves the sense that significant others will not be able to continue providing emotional support, connection, strength, or practical protection because they are emotionally unstable, unpredictable, unreliable, and erratically present; because they will die imminently; or because they will abandon the patient in favor of someone else.

3. **Mistrust/Abuse (MA)**
   One's expectation that others will hurt, abuse, humiliate, cheat, lie, manipulate, or take advantage of him or her. Usually involves the perception that harm is intentional or the result of unjustified and extreme negligence.

4. **Social Isolation/Alienation (SI)**
   The feeling that one is isolated from the rest of the world, different from other people, and/or not part of any group or community.

5. **Defectiveness/Shame (DS)**
   The feeling that one is inwardly defective, flawed, or invalid; that one would be fundamentally unlovable to significant others if exposed; or a sense of shame regarding one's perceived internal inadequacies.

6. **Social Undesirability (SU)**
   The belief that one will inevitably fail, or is fundamentally inadequate relative to one's peers, in areas of achievement (school, career, sports, etc.). Often involves the belief that one is stupid, inept, untalented, ignorant, etc.

7. **Functional Dependence/Incompetence (DI)**
   Belief that one is unable to handle one's everyday responsibilities in a competent manner, without considerable help from others (e.g., take care of oneself, solve daily problems, exercise good judgment, tackle new tasks, make good decisions).

8. **Vulnerability to Harm and Illness (VH)**

   Exaggerated fear that disaster is about to strike at any time (natural, criminal, medical, or financial) and that one is unable to protect oneself. May include unrealistic fears that one will have a heart attack, get AIDS, go crazy, go broke, be mugged, crash, etc.

9. **Enmeshment/Undeveloped Self (EM)**

   Excessive emotional involvement and closeness with one or more significant others (often parents) at the expense of full individuation or normal social development. Usually leads to insufficient individual identity or inner direction. May include feelings of being smothered by or fused with others.

10. **Subjugation (SB)**

    Excessive surrendering of control over one's own decisions and preferences—usually to avoid anger, retaliation, or abandonment. Involves the perception that one's own desires are not valid or important to others. Frequently presents as excessive compliance and eagerness to please.

11. **Self-Sacrifice (SS)**

    Excessive voluntary focus on meeting the needs of others at the expense of one's own needs and preferences. The most common reasons are to avoid guilt, to prevent causing pain to others, to gain in esteem, and to maintain the connection with others perceived as needy.

12. **Emotional Inhibition (EI)**

    Excessive inhibition of emotions or impulses because one expects their expression to result in loss of esteem, harm to others, embarrassment, retaliation, or abandonment. May result in loss of spontaneity and warmth, flatness of affect, mishandling of anger, obsessive-compulsive symptoms, etc.

13. **Unrelenting/Unbalanced Standards (US)**

    The relentless striving to meet high expectations of oneself, at the expense of happiness, pleasure, health, sense of accomplishment, or satisfying relationships.

14. **Entitlement/Self-Centeredness (ET)**

    Insistence that one should be able to have whatever one wants, regardless of what others consider reasonable or regardless of the cost to others. Often involves excessive control over others, demandingness, and lack of empathy for others' needs.

15. **Insufficient Self-Control/Self-Discipline (IS)**

    Pervasive difficulty exercising sufficient self-control and frustration tolerance to achieve one's personal goals or to restrain the excessive expression of one's emotions and impulses.

Once the client begins to recognize situations in which these core beliefs exist, he can be taught to consider alternative inferences.

While most empirical studies of cognitive therapy have been with depression (see, for example, Gottlib & Hammen, 2002; McCollough, 2003), there has been an extension of the aims and principles to other disorders such as anxiety (see, for example, Beck & Emery, 1985), social phobia, social anxiety (Bruch, Heimberg, &

Hope, 1991), and generalized anxiety disorder (Brown, O'Leary, & Barlow, 1993, cited in Barlow, 1993). Cognitive theory has also been especially useful in the treatment of substance abuse and personality disorders (J. Beck, 1995).

Techniques in Practice

Case Example: Cognitive Treatment for Anxiety

The following case illustrates theory and techniques from both Albert Ellis and Aaron Beck.

    The client, Linda, is a 32-year-old woman who functions well in her work and social milieus. However, she described "getting very crazy inside" whenever she was waiting for the appearance of someone important to her, often her boyfriend Carl. She would feel frightened and fantasize various catastrophic events that might have occurred. If in a public place, such as a restaurant, Linda would be able to hide her reactions, but if alone, she would become physically restless, pace, peer out the window, and sometimes survey the phonebook to determine the number of hospitals she would have to call to search for Carl. She also engaged in ritualistic behaviors in attempts to calm herself, such as counting the number of cars passing her window and telling herself, "By the time I get to two dozen cars, Carl will be here."

    Linda had tried to manage these anxious feelings with alcohol and marijuana, but has been sober and in Alcoholics Anonymous for four years. When asked if she could identify any thoughts she had immediately before the anxious feelings began, Linda was able to find a pattern common to these experiences. In session, the worker attempted to help Linda identify her underlying schema, first helping her to relax and then to try to remember the origin of her fears.

Worker: Linda, we're going to work on trying to identify your core beliefs, or schema, that have led to your distressing thoughts. These beliefs originate in childhood, so I'm going to ask you, in a moment, to close your eyes and think of something that happened when you were very young. Does that seem all right with you?

Linda: OK.

Worker: Now just close your eyes and let yourself relax. Picture yourself somewhere in the distant past and describe the scene to me.

Linda: I'm in my living room, with my younger brother, and it is starting to get dark.

Worker: Go on.

Linda: It feels chilly, like November or sometime when the days get shorter.

Worker: Yes.

Linda: I see my younger brother playing with some toy cars. I'm about 7 or 8 years old.

Worker: What are you feeling?

Linda: I think I'm scared. I don't like being alone when it starts to get dark. I'm thinking I want my mom to come home, and what to do if she doesn't.

(continued)

Case Example   Continued

> *Worker:*   And then?
>
> *Linda:*   I'm starting to walk around the house. Like I'm looking for her, even though I know she's not there. I'm trying not to cry, because I don't want my little brother to get scared. I feel it getting darker, and I'm listening for my mom's car in the driveway. I'm looking out the window now, just sitting on the sofa and staring out the window. I feel my heart beating faster, and I'm worried that I'll get sick or something and be all alone.
>
> *Worker:*   How do you feel now?
>
> *Linda:*   Really anxious, like it's happening all over again.
>
> *Worker:*   You've done a good job of visualizing this, Linda. Now in just a moment I will count to three, and you can open your eyes. You'll be here with me in my office and you'll feel very safe.

It was not difficult to see how this anxious thinking began for Linda at an early age and how it would fit into an overall schema Linda had put together around her early experiences of being responsible for her sibling, feelings of abandonment, and the lack of supervision and structure. Using Bricker and Young's schema outline, we could say that Linda's maladaptive schema are in two primary areas: *Abandonment/Instability,* and *Vulnerability to Harm and Illness.* Linda's sequence of events and feelings can also easily be viewed through the format of Ellis's ABC theory of emotions: The *activating event* (A) is that someone important is supposed to be with her at a given time, (B) is Linda's *belief* that she has to know what to do if that person doesn't arrive, and (C) represents the *consequences,* which, for Linda, include uncomfortably high levels of anxiety. Linda also mentioned a tendency to avoid situations that might evoke this sequence.

Linda was acknowledged for her courage in attempting to take on this difficult problem. She was told that her obsessive thinking usually started out as an effort to massage a thought or situation into a less scary shape, but that it then takes on a life of its own and becomes the problem. Our goal, mutually agreed upon, was to break this habit of reacting with obsessive thinking, high anxiety levels, and anxiety-provoked behaviors, and to replace this pattern with more comfortable thoughts, feelings, and actions. When asked what Linda would "like it to look like" when we had met our goal, she said that she wanted to react as most other people did to lateness, specifically, "annoyance at the worst" while being able to relax or use the time spent waiting productively.

Linda was asked to keep a daily record describing the situation, emotion, automatic thought, and actions taken, based on the model described by Beck (1995). She was also asked to rank her emotional state on a scale of 1 to 10, with 1 indicating low emotional arousal, and 10 indicating high emotional arousal. Three events are printed in Linda's daily record; see Figure 9.3 on page 142.

In the next session Linda was asked about her overall experience with completing the thought record. She said that she thought the act of keeping the log had made her very aware of her thoughts and feelings. In two of the episodes recorded that week, the anxious thinking began when Linda noticed that it would soon be time for Carl to come home. In the third instance, she did not begin to worry until his usual time of arrival because she was involved in preparing a complicated dinner and had not noticed the time. Linda's automatic thoughts all centered around the need to know what to do if Carl did not come home. Her behaviors then became anxious; she paced and counted the number of hospital emergency rooms she would call if Carl failed to appear.

Intervention

The core of the treatment process was to have Linda identify her irrational thoughts and underlying beliefs and to debate them for truth or falsehood. The worker would help Linda to discriminate between her rational and irrational beliefs. The underlying schemas that would be addressed would include the beliefs that others cannot be counted on to remain available to support, nurture, or protect her and that disaster could strike at any time. Linda was given other suggestions to interrupt obsessive worrying. She was told to visualize a stop sign in her head and to carry a 3" × 5" card with the word "STOP" written on it to remind her to use this technique. She was also advised that she could wear a rubber band on her wrist and snap it whenever the obsessive thinking started, followed immediately by directing her attention elsewhere. An example would be to pick up a small object and study it (Seligman, 1990).

Exploring Automatic Thoughts in an Interview. The following session demonstrates the process of exploring and disputing automatic thoughts:

Worker: Linda, what about the automatic thoughts, all the need to know what to do? What do you notice as you think about them now?
Linda: Well, it's always the same thing. And it feels really urgent.
Worker: Do you notice anything missing?
Linda: Missing?
Worker: Missing compared to what others might think. You often mention your friend Gerri as being a logical thinker. What would Gerri say back to you, for example, if you were saying those thoughts out loud to her?
Linda: Ha. Well, she'd think I was crazy, but that's why I don't tell her, of course. Hmmm . . . I guess she'd point out that I don't know why he's late, it could be anything. Oh, that never occurs to me, does it?
Worker: Right. Because people are late for all sorts of reasons, even super on-timers like you. (Both smile). So if it did occur to you, what might you come up with for Carl? Or whomever?
Linda: Well, I suppose there are reasons why he usually is late when he's late. With Carl, it's mostly the subway or work. Or sometimes he stops somewhere or forgets to tell me about something.
Worker: What about other people? If they might be late?
Linda: I suppose it would depend on who. If it were Gerri, it's because she's just more casual about time than I. You know "on time" for her means within 5 or 10 minutes after the appointed time. Other people . . .
Worker: Just generic or ordinary reasons why people are late . . .
Linda: Yeah, like the subway or transportation. . . . Why don't I think of things like that?

(continued)

FIGURE 9.3   Linda's Thought Record

Date	Situation	Emotion	Automatic Thought	Action
	Describe the: 1. act or event leading to the anxiety 2. stream of thoughts or fantasies	1. the specific emotion 2. rate the degree on scale of 1–10	1. the thought that precedes the emotion 2. rate belief in the thought on 1–10 scale	Describe what actions are taken.
5/26	*Waiting for Carl. I noticed the time and started to plan how long until I would get really worried, then how long until I would take action.*	*Anxious.* *7*	*What will I do if he doesn't come home? I have to know what I'm going to do.* *9*	*Got physically restless. Could not sit still.*
5/28	*I was on the phone with a friend and noticed the time I couldn't really pay attention to her after that, but Carl came home before I finished the call and I was okay then.*	*Anxious.* *7*	*He's not here. I have to stop talking and figure out what to do if he doesn't come.* *9*	*Started walking around with the phone. Tried to listen to her and listen for him at the same time.*
5/31	*Dinner was almost ready and no Carl. Imagined myself being told Carl had been killed and life without Carl.*	*Anxious and then panicky.* *10*	*What am I going to do if he doesn't come home?* *10*	*Did things with the food, then paced. Looked at the number of hospitals in New York in the telephone directory.*

Case Example   Continued

Worker: Well, you can now. You can begin to tell yourself that kind of stuff. What way of doing this would work for you?

Linda: I could ask myself, "What would Gerri say?" That would be good. Because I know what kind of things she would say. I can even picture how she would feel when she was saying it, you know, by how she looks, just calm and sort of casual.

Worker: You could make yourself a card for your bag: "What to do when someone might be late." What could you tell yourself? The card could ask, "What would Gerri say? And how would she act?"

Linda could now dispute her irrational thoughts by putting herself in the role of Gerri, intuiting her reactions, and putting her answers into action. Linda was also encouraged to ask herself, "What would I be doing if I weren't worrying?" She would then proceed to put the answer into action. Linda was also taught a relaxation technique called "circular breathing." In this technique, Linda counts to eight (or higher as one becomes practiced) on an inhalation, then to eight on the exhalation, but without a pause at the "top." The long "loops" of circular breathing give the body a message of safety. This breathing technique was used in addition to cognitive techniques. Relaxation methods are known to help clients with anxiety disorders. Such clients tend to take shallow breaths when anxious, which increase physical symptoms and escalate anxiety.

Daily Record Sheets.   Linda was given new daily record sheets, which included additional columns for recording her new "rational responses" to automatic thoughts, as described by Beck (1976). See Figure 9.4 (p. 144) for a copy of Linda's completed Daily Record of Automatic Thoughts.

Exploring Underlying Assumptions.   In the following session excerpts, the previously revealed automatic thoughts and underlying assumptions or schemas are explored:

Worker: It's interesting that when people are late, you always start thinking and planning about what you're going to have to do about it.

Linda: Yeah . . . (looks blank).

Worker: You always have to plan that you're going to go into action. It seems there's an assumption underneath those "what-am-I going-to do" thoughts.

Linda: Well, right. I guess I'm assuming it's something really bad, tragic. If someone is late, they must have been in an accident. They've been killed. They aren't coming back. (Linda becomes teary.) Because if it goes on long enough, if I have to wait long enough, I start imagining all of that, you know, the funeral. Even what I'll wear. (Smiles). And what it would be like if they really were dead, how much I'd miss them. Then I'm scared and sad. But nothing has happened yet. It doesn't get that far too often because most of the time they show up before I get to that point. Whew! What a lot of stuff from something that's probably due to a subway delay.

Worker: People suffer a lot from thinking that's just plain illogical. One of the people who writes about this has a chapter title that really fits: It's called "The Alarm Is Worse Than the Fire" (Beck, 1976, p.132).

(continued)

FIGURE 9.4 *Daily Record*

DAILY RECORD

Date	Situation	Emotion	Automatic Thought	Action	Rational Thought	Outcome	Action
	Describe 1. the act or event leading to . . . 2. stream of thought or fantasy	1. the specific emotion 2. rate degree on 1–10 scale	1. the thought that precedes the emotion 2. rate on 1–10 scale	Describe what actions are taken.	1. Write rational responses to the automatic thought. 2. Rate belief in the rational response.	1. Rerate belief in the automatic thought on 1–10 scale. 2. Rate degree of subsequent emotion.	Describe what actions are taken.
6/2	*Meeting Carl at a restaurant and he's not there first. Started to think about how long I should wait until being really scared.*	*Anxiety* 6	*Something might have happened to him (more an image than a thought).* 7	*Clenched hands under table.*	*What would Gerri be thinking? She'd assume he was on his way. The most she'd be worried about was whether he'd be crabby when he got there, from being late.* 5	*Belief = 5* *Anxiety = 4*	*None, because I was in a restaurant.*
6/4	*Waiting for Carl to get home from the gym. I noticed the time and started trying to figure out what was a reasonable time to expect him.*	*Anxiety* 6	*Seeing myself waiting and no Carl. Have to figure out how to find out what happened.* 8	*Started to pace.*	*Did the 3-interp. exercise. Did circular breathing.* 6	*Belief = 4* *Anxiety = 4*	*Cleaned out my junk drawer!*
6/7	*Waiting for my Mom's weekly call. Started thinking about what I'll have to do when she dies.*	*Anxiety* 5	*If she doesn't call, what should I do to find out if she's okay.* 7	*Was restless, but didn't do anything in particular.*	*Told myself she often calls late and she doesn't know I worry.* 4	*Belief = 4* *Anxiety = 3*	*Watched a video.*

144

Case Example Continued

Linda: Yeah, you're right. I guess an accident could happen. I mean, they do happen to people. But I'm setting off the alarm every time somebody lights a match, aren't I?

Worker: Right. What you automatically imagine is always a catastrophe.

Linda: So it's not just, "If they're late, I have to know what to do." It's "If they're late, something really bad happened." Really bad, because if it goes on long enough, I always get to the seeing myself at the funeral part. I plan as if well, if they're late, they're dead. But that doesn't follow. And you're right, I do at least partly know it doesn't make sense, because I could certainly never say that aloud to anyone. (Smiles).

This session demonstrated that Linda has understood the underlying beliefs driving her obsessive planning. Her ability to smile at herself is a sign that she knows there is irrationality behind her obsessive thinking. The worker points this out and acknowledges Linda's hard work.

Conclusion

Linda's therapy was completed in six sessions. Using single-subject design methodology to demonstrate effectiveness, the worker created a graph measuring Linda's anxiety, the frequency of her thoughts, and her belief in these automatic thoughts.

The two baseline weeks (B) measure weekly frequency of occurrence and levels of anxiety and of belief in the automatic thoughts. The two intervention weeks (I) measure frequency and Linda's degree of anxiety and belief in the automatic thought following her use of one or more of the interventions. The graph in Figure 9.5 shows that the levels of belief in the automatic thoughts and the degree of anxiety seem to parallel. The limitations of this study are that the worker was only able to obtain 2 to

(continued)

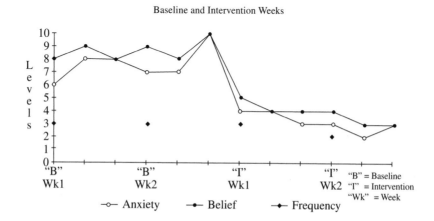

Baseline and Intervention Weeks

FIGURE 9.5   *Linda's Automatic Thoughts*

Case Example   Continued

4 baseline points (7 to 10 are considered desirable to ensure that the baseline is stable, as problems do fluctuate over time (Bloom & Fischer, 1982), and there are no statistical calculations to help analyze the data. However, a quick "eyeballing" of the graph below notes a clear reduction in anxiety and belief levels following the interventions and a one-third decrease in frequency. In order to achieve pervasive and long-lasting change, Linda will be assisted, in future sessions, in revealing and understanding the ways in which this particular cognitive error fits in with her overall schemata. It is possible that a core belief underneath her feeling that "If they are late, they must be dead." is, perhaps, "If they don't come home, I'll die." If so, disputing it will help Linda to understand that today, as an adult, while the death of a loved one would be painful and tragic, it would not threaten her existence. Linda can come to further appreciate her own very real and well-developed capacity to survive.

Source: Case material supplied by Catherine Boyer.

Summary

Cognitive therapy is a skills-based therapy. Clients are given techniques that help them to change their thought processes so that they can perceive reality more accurately. These tools help them to acquire healthier ways of thinking and communicating. Cognitive theory is well suited for contemporary clinical social work practice. Depression and anxiety are common clinical syndromes experienced today by many clients from many different cultures, and the empirical evidence demonstrates that cognitive theory is an effective means of intervention with clients suffering from these mood disorders (see, for example, Beck & Emery, 1985; Brown et al., 1993; Young, Beck, & Weinberger, 1993). Because cognitive therapy is a structured approach, it provides a focus for both the clinician and the client as they work together to prioritize problems and set therapeutic goals. Finally, cognitive therapy enables clients to achieve a sense of mastery as they continue to use the techniques they have learned after the therapeutic relationship has ended.

Learning Assignments

1. Select a client who might benefit from cognitive therapy. Using the Daily Record of Dysfunctional Thoughts developed by Beck and colleagues (1979), have the client record the situation, emotion, and automatic thoughts for seven days. Have the client rate the belief in each automatic thought on a scale of 1 to 10.

2. Use this client record in class with a partner. Have the partner play the client, and you play the therapist. The therapist must dispute and challenge the client's irrational thoughts and help the client to come up with the rational response. Switch roles halfway through the exercise. Be sure to have the client rerate the

belief in the automatic thoughts after the intervention.

3. Discuss a plan to evaluate the effectiveness of the above intervention.

4. Try to learn about your client, friend, or self using a schema therapy approach.

Have the subject identify his or her schemas by closing his or her eyes and imaging a scene from childhood that has left a lasting impression. List those schemas that are influential and that need to be the focus of attention in treatment.

References

Adler, A. (1964). *Social interest: A challenge to mankind.* New York: Capricorn.

Barlow, D. H. (Ed.). (1993). *Clinical handbook of psychological disorders* (2nd ed.). New York: Guilford.

Beck, A. T. (1961). A systematic investigation of depression. *Comprehensive Psychiatry, 2,* 305–312.

Beck, A. T. (1976). *Cognitive theory and emotional disorders.* New York: International Universities Press.

Beck, A. T., & Emery, G. (1985). *Anxiety disorders and phobias.* New York: Basic Books.

Beck, A. T., & Hurvich, M. (1959). Psychological correlates of depression. *Psychosomatic Medicine, 21,* 50–55.

Beck, A. T., Rush, A. J., Shaw, B. F., & Emery, G. (1979). *Cognitive therapy of depression.* New York: Guilford.

Beck, A. T., & Ward, C. H. (1961). Dreams of depressed patients: Characteristic themes in manifest content. *Archives of General Psychiatry, 5,* 462–467.

Beck, A. T., & Young J. E. (1985). Depression. In D. H. Barlow (Ed.), *Clinical handbook of psychological disorders: A step-by-step treatment manual* (pp. 206–244). New York: Guilford.

Beck, J. S. (1995). *Cognitive therapy: Basics and beyond.* New York: Guilford.

Bloom, M., & Fischer, J. (1982). *Evaluating practice: Guidelines for the accountable professional.* Englewood Cliffs, NJ: Prentice-Hall.

Bricker, D., Young, J., & Flanagan, C. (1993). Schema focused cognitive therapy: A comprehensive framework for characterological problems. In K. T. Kuehlwein & H. Rosen (Eds.), *Cognitive therapies in action: Evolving innovative practice* (pp. 88–125). San Francisco: Jossey-Bass.

Brown, T. A., O'Leary, T. A., & Barlow, D. H. (1993). Generalized anxiety disorder. In D. H. Barlow (Ed.), *Clinical handbook of psychological disorders* (2nd ed., pp. 137–188). New York: Guilford.

Bruch, M. A., Heimberg, R. G., & Hope, D. A. (1991). States of mind model and cognitive change in treated social phobics. *Cognitive Therapy and Research, 15,* 429–441.

Carr, A. (Ed.). (2000). *What works with children and adolescents? A critical review of psychological interventions with children, adolescents, and their families.* London: Routledge.

DeRubeis, R., & Beck, A. (1988). Cognitive therapy. In K. Dobson (Ed.), *Handbook of cognitive-behavioral therapies* (pp. 273–306). New York: Guilford.

Dobson, K. (Ed.). (1988). *Handbook of cognitive-behavioral therapies.* New York: Guilford.

Ellis, A. (1962). *Reason and emotion in psychotherapy.* New York: Stuart.

Friedberg, R. D., & McClure, J. M. (2002). *Clinical practice of cognitive therapy with children and adolescents: The nuts and bolts.* New York: Guilford.

Gallagher-Thompson, D., Hanley-Peterson, P., & Thompson, L. W. (1990). Maintenance of gains versus relapse following brief psychotherapy for depression. *Journal of Consulting and Clinical Psychology, 58*(3), 371–374.

Gottlib, I. H., & Hammen, C. L. (2002). *Handbook of depression.* New York: Guilford.

Hollon, S. D., & Kriss, M. R. (1983). Cognitive factors in clinical research and practice. *Clinical Psychology Review, 4,* 35–76.

Horney, K. (1950). *Neurosis and human growth.* New York: Norton.

Kendall, P. (Ed.). (2000). *Child and adolescent therapy: Cognitive-behavioral procedures* (2nd ed.). New York: Guilford.

Klosko, J. S., & Sanderson, W. C. (1999). *Cognitive-behavioral treatment of depression.* Northvale, NJ: Jason Aronson.

Mahoney, M. J., & Freenab, A. (Eds.). (1985). *Cognition and psychotherapy.* New York: Plenum.

McCollough, J. P. (2003). *Treatment for chronic depression: Cognitive-behavioral analysis system of psychotherapy (CBASP).* New York: Guilford.

Persons, J. B., & Burns, D. D. (1985). Mechanisms of action in cognitive therapy: The relative contributions of technical and interpersonal interventions. *Cognitive Therapy and Research, 9,* 539–557.

Reinecke, M. A., Dattilo, F. M., & Freeman, A. (2003). *Cognitive therapy with children and adolescents: A casebook of clinical practice* (2nd ed.). New York: Guilford.

Safron, J. D., & Segal, V. (1996). *Interpersonal process in cognitive therapy.* Northvale, NJ: Jason Aronson.

Seligman, M. E. (1990). *Learned optimism.* New York: Alfred A. Knopf.

Turner, F. (1986). *Social work treatment: Interlocking theoretical approaches* (3rd ed.). New York: The Free Press.

Young, J., Beck, A., & Weinberger, A. (1993). *Depression.* In D. H. Barlow (Ed.), *Clinical handbook of psychological disorders* (2nd ed.). New York: Guilford.

10

Behavior Therapy

A Structural Approach

Definition

Behavior therapy refers to the systematic application of techniques that facilitate behavioral change. The word "systematic" is key, for it is the planned arrangement of behavioral contingencies (those events that happen before and after specific behaviors) in relation to specific goals, and the evaluation of outcomes, that characterize a behavioral model.

In behavioral therapy there are no differences between what is labeled normal or abnormal behavior. The same learning principles give rise to both. Human behavior is viewed largely as a function of past and present circumstances, and emotional problems are seen as problems in living or maladaptive ways of behaving. Since behaviors are learned, they can be unlearned, and therapy is, essentially, a learning process. Behavioral therapy is therefore an empowerment therapy: Clients gain mastery over their lives and increase self-esteem through their own actions that bring about behavioral change.

Behavioral techniques are based principally on learning conditioning theories. B. F. Skinner is considered to be the father of behavioral theory, and he and his followers developed radical behaviorism, which is the philosophy of science that underlies behavioral work. At the heart of Skinner's theory is the concept of reinforcement. Skinner and his followers state that the operant (or voluntary) behavior of a person can be increased in frequency if it is positively reinforced. Alternatively, the frequency of a behavior could be decreased by either administering punishment or withholding reinforcement, a process referred to as extinction. The essence of the Skinnerian, or operant model of human behavior, relied heavily on an understanding of the environmental (behavioral) events that preceded and/or followed the behavior(s) under consideration (Thomlison & Thomlison, 1996).

Another important name in behavioral theory is Pavlov, whose work with salivating dogs is well known to undergraduate psychology students. Pavlov's behavioral learning process is referred to as respondent conditioning, which remains as the fundamental theoretical explanation for a variety of anxiety and phobic disorders. Pavlov developed his theory by placing food (an unconditioned stimulus) in view of a dog. Salivation (the conditioned response) was elicited by the arbitrary event of ringing a bell. Over a number of such pairings, the bell (conditioned stimulus) took on the power to elicit the response of salivation (conditioned response; Thomlison, 1984). Although both of these explanations of human behavior have been refined as a result of research and clinical experience, the interaction between behavior and the events that precede and follow the behavior remains the foundation of most contemporary behavior therapy.

Behavioral Assessment

Behavioral assessment consists of a thorough evaluation of behaviors that either need to be increased or shaped (e.g., lack of assertiveness), or behaviors that need to be extinguished (e.g., temper tantrums). Assessment and selection of intervention methods are closely related in behavioral therapy. Quantitative data about the frequency, magnitude, or duration of a behavior, thought, feeling, or other outcome is collected before intervention and is then compared with the frequency, magnitude, or duration after the intervention. Standardized tests (such as depression and anxiety scales) as well as subjective measures (i.e., client logs, diaries, and charts) are good assessment tools. Behavioral therapy is ideally suited to evaluation, because clients can act as their own evaluators by gathering data on their problem behaviors before, during, and after an intervention. Behavioral treatments are individually tailored; there is a specificity of treatment approaches for each subproblem. Social workers practicing behavior therapy can, therefore, go to the literature on the problem at hand (e.g., social phobia) and follow the treatment protocol verbatim to achieve results.

The Therapeutic Relationship

In behavioral therapy, the therapist is viewed as a consultant, teacher, and trainer who is there to help clients learn about themselves and change maladaptive behavior patterns. Corrective learning experiences are emphasized. Clients acquire new coping skills and improved communication competencies, or learn how to break maladaptive habits and overcome self-defeating emotional conflicts. Behavioral therapists have not consistently credited the relationship as an important variable in behavioral change, but there is a growing empirical literature that demonstrates that clients perceive the relationship as crucial. Safron and Segal (1996) cite the following works: Sloane and colleagues (Sloane, Staples, Cristol,

Yorkston, & Whipple, 1975), who found that patients successful in behavior therapy felt that the personal interaction with the therapist was the single most important element in the treatment; Agras and colleagues (Agras, Alexander, Leitenberg, & Barlow, 1968), who found that relationship variables contributed significantly to outcome in the behavioral treatment of delinquents and their families; Rabavilas, Boulougouris, and Perissaki (1979, cited in Safron & Segal, 1996), who correlated therapists' attitudes of understanding, interest, and respect with favorable outcome in the treatment of thirty-six obsessive-compulsive patients; and Johnston and coworkers (Johnston, Lancashire, Matthews, Munby, Shaw, & Gilder, 1976), who studied agoraphobic patients and ranked their therapists' encouragement and sympathy as more important than the practicing component of the treatment.

Cognitive Behavior Therapy

In cognitive behavioral therapy, the added emphasis is on cognition. Cognitive behavioral therapy resulted from an integration of three schools—behavior therapy, cognitive therapy, and cognitive and social psychology. Cognitive behavioral theory is built on the framework of social learning theory (Bandura, 1977, 1986). The basic tenet of social learning theory is that it is partly through their own actions that people produce the environmental conditions that can affect their behavior in a reciprocal fashion. Behaviors that are the focus of change are known as *target behaviors. Antecedent behaviors* are events that precede the problematic behaviors. Events that follow are known as *consequences.* These elements interlock. The use of positive consequences (reinforcement) to change maladaptive behaviors is at the crux of social learning theory. The experiences generated by behavior can also partly determine what individuals think and can do, which, in turn, affects their subsequent behavior, cognitive processes, and environmental factors. In social learning theory, thoughts and feelings can both cause and explain behavior. This is in contrast to radical behaviorism, which views thoughts and feelings as covert behaviors that may be part of chains of behavior but do not have an initiating role. In social learning theory, thoughts and feelings may elicit emotional reactions, or provide discriminative cues for operant behaviors or negative or positive consequences (Gambrill, 1994).

There are three overlapping schools of cognitive behavioral therapy: RET (Ellis, 1962), cognitive therapy (Beck & Emery, 1985; Beck, Rush, Shaw, & Emery, 1979), and self-management strategies. The first two schools are detailed in the chapter on cognitive theory. Self-management strategies have a conceptual scheme of self-efficacy (Bandura, 1977, 1980) and self-instructional training, developed by Meichenbaum and his colleagues (Meichenbaum, 1977; Meichenbaum & Goodman, 1971), and will be discussed here in some detail. Self-instructional training emphasizes teaching clients coping statements and strategies. The major application of self-management strategies has been to problems of impulse control (e.g., weight, alcohol, drugs, impulsive children).

Self-Management Strategies.   Bandura (1977) suggests that people who have a high degree of perceived self-efficacy believe that they can master difficult tasks. Repeated successes in particular situations give rise to self-efficacy expectations, while failures tend to lower them. Observing another person performing the behavior of interest can also influence a person's efficacy expectations. Verbal persuasion is also a valuable tool in changing a person's efficacy expectations; however, because it is not founded on experience, it may be easily dismissed by the client (Rehm & Rokke, 1988). Bandura and his colleagues have conducted several studies that show a strong association between perceived self-efficacy and the subsequent level of performance accomplishment (Bandura, Reese, & Adams, 1982). Bandura believes psychological treatment of any form is successful in part because it alters a person's expectations of personal self-efficacy. Self-management approaches teach skills that can be implemented on one's own. For example, one of the most useful coping strategies taught by those who work with alcoholics using a coping skills model is the toleration of a certain amount of anxiety without giving into temptation (Chaney, O'Leary, & Marlatt, 1987).

Self-instructional training is a form of self-management that focuses on the importance of a person's self-statements, as maladaptive self-statements may contribute to a person's problems. The learning and application of more adaptive self-instructions is the goal of self-instructional training (Rehm & Rokke, 1988). Meichenbaum (1977) describes imaginal techniques to help the worker assess the client's self-statements. The client, with eyes closed, is asked to imagine a difficult situation and to describe her internal dialog to the social worker. They then discuss the quality of these self-statements and how they affect the behavior. Self-monitoring can be used with more formal record keeping or simply by telling the client to listen to herself. Conducting initial sessions in this way enables the therapist and client to conceptualize the problem and introduce a credible treatment rationale.

The second phase of self-instructional training is called "trying on," or allowing the client to test the logic of the rationale to see if it applies. The essence of the treatment is to teach the client more adaptive self-statements so that the problem can be changed. The third stage of treatment is directed toward promoting change. The client and social worker together develop some self-statements that are conducive to coping, to replace the maladaptive self-statements that promote negativity and hopelessness. Meichenbaum and Goodman (1971) outlined their procedures for training impulsive children in self-instructional techniques. This was a five-step process. First, an adult modeled a task while talking to himself out loud, thus modeling self-statements to the child. The child performed the same task under the therapist's direction (using the same or similar statements). The child then performed the task while instructing himself out loud. The self-instruction was gradually faded so that the child repeated the task while whispering the instructions to himself, and finally while guiding his performance by private (covert) speech.

One of my favorite methods of instructing children to resist their impulses, developed by Meichenbaum and Goodman (1971), is called "The Little Turtle

Story." It goes something like this: "The little turtle didn't like school and vowed to stay out of trouble but always found it. Then he'd get angry and rip up his papers. Luckily, he met a tortoise who told him that he was carrying the answer to his problem in his shell. He could hide in the shell whenever he got the feeling that he was angry. Then he could rest a moment and figure out what to do." The therapist or teacher can then demonstrate the turtle reaction. Relaxation skills can be taught to the child, to be used while in his or her "shell." Counting from 1 to 10 while tensing and relaxing muscles can help to control strong feelings. The turtle method is combined with problem solving—once safely inside the "turtle shell," the child then thinks of an appropriate way to handle the situation. This might include *self-instructional training*, such as having the child talk to himself in his head, using language such as "I'm going to cool down now. Getting all upset about this never works, it just makes things worse. I don't need to let my anger get the best of me; I can keep cool, relax, and think of what to do." Meichenbaum and Goodman (1971) found that self-instructional procedures, compared to placebo and assessment control conditions, resulted in improved performance for impulsive children on the Porteus Maze, the Performance IQ, the WISC, and on a measure of cognitive impassivity.

These self-instructional procedures can be applied to adults with a variety of problems such as anger, anxiety, pain, and schizophrenia (Meichenbaum, 1977). The most important features of self-instructional training are the education about the specific problem and the modeling and rehearsal of relevant behavioral and cognitive skills. Strategies such as relaxation training, systematic desensitization, and assertiveness training could all include a self-instructional component.

A Typical Cognitive Behavioral Approach.   Included in a typical CBT assessment and intervention includes the following steps:

1. Specifying the problematic behaviors. Here one needs to be as specific as possible as to the "target" (key) behaviors that are to be the focus of change. Indicate which behaviors are excessive and need to be extinguished (i.e., temper tantrums, overeating, smoking) and those behaviors that are underdeveloped and that need to be shaped (developed), such as lack of assertiveness, too little motivation.
2. Collecting data. Assessment includes monitoring of behaviors that require attention by keeping logs, journals, or note cards on a daily basis and looking at the antecedent events that arouse the behaviors and their consequences. Clients need to learn to evaluate their behavior, monitor their behavior, read signs of their own feelings (anger and hostility), label their feelings, and evaluate their acts as social or antisocial. This also includes identifying patterns and themes that have occurred. Diaries are useful tools wherein the client can write what happened, what was said, what she did, and how comfortable she was with the results. Scaling (applying a numerical value from 0–100) can help the client to identify the intensity of the response. The client can then evaluate how satisfied she was with her actions, and what she

would do differently if that event was to occur again. Additional comments can be recorded if applicable, such as thoughts and feelings. Therapists can also monitor the therapist–client interactions, as can others in the client's life such as a parent or teacher. Standardized tests are also useful monitoring tools.

3. Goal setting. The therapist and client work collaboratively to set goals for change.

4. Intervention. Behavioral interventions include numerous techniques that are specifically tailored to enable the client to reach the goal that has been set. Many existing protocols can be found in the literature, and can be accessed by problem definition or clinical syndrome.

5. Homework. Giving homework assignments helps clients practice the skills they are learning in therapy and provides continuity from session to session.

6. Reinforcement for change. The acquisition of new, positive behaviors needs to be met with positive reinforcement. This is usually done by significant others, but clients can be their own reinforcers by giving themselves rewards for engaging in new behaviors. Behavioral clinicians and researchers have taken a leading role in designing intervention methods that only use positive reinforcement, and in advocating against the use of aversive methods that inflict unnecessary stress or physical discomfort upon the client (LaVigna & Donnellan, 1986; Meyer & Evans, 1989, cited in Gambrill, 1994).

7. Taking credit for change. Clients need to credit themselves with change that takes place, instead of attributing the change to the therapist. In this way, they learn to feel that they can engage in changing behavior on their own, which leads to greater self-control, mastery, and self-esteem enhancement.

8. Relapse prevention. It is much more difficult to break a habit than to form one. Plus, old habits tend to come back, particularly when a person is under stress. Clients need to be prepared for the possibility of relapse and strategize as to how they will handle slipping when it does occur. This is common in treatment of problems of impulse control regarding drinking, overeating, and smoking. Self-management strategies such as coping skills training and using self-statements help to prevent relapse.

Some of the more common behavior therapy techniques that can be utilized within specific interventions are the following:

1. Reinforcement. Positive reinforcement is something the person wants, like praise. It increases the probability that the behavior will occur again. In behavior therapy, the therapist and client both create opportunities for the client to receive rewards for the new behaviors. For some clients, just engaging in new, positive behaviors has merit of its own. Sometimes reinforcements have to be earned, as with token economies—a work payment incentive system in which the participants receive tokens when they display appropriate behavior. At some specified time, these tokens are exchanged at an agreed tariff for a variety of backup reinforcers—items and activities. Tokens such as stickers are used in classrooms to help

children earn points that can later be exchanged for small toys, treats, and other rewards. They are used with great success in special settings with handicapped or retarded children, and with chronic emotionally disturbed patients in mental hospital settings (five days of earning tokens for appropriate behaviors might be exchanged for a pass to go off grounds).

2. Punishment. This is a controversial technique that requires some consideration. An extreme form of punishment, known as aversion therapy, has been used with injurious behaviors to self and/or others, such as head banging, induced vomiting, self-mutilation, and child molesting. However, punishment not only goes against social work ethics, it is generally not effective. Because punishment doesn't usually coincide with the actual behavior, but happens afterward, the subject doesn't connect punishment with the deed. Punishing rewards the punisher, helps to maintain dominance, and induces guilt and shame (Pryor, 1985). Negative reinforcement, more acceptable than aversion therapy, differs from punishment in that it occurs during the behavior, and the consequence is immediate. (Time out for a disruptive child is a negative reinforcer. This procedure has been used quite effectively and is well known to most parents and practitioners.)

3. Social skills training. This is a technique that is frequently used to coach children in a variety of socially acceptable skills. The skills usually covered are listening, speaking, and verbal and nonverbal communications (Pryor, 1985). Popular children are socially sensitive children. Training in social skills teaches children to see others' points of view. Prosocial behavior is modeled, such as making positive comments to another child who is playing constructively. Praise is given for appropriate social behavior that is initiated, and the child is encouraged to adopt a sociable personality. (For example, "Let's talk about some ways to have fun with other children when you play games. One way is for everyone to take turns." The therapist then clarifies what "taking turns" means.) The child is also encouraged to identify some good and bad examples. (For example, "waiting until others have finished before you begin" would be a good example of how to take turns. "Always trying to go first" is not a good example of how to take turns.) The child receives feedback about what she has learned and how she performs.

4. Assertiveness training. These skills help clients to accurately discriminate between aggression, assertiveness, and slavish conformity or deference. Clients practice assertiveness training by making statements that are direct and to the point, firm but not hostile, considerate, and respectful. They are taught to recognize the other person, accurately reflect their goals, and offer a short explanation rather than a series of excuses. They are helped not to include sarcasm, pleading, or whining, and not to blame others.

5. Relaxation training. This technique is useful with clients suffering from anxiety disorders and panic attacks. Different scripts abound, but most include progressive muscle relaxation where the client, with eyes closed, focuses on the different parts of the body while tensing and relaxing the muscles for 15 to 20 minutes.

We have noted only a few of the more common behavioral techniques used in practice. There is a breadth of behavioral interventions specific to clinical syndromes such as generalized anxiety disorder, depression, panic disorder, agoraphobia, social phobia, and social anxiety, obesity, and eating disorders. We refer you to a comprehensive text offering specific protocols, *Clinical Handbook of Psychological Disorders,* by David H. Barlow (2001). Barlow's contributors give thorough assessment and research evaluation information, plus step-by-step instructions on how to intervene with a wide range of psychosocial disorders.

Case Example: A Behavioral Approach to Obsessive-Compulsive Disorder

The following case illustrates behavioral treatment of a client with obsessive-compulsive disorder. Several behavioral techniques are demonstrated: modeling, exposure, response prevention, the construction of an anxiety hierarchy, use of client self-statements, homework, and self-monitoring. Single-subject design methodology was used to evaluate the effectiveness of the interventions.

The client, a 26-year-old woman, was handicapped by severe washing, checking, and counting rituals. During the course of a typical day, she performed approximately fifty-four rituals, which impaired her ability to function vocationally and socially and caused her great suffering and misery. She told me that she had to awaken at 4 A.M. in order to do all her morning rituals and still be at work by 9 A.M. Not surprisingly, she was frequently late for work. Although she recognized that her ritualizing was senseless, she felt compelled to continue to do so. Originally treated with psychodynamic psychotherapy for several years, she experienced no relief in symptom reduction. I treated her psychodynamically for two additional years, with no change in her ritualizing behavior. Depressed and discouraged, the client happened upon a television program on obsessive-compulsive disorder that spoke of a successful behavioral treatment. She asked if I could help her with the approach described on the show. As I was not a behavioral therapist at the time, I began my own research and discovered some protocols on the treatment of obsessive-compulsive disorder. The result was astounding—after nearly five years of psychodynamic therapy, the change in approach in favor of behavioral treatment resulted in an elimination of the client's rituals in just eight weeks.

Assessment Phase

To prepare for the behavioral treatment, I discussed the rationale for the protocol with the client: Obsessive-compulsive disorder is considered an anxiety disorder. Some people feel that it is biological in nature and that it has to do with the uptake in the brain of a chemical called serotonin. Others believe that it is a maladaptive way of managing anxiety—that sometime in the past you made an association between a behavior that you participated in and a feeling of calm. Perhaps you were feeling anxious one day, and you washed your hands and felt better. So the next time you felt anxious you washed your hands, and this pattern continued until suddenly, without thinking about it, you were washing your hands all the time. Then this washing behavior began to enter into other aspects of your life. Soon you started showering for longer periods of time. The ritual seemed to grow in size as well as frequency, until it took on a life of its own. Now, instead of feeling less anxious, you begin to feel more anxious because of all the time you were spending washing in an attempt to ward off bad feelings. That is what happens with OCD—the ritualizing begins to spread into other areas of your life. Pretty soon, you forget the reason that you started ritualizing in the first place. The treatment we will undertake is called exposure and response prevention. I will expose you to those things that you fear, and help you to face your fears. By preventing you from ritualizing we will break the automatic bond between the discomfort and the ritual. It won't be easy, but I will be here to help you each step of the way.

The client was given some reading material on OCD and behavior therapy, and after she consented to this change in the treatment approach, we started the assessment process. This entailed looking at all of the external stimuli that gave rise to obsessive-compulsive behavior, the content of the rituals, the length of time taken to perform them, the sequence in which they were performed, and the situations that were avoided to prevent ritualizing. An easy way to do this is to ask the client to describe a typical day, giving details of all the rituals she performs from the time she awakes until the time she goes to sleep. The client identified fifty-four rituals that she performed with regularity. Some examples included glancing into cups, glasses, and the corners of doorposts of a room; looking up common words in a dictionary when writing to ascertain that they were spelled correctly; and counting the number of times she swallowed or gulped while drinking a beverage. Using a method described by Emmelkamp (1982), we constructed a hierarchy of anxiety. This was done by asking the client to rank on a scale from 0 to 100 how anxious she would feel as she was confronted by each item that engendered the urge to ritualize. Then these items were listed in a hierarchy ranking from 0 to 100 (0 on the scale indicated no anxiety, and 100 signified intense anxiety). From this hierarchical list the worker developed assignments to eliminate the rituals. To determine the effectiveness of the treatment, I selected three rituals for monitoring: (1) repetitively opening and shutting makeup cases, which she did after daily use to listen for a clicking sound that would indicate that they were closed; (2) excessive rinsing in the shower after soaping, which lengthened her shower time to over an hour; and (3) counting her belongings (for example, tote bag and pocketbook) each time she carried them from place to place. The client predicted that the anxiety she would have if faced with the first item while not being allowed to ritualize would cause her to experience a discomfort level of 30 to 40 on the anxiety hierarchy. The assignment developed for eliminating the ritual became "Open and close makeup cases only once, and don't listen for a click or other signs that they are closed." According to the client, lowering the rinsing time (item #2) in the shower to 15 minutes (considered normal) would result in an anxiety level of 50 to 60. I developed an assignment accordingly. The client rated eliminating the counting of belongings at a discomfort level of 90 to 100. The assignment for extinguishing this ritual was stated as, "When you move from place to place and carry your belongings, do not count them." As can be noted, there is no particular reason why the elimination of one ritual would cause more anxiety than another—it is all part of the senseless nature of the disorder.

(continued)

Case Example   **Continued**

The Measurements

A single-subject design with a multiple-baseline approach was used to monitor the effectiveness of the treatment. The client identified fifty-four rituals that she regularly performed. The three target behaviors mentioned above were systematically monitored, although the intervention addressed all fifty-four items.

The Behavioral Techniques

Modeling, exposure, and response prevention were the three treatment techniques applied. First, I modeled (demonstrated) the appropriate way that a person would respond in different situations (for example, when putting on makeup). Then, the client was confronted with the item that caused her fear and created the urge to ritualize (exposure). The client would be exposed to a makeup item such as mascara and then instructed to perform the task of applying the mascara, replacing the wand in the tube, and refraining from ritualizing (response prevention). The client was exposed, in sessions, to those items that caused her to ritualize. In one instance, she was told to bring to session her makeup and the makeup cases. I showed her how I applied each makeup item, closing each case only once (modeling). The client was then instructed to do the same. This, at times, engendered considerable anxiety, as noted in the following dialog from an early session:

Worker: Now I will put on mascara. (I begin to do so.) Notice how I open the wand, apply the product to my eyelashes, close the wand, and return it to my makeup case. Now you do the same. (I hand her the wand.)

Client: No, I can't do it.

Worker: Yes, you can. I know it's hard, but I assure you, nothing bad will happen. I did it just a moment ago, and nothing bad happened to me.

Client: That's easy for you to say. What if something does happen? It's too difficult for me, I need more time. I'll do it next week. I need to think about it.

Worker: We've already thought about it, and you've come to recognize that these rituals don't make any sense. You think they will comfort you, but in actuality, you have become much more anxious since taking them on. Here, take the mascara; I know you can do it.

Client: (becoming more frightened now) No, I can't. You can't make me. It's all too much for me. I should never have let you talk me into this. Stop pushing me. I need more time.

Worker: We could put it off, but it won't get any easier. Sometimes you just have to forge ahead. Just think about how good you will feel when you can put on your mascara like everyone else. Remember, no harm will come to you. I'm living proof that a person can put on mascara and not have anything bad happen. Just take my example. I have complete confidence in you. (I again hand her the wand.)

Client: (takes the wand and looks at it)

Worker: That's the way. Now just apply it to your eyelashes. Just remember, worrying about things like mascara takes too much time and energy. What's the worst thing that will happen? Maybe some will spill. Maybe you'll have to clean it up. But you can't spend your days worrying about every little thing.

The client takes the wand and finally applies her mascara.

Client: See, I did it. Are you happy now?

Worker: You did a very brave thing. I know how hard that was for you. Now let's see if we can apply the other makeup items.

I then proceeded to expose her to the other makeup items that caused her to ritualize. She was able to follow my example and apply each item, with considerably less anxiety than she had first experienced. Homework was assigned, consisting of daily practice sessions of exposing herself to her makeup and applying it without ritualizing, for a total of 40 minutes of practice time Monday through Friday. Self-instructional training was also used, and together the client and I constructed a script that she would practice and say to herself when she became anxious. Included in these self-statements were some of the following:

"There's no need to feel anxious now. I know the correct way to put on makeup. I know how to close the case just once. What difference does it make if I don't close it perfectly? What is the worst that could happen? So maybe a little bit of makeup will spill inside the bag. So what? It's not a catastrophe. It won't hurt anyone. All this closing and listening is senseless, just time-consuming nonsense that prevents me from doing important things. I will choose to stop this ritualizing. I can do it. It might be hard, but I can do hard things."

The client was also instructed to practice correctly closing, pressing, and twisting items such as bottles, jars, and containers, to foster generalization from makeup items to other items that required closing. The client kept a homework book and recorded exactly how, and how often, she practiced each item. After intervention, self-monitoring (recording) continued for each targeted ritual six more times over six weeks, as an after-measure. This continuation of self-monitoring provided a basis for measuring change between the pretreatment and posttreatment phases, and gave me feedback on the success of the treatment. Followup reporting took place at 3- and 6-month intervals. At both followup sessions the client reported that ritualizing remained extinguished for makeup cases. The same treatment principles were applied to all fifty-four items on the list, in order to eliminate all ritualizing behavior.

Conclusion

Complete data analysis with graphs is found in Chapter 14, Integrating Research and Practice. The official behavioral therapy protocol ended after eight sessions. Talk therapy continued, and together we worked on reducing the frequency of the twelve remaining rituals, and in the next two months, nine of the remaining rituals were reduced by half and three were eliminated completely. Treatment then terminated, as the client had reached her goal. By the three-month followup, forty-five of the fifty-four rituals had been eliminated. The nine that remained were reduced in frequency by at least half. All of the target rituals had been eliminated. Of the fifty-four rituals, forty-six were gone within six months. The original eight that had remained were reduced by at least half, and the client had eliminated one ritual on her own. The client was extremely pleased with her progress and felt that for the first time in years she was leading a normal life.

The treatment protocol for obsessive-compulsive disorder has been established to be effective (Clark, 2003; Swinson, Antony, Rachman, & Richler, 2001). The over-

(continued)

Case Example   Continued

all success for the combination of exposure and response prevention has been consistently high—about 75 percent of patients have markedly improved (Steketee, 1987). What is unique about this case is that the client and I had a two-year psychotherapeutic relationship before the behavioral treatment was introduced. She had already established trust and had made a commitment to the therapy. These relational factors cannot be overlooked in evaluating her progress.

Source: Cooper, M. (1990, June). Treatment of a client with obsessive-compulsive disorder. *Social Work Research & Abstracts, 26*(2), 26–32. Copyright © 1990, National Association of Social Workers, Inc. Social Work Research & Abstracts.

Summary

Behavior theory has value for social workers because of its practical application to case situations. It is particularly useful when working with children, who respond extremely well to positive reinforcement techniques. Social workers can teach behavioral strategies to parents and teachers, who can then use them with children at home and in school. A behavioral assessment requires the worker and client to specify problems and goals. It is a collaborative process that requires focus. Interventions are systematically applied. This highly structured arrangement is comfortable for both clients and workers. In addition, social workers can immediately learn the effectiveness of the treatment. Finally, behavioral practice lends itself to evaluation, as noted in the single-subject design method described in this chapter. Behavioral practice is, therefore, evidence based—a concept of growing importance as social workers are being urged to become more rigorous in examining their practice.

Learning Assignments

1. Pick a habit that you have that bothers you or someone else. Try to break the habit. Write up your results.

2. Pick a subject who might benefit from behavioral therapy. If you do not have a client, consider using a friend, or yourself. Define the target problem for intervention and the particular behavioral technique that you would use.

3. Intervene with your subject and discuss your results.

4. Working in pairs, have one person role-play the client and the other role-play therapist. Develop a scenario in which the client has a homework assignment to do. Discuss the assignment with the client. Have the client return the following week without having the assignment completed. How should the therapist handle this?

References

Agras, S., Alexander, J. F., Leitenberg, H., & Barlow, D. H. (1968, October). Social reinforcement in the modification of agoraphobia. *Archives of General Psychiatry, 19*(4), 423–427.

Bandura, A. (1977). *Social learning theory.* Englewood Cliffs, NJ: Prentice-Hall.

Bandura, A. (1980). Gauging the relationship between self-efficacy judgment and action. *Cognitive Therapy and Research, 4,* 263–268.

Bandura, A. (1986). *Social foundations of thought and action.* Englewood Cliffs, NJ: Prentice-Hall.

Bandura, A., Reese, L., & Adams, N. E. (1982). Microanalysis of action and fear arousal as a function of differential levels of perceived self-efficacy. *Journal of Personality and Social Psychology, 43,* 5–21.

Barlow, D. H. (Ed.). (2001). *Clinical handbook of psychological disorders* (3rd ed.). New York: Guilford.

Beck, A. T., & Emery, G. (1985). *Anxiety disorders and phobias.* New York: Basic Books.

Beck, A. T., Rush, A. J., Shaw, B. F., & Emery, G. (1979). *Cognitive therapy of depression.* New York: Guilford.

Chaney, E. F., O'Leary, M. R., & Marlatt, G. A. (1987). Skill training with alcoholics. *Journal of Consulting and Clinical Psychology, 46,* 1092–1104.

Clark, D. A. (2003). *Cognitive-behavioral therapy for OCD.* New York: Guilford.

Ellis, A. (1962). *Reason and emotion in psychotherapy.* Secaucus, NJ: Lyle Stuart.

Emmelkamp, P. (1982). *Phobic and obsessive-compulsive disorders: Theory, research and practice.* New York: Plenum.

Gambrill, E. (1994). Concepts and methods of behavioral treatment. In D. Granvold (Ed.), *Cognitive and behavioral treatment* (pp. 32–62). Pacific Grove, CA: Brooks/Cole.

Johnston, D. W., Lancashire, M., Matthews, A. M., Munby, M., Shaw, P. M., & Gilder, M. G. (1976, October). Imaginal flooding and exposure to real phobic situations: Charges during treatments. *British Journal of Psychiatry, 129,* 372–377.

LaVigna, G. W., & Donnellan, A. M. (1986). *Alternatives to punishment: Solving behavior problems with nonaversive strategies.* New York: Irvington.

Meichenbaum, D. (1977). *Cognitive behavior modification: An integrative approach.* New York: Plenum.

Meichenbaum, D., & Goodman, J. (1971). Training impulsive children to talk to themselves: A means of developing self-control. *Journal of Abnormal Psychology, 77,* 115–126.

Meyer, L. H., & Evans, I. M. (1989). *Nonaversive intervention for behavior problems: A manual for home and community.* Baltimore: Paul H. Brookes.

Pryor, K. D. (1985). *Don't shoot the dog. The new art of teaching and training.* New York: Bantam.

Rabavilas, A. D., Boulougouris, J. C., & Perissaki, C. (1979). Therapist qualities related to outcome with exposure in vivo in neurotic patients. *Journal of Behavior Therapy and Experimental Psychiatry, 10,* 293–299.

Rehm, L., & Rokke, P. (1988). Self management therapies. In K. D. Dobson (Ed.), *Handbook of cognitive-behavioral therapies* (pp. 136–166). New York: Guilford.

Safron, J. D., & Segal, V. (1996). *Interpersonal process in cognitive therapy.* Northvale, NJ: Jason Aronson.

Sloane, R. B., Staples, F. R., Cristol, I. H., Yorkston, N. J., & Whipple, K. (1975). *Psychotherapy versus behavior therapy.* Cambridge, MA: Harvard University Press.

Steketee, G. (1987). Behavioral social work with obsessive-compulsive disorders. *Journal of Social Service Research, 10,* 53–73.

Swinson, R. P., Antony, M. M., Rachman, S. & Richler, M. A. (2001). *Obsessive compulsive disorder: Theory, research, and treatment.* New York: Guilford.

Thomlison, B. (1984). Phobic disorders. In F. Turner (Ed.), *Adult psychopathology: A social work perspective* (pp. 280–315). New York: The Free Press.

Thomlison, B., & Thomlison, R. (1996). Behavior theory and social work treatment. In F. Turner (Ed.), *Social work treatment: Interlocking theoretical approaches* (4th ed.). New York: The Free Press.

11

Narrative Therapy

A Postmodern Approach

Narrative theory is a postmodern theory, similar to postmodern literary criticism, where the story line is deconstructed and the plot, characters, and timeline are reassessed for meaning (Kelly, cited in Turner, 1996). Narrative therapy began with the family therapists in Australia and New Zealand, originating with the work of White and Epston in the 1980s. Their approach became popular in North America with the 1990 publication of their book, *Narrative Means to Therapeutic Ends*.

Narrative therapy is a brief treatment modality. It can be accomplished in seven or eight sessions, but does not have to be limited to that time frame. The emphasis in narrative therapy is on understanding and meaning, which makes it particularly relevant to social work practice with diverse populations. This is true since the clinician does not presume a way of being, but instead aims to understand the client's reality within the client's social and cultural contexts. Narrative theory is strengths based, and thus bears resemblance to the solution focused therapy of Berg and de Shazer (de Shazer, 1991). Narrative therapy is about knowledge and how the client has "storied" her life to make sense of it. Often this story is "saturated" with problems. Through a process known as "deconstruction," the dominant dysfunctional story line is given new meaning, based on an understanding of other truths and alternative realities (Drewery & Winslade, 1997; Morgan, 2000).

Constructivism as a Conceptual Framework for Narrative Therapy

Constructivism is a conceptual framework that informs the narrative approach to clinical practice. Constructivism emphasizes the importance of the client's subjective perception and experience of a problem. Philosophically, constructivism is concerned with the nature of reality and being (metaphysics and ontology) and the nature and acquisition of human knowledge (epistemology; Carpenter, cited in Turner, 1996; Dean, 1993). Constructivism is rooted in postmodern thinking—which assumes that there are no universal truths and that there are as many realities as there are perceivers of reality. Constructivism asserts that (1) individuals are active participants in the construction of their reality; (2) cognition, affect, and behavior are interactive; (3) an individual's development across the life span is significant; and (4) internal cognitive and affective structures (including meaning systems, narrative and life stories) determine behavior and behavioral change (DiGiuseppe & Linscott, 1993; Mahoney, 1988; Neimeyer, 1993, cited in Franklin & Nurius, 1996, p. 323).

Constructivism places great emphasis on the development of a caring, respectful, understanding, and trusting therapeutic relationship. The practitioner is the learner and the facilitator of new stories that are more empowering and more hopeful than the problem-saturated story that has dominated the client's life. The client is the teacher who brings as much of her world to the treatment arena as possible. Narrative therapists enlist the client's problem-solving capacities by focusing on successful ways that she has coped in the past.

The Language of Narrative

The use of language plays a central role in the postmodern paradigmatic shift from objective to subjective reality because reality is constructed through social discourse (Real, 1990). Rather than acquiring the *facts* about the client's life (taking a psychosocial history), the therapist listens to the client's *stories*. Therapeutic dialog becomes a conversation as the therapist and client are engaged in the making of a new story called "meaning making or narrative creation" (Peller & Walter, 1998, p. 74). Postmodern language is colorful. Words often change from nouns into verbs; for example, the word "language" (a noun) becomes "languaging" (a verb) to more accurately describe the active, creative *process* of therapy (Neimeyer, 1993). Language is used to build on client's strengths, not to correct pathology or cognitive distortions.

The Structure of Narrative: Narrative as Metaphor

Narratives are reformulations or constructions of memories in the client's life that change over time. They form the center of treatment from a constructivist perspective. The process of understanding and organizing life events and experiences (whether historical or current) within their social and cultural contexts constitutes a narrative. Narratives provide structure and meaning that help people understand their own roles in relation to the wider social and cultural environment. The individual's self (identity) develops within this context. The use of the story metaphor instead of history has several implications. First, we are hearing a reformulation of the client's memories and not necessarily the historical truth. The therapist assumes that every person's life story is filled with contradictions and makes use of that fact in therapy. Second, narratives about the same event can change over time. Finally, the telling of the narrative is influenced by the therapist's participation in the process as a "participant observer" (Anderson & Goolishian, 1988, p. 384) and the context in which the narratives are told and heard. The therapist tries to ask questions that expand upon the client's story and, when relevant, attempts to clarify the story in ways that may be important to the client. This "discourse-sensitivity" (Lowe, 1991, p. 43) assumes center stage in narrative therapy where attention is focused on the ways in which the conversation between the therapist and the client unfolds. In this interpersonal relationship between the therapist and the client, the client's narrative or life story will change in meaningful ways. Hoffman (1992, p. 78) describes the therapeutic encounter in narrative practice as a dialectic process between the activity of patients constructing problems in their lives, the social and environmental forces contributing to and/or encasing these problems, and the patients' present experiences (in the immediacy of the relationship with the therapist). Real (1990, p. 260) describes the collaborative process of conversing, stressing both the facilitative and participatory role of the therapist in "the process of change through conversation."

The Deconstruction of Narrative

Narrative therapy views the client's problems as products of discourse that have placed her in problematic positions in the story she is telling about her life. The narrative counselor looks for alternatives to the problem story, and in so doing, helps the client to develop a clearer perspective, which allows the client to reposition or reclaim her own voice. The process of listening to the client's story in this way is called deconstruction.

An important component of the deconstruction of narrative is the deconstruction of social power that dominates people's lives in more ways than they often realize. Clients are invited to talk about the effects of these familiar practices of power and the hold that they have on their lives—what these practices have caused clients to feel about themselves and their relationships with others. In this way, clients come to appreciate the degree to which these practices of power influence and diminish their lives and the lives of those around them (White, 1995).

In the deconstruction stage, the client is encouraged to take responsibility for her own behaviors and to fight the effects of the problem. The narrative therapist does not assume that there are secondary gains to having the problem, or that the problem serves a function. Clients are not seen as "resistant" or "unmotivated." It is essential that the therapist believe and respect the client's words and not dispute the story as untrue. It is through discussion, analysis, and interpretation that the story is given meaning (White, 1986, 1988b).

Externalizing Conversations

One of the distinctive qualities of narrative therapy (and the deconstruction of narrative) is the use of externalizing conversations (Nylund, 2000; White & Epston, 1990). Through this process, the problem becomes objectified—placed outside the person—rather than internalized. The use of externalizing conversations as a language provides a powerful linguistic shift that enables the individual and family members to collaborate on solving the problem in a unified way. The therapist encourages the client to trace or understand the influence that these perceptions have had on her life, her view of herself, and her relationships with others. The therapist tries to understand the client's perceptions of the problem, and how other persons may have been recruited (or drawn) into sharing these same views. Separating the client from the problem helps the client to explore alternative, more positive experiences and gain self-knowledge. She is now open to the many possibilities of whom she might become. For example, in working with a young child who experiences urinary frequency, Epston (1997, p. 64) writes, "your habit is trying to trick you into thinking you are a weakling . . . it is not so! You are a powerful young man, but your problem is weakening you and making you miserable, making you not sleep at night." Another example of how the concept of externalizing is used in narrative practice is illustrated in White's (1991, p. 24) work with a couple experiencing marital discord. White says he needs the couple to "help me understand how they had been recruited into this pattern of responding to differences of opinion over particular issues. . . ." This allows the clients to unite in challenging the problem, instead of fighting and blaming each other.

Therapeutic Strategies

Real (1990, p. 270) discusses five techniques used in postmodern therapy. Since these strategies are not linear, they can be used at any time during a therapy session.

1. The *eliciting stance.* Here, the therapist invites the client to share his ideas about the presenting problem and shows curiosity about aspects of the problem definition that may have previously received little attention. Real suggests that the therapist use questions that would encourage the client to expand on his thinking. A parent came to me recently. Her 11-year-old son had been stealing money from her purse and was being disruptive in school. She was at her "wits end" because she had taken away many of his privileges—all to no avail. I asked, "What's your thinking about what is happening with your son at this time?" She replied, "I don't know, I think he's angry." I asked, "What might he be angry about . . . do you have any ideas?"

   She replied "I just think he's angry and trying to get attention. . . . I work long hours and he doesn't like that."

2. The *probing* stance. The therapist offers alternative descriptions to those offered by the client. These descriptions are discrepant enough from preexist-
ing descriptions so as to be useful, but not so wildly discrepant as to be
offensive and therefore rejected out of hand. Continuing with the above dialog, the therapist uses a probe, "I'm wondering if John's behavior could be
sending you a message that he is sad, as well as angry?"

3. *Contextualizing.* In this stance, the therapist moves away from language that
focuses on the individual client and moves toward language that connects
the client to others in her life. The focus moves from a state of "being" to a
state of "showing"; for example, "When your son is angry, to whom does he
show his anger?" "What happens then?" "What would happen if your son
showed his anger to . . . (another person)?"

4. The *matching* or *reflecting* stance. In this intervention, the therapist mirrors
back what has been told to her: "I see, you're worried about there being
more tension in the family if your son's behavior continues."

5. The *amplifying* stance. Here, the therapist attends to a particular emotion, behavior, or idea that has worked well for the client in the past. "I am im-
pressed that in spite of your fears about further tension in the family, your
concern for your son has prompted you to get some help."

Reauthoring

The narrative therapist invites the client to evaluate alternative outcomes. He asks
if the client considers them to be significant and preferred and the reasons why
this may be so. The therapist assumes a position of not knowing. Genuinely curious about these alternative outcomes, he engages the client in a retelling of her
original story, called "new meaning making." The client assumes the role of primary author. The therapist becomes the coauthor whose participation depends on
important information and feedback from the client about her experience with the
therapy. The therapist asks the client directly why certain ideas that have emerged
during the therapy are of more interest to her than others. The client is encouraged to evaluate how therapy has affected her life and her relationships to others.
She is also asked if her current relationships are preferable to those that she had
before entering therapy, and to what extent. The therapist engages in different
types of questions in this process of reauthoring:

1. **Landscape of action questions.** These are questions that can address the
past, present, and the future. For example, questions referencing the past are
raised to generate new meanings of a client's history (other than the problem-
ridden perception she may have about her life). White (1991, p. 31) provides
some useful examples of questions that generate "alternative historical landscapes."

"What can you tell me about your history that would help me to understand how you managed to take this step?"

"Are you aware of any past achievements that might, in some way, provide the backdrop for this recent development?"

"I would like to get a better grasp of this development. What did you notice yourself doing, or thinking, as a younger person, that could have provided some vital clue that this development was on the horizon of your life?"

2. **Landscape of consciousness questions.** These questions encourage the client to verbalize and try out alternative or preferred personal and relational qualities, beliefs, and meanings about her life. Such questions generate an optimism as clients are encouraged to reflect on their life stories. Examples of useful questions include the following (White, 1991, p. 31):

"What do these developments inform you about what suits you as a person?"

"Let's reflect for a moment on these recent developments. What new conclusions might you reach about your tastes; about what is appealing to you; about what you are attracted to?"

"What do these discoveries tell you about what you want for your life?"

3. **Experience of experience questions.** These questions help the client reflect on another person's experience of him. They can be oriented to alternative landscapes of action or alternative landscapes of consciousness (as discussed above). They can encourage the client to consider future developments in these two realms. For example (White, 1991, p. 32),

"If I had been a spectator to your life when you were a younger person, what do you think I might have witnessed you doing then that might help me to understand how you were able to achieve what you have recently achieved?"

"How do you think that knowing this has affected my view of you as a person?"

"Of all the persons who have known you, who would be the least surprised that you have been able to take this step in challenging the influence of problems in your life?"

Positions

Narrative theory posits that it is possible for an individual to hold more than one position within each discourse (or conversation), each with a different meaning. A sister and daughter, for example, would be two different *positions* within the single *discourse* of a family. This is complicated by the fact that an individual may also hold positions with different discourses at the same time. (For example, the sister/daughter may have a position in a school in addition to her position in a family.) These different *positions* or *discourses* may hold different sets of *expectations*, which may be in conflict with each other. In the case that follows, Mrs. G. is a daughter to a mother *(position within her family of origin)* who struggled with mental illness and was abusive toward her. She is a student *(position within educational institution),* working toward a degree in human services, and she is the mother of two adolescent children *(position within current family).* We include a genogram and an ecomap in this chapter to illustrate Mrs. G.'s many positions within her family and the other varied discourses in her life.

Narrative therapy suggests that individuals do not always have control over the positions or discourses wherein they find themselves. Unfortunately, these stories, developed from the positions available to individuals, can lead to difficulties contemplating other stories. The conflict and stress that result are often what bring individuals into therapy.

Definitional Ceremony

Narrative therapy is structured as a context for "thick description" of people's lives. Thick description is achieved through tellings and retellings of life stories. There will be an initial telling, a retelling of the telling (first telling), a retelling of the retelling (second retelling), and so on. Through these retellings, people's lives are "thickened," shared themes emerge, and alternatives are generated. This process contributes an understanding about their lives that would otherwise be inaccessible. The therapist and the client discuss who else in the client's life might be invited to participate in the definitional ceremony as affirming witnesses to the client's preferred claims about herself. The therapist (and any other outsider witnesses) engage with the client (and with each other) in conversations about what they heard and their responses. This provides the opportunity for each of the participants (including the therapist) to participate in a new experience—one that hopefully contributes to their emotional growth.

Therapeutic Documents

A "therapeutic document" (White, 1995, p. 199) can be a letter written by the therapist, a statement of position written by the client, or a letter of reference from an affirming person in the client's life. The worker and client discuss confidentiality concerns and determine who should be involved in preparing the document. Additional decisions to be made are who reads the document and under what circumstances and when might the document be consulted. (See, for example, the narrative letter(s) in this chapter written by the therapist to the client between sessions as a source of affirmation and support. The client can consult this letter during periods of self-doubt or stress.) The therapist invites the client to consider the consequences of consulting the therapeutic document by asking "What effect do you imagine this consultation could have on your responses to the problem and on your relationships in general?" (White, 1995, p. 211). Events that take place between sessions are explored to identify those times when the client felt a need to consult the therapeutic document. The client is asked to consider how her prediction about these consultations (e.g., Will it be helpful?) compares to the actual events that occurred (e.g., Was it helpful?). If the predictions were accurate, the client is asked to reflect on the significance (e.g., the letter did help; the letter helped because . . .; the letter did not help; the letter did not help because . . .) If a review of events contradicts the client's predictions, the therapist and client can discuss what important information may have been missing from the documents and how these documents might be revised in the future. Some clients report that each narrative letter is worth as many as four therapy sessions (White, 1991). These letters can also be used as case notes for the clinician.

Cross-Cultural Counseling

Steier (1991, p. 4) defines an individual as "a person in a culture," whose self-definition is influenced by the way in which she is viewed by others in that culture. Narrative therapy has been considered effective in cross-cultural counseling (see Chapter 5) because this therapeutic framework views identity as a socially constructed phenomena (Lee, 1996). In narrative therapy, the client's *way of seeking help* is understood within a sociocultural context. Lee and Greene (1999, p. 30) discuss this as "accessing the culturally embedded, unique meaning of the client's perceived problem and solution . . ." Solutions generated between the therapist, the client, and the therapist's professional values are offered in ways that are both culturally specific and culturally respectful.

Case Example: The G. Family

The following case demonstrates a narrative therapy approach that extended over a period of eight months. The therapist is an Anglo male and the client is a Latina female. Each was raised and educated within different sociocultural contexts, making the choice of narrative therapy a good one. Although the therapy was conducted primarily in English, both the client and the therapist were bilingual, and they were able to introduce Spanish words when English was not sufficiently descriptive. As the Latino definition of self is one of being in relation to family (Garcia-Petro, 1982; Lee, 1996; Lee & Greene, 1999), individual and family interventions were combined.

Mrs. G. is a 45-year-old woman who grew up in a small town in Puerto Rico. She lived with her parents and two other siblings until the death of her father, which occurred when the client was 13 years old. Her father was described as "abusive" and "an alcoholic," and Mrs. G. felt life as a child was chaotic since the family often moved. Mrs. G. migrated to mainland United States in 1990, after experiencing dissatisfaction and disappointment in her marriage. She is the only family member to have left Puerto Rico. (See Figure 11.1 on page 170 for a genogram of Mrs. G.'s family of origin and Figure 11.2 on page 171 for a diagram of Mrs. G.'s family upon marriage.) Since living in the United States, Mrs. G. has become fluent in English. She graduated from college with a degree in human services and refers to this as "my one achievement in life." (See Figure 11.3 on page 172 for an ecomap of Mrs. G.'s family.)

Mrs. G. went to counseling to seek help in parenting her two adolescent children: a daughter, age 16, and a son, age 13. She felt overwhelmed by her son's school

(continued)

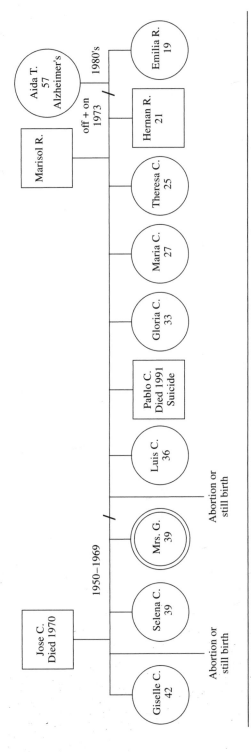

FIGURE 11.1 *Genogram of Mrs. G.'s Family of Origin*

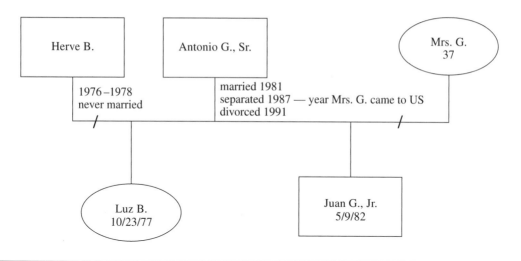

FIGURE 11.2   *Mrs. G.'s Family (Upon Marriage)*

Case Example   Continued

difficulties and out-of-control behaviors and her daughter's incessant demands. The therapist chose narrative therapy as the modality and introduced the use of therapeutic documents, specifically narrative letters, as an important component of the work. The narrative letter is a "record of a session or sessions and its impact on the client, in addition to an account of the client's abilities and talents as identified in the session. The letter emphasizes the client's struggle and draws distinctions between the problem story and the developing preferred story" (McKenzie & Monk, 1997, p. 111). Mrs. G. was able to consult these concrete affirmations of the positive elements of her life story at times when she began to doubt herself.

Using the Narrative Letter

Session with Mrs. G.: Preparing for a School Conference.   After several initial sessions, the therapist and Mrs. G. met prior to a school conference to discuss the difficulties her son was having in school, including explosive and unpredictable behavior, the need for one-on-one support, his tendency to get into various kinds of trouble, and an unwillingness to do the work. The therapist notes:

"Mrs. G. felt very pessimistic about getting change from the school today. We discussed various aspects of that. . . . She doesn't want to get out of control and become emotional." Dialog from the therapeutic letter he writes after the session illustrates how the therapist asks questions that help the client reauthor her story.

The Narrative Letter.   "In our conversation today, we covered several important issues of concern to you. You told me how lonely you feel when you confront situations, such as the school conference for Juan, which you felt you could not handle. You remarked, 'I miss my family' for the 'boundary' it provides. You are indeed far

(continued)

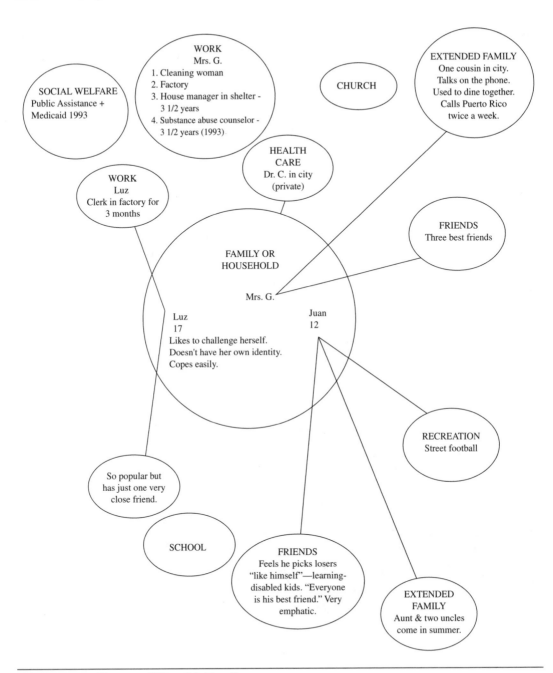

FIGURE 11.3   *Ecomap of Mrs. G.'s Family*

Case Example   Continued

from your family in Puerto Rico. Many people are able to hold powerful images in their mind of those they miss, which enable them to get through tough situations. *I'm wondering how you will view your difficulties and what images you will choose to help you.*"

Here, the therapist assumes an *eliciting stance* (inviting the client to share her ideas about the presenting problem) and uses a *landscape of action question* (addressing the future). These questions are framed so as to suggest that Mrs. G. may be able to construct new meaning—a meaning that will help her to feel secure.

The Narrative Letter Continues.   "How extraordinarily special you are to your mother that she always knows when you will call. What joy to hear her laughter with Juan! There is a deep and rich connection of joy and sharing between three generations. This is the positive side of your relationships. The idea of possible inherited mental illness continues to worry you. I want to remind you of all the ways you are different from your mother and how you are *not* crazy. You worry that Juan may have inherited some of your mother's characteristics. I'm wondering if it would be helpful to examine Juan and his ancestors by asking yourself, *'How is Juan different from his relatives who have suffered from mental illness?'* "

Here, the worker is *probing* (helping the client to find alternative explanations) and *contextualizing* (using language that connects her to others in her life). He is again using a *landscape of action* question (this one addresses the past) as he tries to help Mrs. G. consider an alternative way of storying her family background. He encourages a strengths model, rather than a deficits perspective, which Mrs. G. finds empowering.

In another session, Mrs. G. shared some painful feelings about her relationship with her son. Following the session, the therapist wrote this letter to her:

The Narrative Letter.   "You talked about the difficult transition Juan is facing in his new behavioral class and of your continuing effort to help Juan be successful in his new school. How painful it was for you to have Juan openly say 'I hate you' during your school visit. You requested that I speak with him, and I will soon schedule a visit to your home. I continue to be amazed by your growing *confianza* in me. You are indeed very committed to the process of counseling to help you unravel the difficulties that confront you and your children.

"*How have you talked to Juan this week about his anger? What did you discover about your relationship with Juan? What do these discoveries tell you about what you want for your life?*"

The therapist is now *amplifying* (attending to a particular emotion—Juan's anger) with a *landscape of consciousness* question (engaging her to verbalize and reflect on alternative meanings and beliefs). This encourages Mrs. G. to verbalize and consider preferred ways of interacting with her son.

Home Visit

The therapist made a home visit to the G. family and met with Mrs. G., her daughter, Luz, and her son, Juan. The purpose of the visit was to facilitate communication between family members, particularly between Mrs. G. and Juan. The hostility between

(continued)

Case Example   Continued

mother and son was immediately evident. Mrs. G. repeatedly interrupted the therapist in his conversation with Juan, making critical comments about the boy. Luz twice
sided with her mother. Success came when Juan's cousin and best friend, Jose, came
to visit. The therapist asked Jose to join the meeting (with the family's permission)
and attempted to recruit him as an ally who might be more affirming of Juan. During
this family meeting, Mrs. G. noted that Juan reminded her of his father. Juan's father
left her because he could not live up to "her high expectations."

Narrative Letter Following Home Visit.   "Mrs. G., in the past you shared with
me some of your emotional experience of childhood. 'I wasn't showed how to love
anybody. I wasn't taught to love, just to survive. I think I'm the only one in the family who expresses feelings.' Then you connected this to your daughter Luz. 'I feel
overwhelmed when Luz gets so close to me. She demands too much.' Your ability to
build deep and lasting relationships is extraordinary—precisely because you continue
to believe quite often that you are unlovable or isolated. You wonder how capable you
are of being loved. I don't think these beliefs are part of your real and authentic self.
Where do these ideas come from? You will be able to more readily determine the answer when you are speaking for yourself than when that belief is running the show.
*I wonder if you feel Juan demands too much, in different ways that also touch on your childhood
experience of love?*"

In this example, the therapist is *reflecting, contextualizing,* and *probing* and poses a
landscape of consciousness question to try and help Mrs. G. consider new ways of thinking about her past. He writes, "You are so often able to see connections and apply
what you experience in one part of your life to another. We have spoken in the past
of your relationship with Juan. I asked if your conflicts with him might in some way
be related to your profound hurt and disappointment about his father. You did not
feel this to be so. You are so often able to see connections and apply what you experience in one part of your life to another. You have 'been there' for Pablo (a friend of
Mrs. G.'s). You said, 'By expressing how strongly I'm there for him, how much I care
for him, I have seen how important these expressions are. So I now support my children and express my love to them.' You continue to evaluate your present and past
relationships. It will be fascinating to listen to this dialog with yourself and see where
you go. As you said, 'My goal is peace of mind.' *Would it be helpful to explore your relationship with each of your children through the theme of expectations? You spoke of how Luz
'lived up to my expectation.' You feel 'so proud of her . . . so close.' How has Juan's inability to
live up to your expectations changed your relationship with him? How has it affected his relationship with himself (with how he feels about himself), and how he feels toward you? How can
you act now, Mrs. G., to improve this? How can I help you?*"

The therapist continues *probing* and *amplifying;* this series combines *landscape of
consciousness* questions, *landscape of action* questions, and *experience of experience* questions (helping the client reflect on another's experience of her) as he ties Mrs. G.'s past
to her present and gives her optimism for the future.

In another session, Mrs. G. tells the therapist that she is thinking of putting Juan
in foster care because she cannot handle both him and the stress of her new job. After
the session, the therapist writes the following:

Narrative Letter.   "You certainly face very difficult decisions at home. You are determined not to lose your job because it is so central to your definition of yourself. You have said, 'If I have to quit because of Juan, I will be a complete failure.' I sense your despair of being trapped by a deficit model, a half-empty glass. This feeling is very much underscored by our culture and the values that are dominating the political process in our country, tending to be destructive to the poor and working class of this country. You seem to feel that there is only enough of you to either succeed at work or to hold things together unhappily at home. You told me, 'I will give up Juan before I give up my job. I have no one to care for me. I will not go back on welfare. Juan has disability insurance,' implying that he will be okay because he will have financial support. How sad for parents to have to think about choosing between keeping their children and keeping a job they love. Your lack of practical resources has you facing this choice. For next week, I would like you to do an experiment on alternate days. One day you will think and feel as if you have given up Juan. The next day you will think and feel as if you have decided to keep Juan and have found a way to combine work and family. Then go back to thoughts of giving up Juan. It will be important for you to write down your thoughts, ideas, and feelings each day. The forces of despair will try to convince you that you could never successfully combine work and family (days 2, 4, and 6). Don't let them fool you! Call me if you need reinforcing."

Following the letter, Mrs. G. tries to get Juan's father to take charge of him for a while. When the father refuses to help, she makes the decision, in spite of her frustration, to keep him at home with her. She does not feel that she can give up on him. As the situation develops, Juan does better in his new school, and because Mrs. G. learns to modify her expectations, set limits, and be more expressive of her love for him, their relationship improves. As the client's goals have been reached, the worker moves toward termination.

Narrative Letter Following Termination.   "As we talked about the end of our work, you have been able to describe the remarkable progress you have made in our eight months together. You described some of the powerful decisions that you have been able to make:

1. You confronted Juan's father.
2. After months of consideration, you make the decision to leave Pablo and you found a new apartment.
3. You didn't let Luz and Juan 'walk' all over you.
4. You learned to tell yourself, 'I'm not a supermom, I guide my children, but I can't control their choices. . . . I'm not going to take responsibility for their actions.' I asked you if this was tough love and you replied, 'No, it's real love. I think I have found myself.'

"What rich roots have you rediscovered that have nurtured your rapid growth these last few months? What experiences have you had in the past that made it possible to predict these recent changes, that let you know you were capable of these many recent changes? What new knowledge of yourself do you have that makes growing easier and easier? What are you learning about the process of making life-changing decisions? How can you make it easier on yourself to make such decisions?"

(continued)

Case Example   **Continued**

As therapy with Mrs. G. terminates, the therapist continues *amplifying* and *contextualizing* and introduces several *landscape of consciousness* questions to review the past work and empower Mrs. G. to think about the future.

The Narrative Letter Continues.   "You have long struggled with a deeply felt sense of aloneness. The end of my work with you, of course, raises these feelings again. But during your time alone this summer, you went from feeling empty to being able to make a triumphant statement, 'I'm me alone.' Do you understand the power of that statement? You are whole; you are complete. You went on to say, 'I want to be alone, to explore myself, to be independent.' When we meet for our last counseling session, I will read this letter and we can reflect on it further. I suggest that we try to talk more fully about my leaving and how that makes you feel. While I am leaving you, I am NOT leaving without telling you. I continue to be amazed by your skillful sculpting of your future. *Is that a useful analogy, of yourself as a sculptor, carving yourself in a new image?"*

The therapist concludes therapy with Mrs. G., *reflecting, contextualizing,* and *amplifying* their work together. He uses *experience of experience* questions, encouraging Mrs. G. to give new meaning to her history, her current life, and her future.

Research Perspectives

Narrative research would value difference, thick description, metaphor, individual preception, and the voice of the client over the voice of the researcher (Carlson & Kjos, 2002). Narrative research would not care about cure rates, as studies using measurement are not what narrative is about. Rather, qualitative approaches that honor the assumptions of the narrative perspective and that thicken description and capture diversity would be consistent with the narrative perspective. Citing Gergen (1999), Carlson and Kjos state:

> Required are the kinds of analysis that enable us to understand what is taking place from multiple standpoints, that will help us engage in dialogue with others from varied walks of life, and that will sensitize us to a range of possible futures. Most important, social analysis should help us generate vocabularies of understanding that can help us create our future together. For the constructionist, the point of social analysis is not then to "get it right" about what is happening to us. Rather, such analysis should enable us to reflect and create. (p. 195)

Summary

This case example illustrates the concepts of narrative therapy and, in particular, the use of the narrative letter as a therapeutic tool. These narrative letters advance the work of the therapy between sessions, affirm the client, and enable her to re-frame the "problem saturated story" into a new and empowering narrative. The therapist's respect for the client's culture is evident as he helps Mrs. G. to address conflicts with family members in ways that continue to strengthen her connection to them. He also respects her self-determination, for example, when she struggles with decisions concerning foster care for Juan. Through the use of externalization, Mrs. G. is able to experience the problem as the adversary and work with the therapist to fight and challenge her difficulties. The therapist regards Mrs. G. as the expert on her life, even when it might have been tempting to offer his own assessment or advice (as evidenced in the home visit). His language is empowering of Mrs. G.'s strengths and is never judgmental when she falters.

Many qualitative researchers do not subscribe to the postmodernist approach. They disagree with the notion that all information is interpretation. Padgett (1998, p. 7), in taking up this point, states, "Clearly, the logic of postmodernism and cultural relativism can be taken to an extreme; the 'many realities' approach becomes a hall of mirrors where all knowledge is suspect. In this context, we can never verify how many died in the Nazi Holocaust or in the Serbian massacres in Bosnia in the 1990s because these horrific incidents can be seen via many interpretive standpoints—none being privileged." Citing Lofland and Lofland (1995), she continues, "This statement may seem far-fetched but it follows a line of reasoning consistent with postmodern assertions regarding the fictitiousness of facts."

The narrative therapist accepts that there are multiple versions of reality. We underscore that this does not mean accepting everything that the client might say or want to do. Carpenter (citing Colapinto, 1985, p. 30, in Turner, 1996) points out that we may choose not to accept versions that are congruent with the perpetuation of racism, domestic violence, school dropouts, runaway teenagers, and other destructive interactions and try to change "uglier versions of reality." This is consistent with our social work mission and the value base of our profession. Equally important is that we don't deny the harsh realities of our clients' lives. We must help them to find the strengths and coping capacities that have been ignored in their problem-saturated dominant story line and to challenge the power that these harsh realities have been given. Such is the work of creating new narratives.

Learning Assignments

1. Reflect on a recent session you had with a client. Practice writing the client a narrative letter that you think would be helpful.

2. Working in small groups, discuss the use of "externalizing conversations" in narrative therapy. Role-play a conversation with a client, practicing the concept of externalizing.

3. Working as a class or in small groups, select two individuals to role-play the client and the therapist. Assign others in the class or group to record their observations of the conversation between the two.

Practice using different strategies such as *eliciting, probing, contextualizing, reflection,* and *amplifying*. As a group, discuss the language used by the therapist and its impact on the therapeutic process.

4. Working in pairs as the therapist and client (being sure to switch roles at some point), plan a *definitional ceremony*. Discuss the purpose and who might be invited to attend. Select others in the class to role-play those persons whom you have decided to invite as witnesses. Practice calling the witnesses and informing them of the intent of the definitional ceremony. Finally, role-play the definitional ceremony including the therapist, the client, and the witnesses.

References

Anderson, H., & Goolishian, H. A. (1988). Human systems as linguistic systems: Preliminary and evolving ideas about the implications for clinical theory. *Family Process, 27*, 371–393.

Carlson, J., & Kjos, D. (2002). *Theories and strategies of family therapy*. Boston: Allyn and Bacon.

Carpenter, D. (1996). Constructivism and social work treatment. In F. Turner, *Social work treatment: Interlocking theoretical approaches* (4th ed.). New York: The Free Press.

Colapinto, J. (1985, May–June). Maturana and the ideology of conformity. *The Family Therapy Networker*.

Dean, R. G. (1993). Constructivism: An approach to clinical practice. *Smith College Studies in Social Work, 63*(2), 129–146.

de Shazer, S. (1991). *Putting difference to work*. New York: Norton.

DiGiuseppe, R., & Linscott, J. (1993). Philosophical differences among cognitive-behavioral therapists: Rationalism, constructivism, or both? *Journal of Cognitive Psychotherapy, 7,* 117–130.

Drewery, W., & Winslade, J. (1997). The theoretical story of narrative therapy. In G. Monk, J. Winslade, K. Crocket, & D. Epston (Eds.), *Narrative therapy in practice: The archaeology of hope* (pp. 32–53). San Francisco, CA: Jossey-Bass.

Epston, D. (1997). "I am a bear"—Discovering discoveries. In C. Smith & D. Nylund (Eds.), *Narrative therapies with children and adolescents* (pp. 53–71). New York: Guilford.

Franklin, C., & Nurius, P. (1996). Constructivist therapy: New directions in social work practice. *Families in Society: The Journal of Contemporary Social Work Practice, 77*(6), 323–325.

Garcia-Petro, N. (1982). Puerto Rican families. In M. McGoldrick, J. Pearce, & J. Girodano (Eds.), *Ethnicity and family therapy*. New York: Guilford.

Gergen, K. J. (1999). *An invitation to social construction*. London: Sage.

Hoffman, L. (1992). Some practical implications of a social constructivist view of the psychoanalytic situation. *Psychoanalytic Dialogues, 2*(3), 287–304.

Kelly, P. (1996). Narrative theory and social work treatment. In F. Turner (Ed.), *Social work treatment: Interlocking theoretical approaches* (4th ed.). New York: The Free Press.

Lee, M. (1996). A constructivist approach to the help-seeking process of clients: A response to cultural diversity. *Clinical Social Work Journal, 24*(2), 187–202.

Lee, M., & Greene, G. J. (1999). A social constructivist framework for integrating cross-cultural issues in teaching clinical social work. *Journal of Social Work Education, 35*(1), 21–37.

Lofland, J., & Lofland, L. (1995). *Analyzing social settings: A guide to qualitative observation and analysis* (3rd ed.). Belmont, CA: Wadsworth.

Lowe, R. (1991). Postmodern themes and therapeutic practices: Notes towards the definition of "family therapy" (Part 2). In *Dulwich Centre Newsletter, 3*, Publication No. SBG 1093, pp. 41–51. Adelaide, Australia: Dulwich Centre Publications.

Mahoney, M. J. (1988). Constructive meta-theory: Basic features and historical foundations. *International Journal of Personal Construct Psychology, 1*(1), 1–35.

McKenzie, W., & Monk, G. (1997). Learning and teaching narrative ideas. In G. Monk, J. Winslade, K. Crocket, & D. Epston (Eds.), *Narrative therapy in practice: The archaelogy of hope* (pp. 82–121). San Francisco, CA: Jossey-Bass.

Morgan, A. (2000). *What is narrative therapy?* Adelaide, Australia: Dulwich Centre Publications.

Neimeyer, R. A. (1993). An appraisal of the constructivist psychotherapies. *Journal of Consulting and Clinical Psychology, 61*, 221–234.

Nylund, D. (2000). *Treating Huckleberry Finn: A new narrative approach to working with kids diagnosed with ADD/ADHD*. San Francisco, CA: Jossey-Bass.

Padgett, D. K. (1998). *Qualitative methods in social work research*. Thousand Oaks, CA: Sage.

Peller, J., & Walter, J. J. (1998). Solution-focused brief therapy. In R. A. Dorfman (Ed.), *Paradigms of clinical social work* (pp. 71–93). New York: Brunner/Mazel.

Real, T. (1990). The therapeutic use of self in constructivist/systemic therapy. *Family Process, 29*, 255–272.

Steier, F. (1991). Introduction: Research as self-reflexivity, self reflexivity as social process. In F. Steier (Ed.), *Research and reflexivity* (pp. 1–11). Newbury Park, CA: Sage.

Turner, F. J. (1996). *Social work treatment: Interlocking theoretical approaches* (4th ed.). New York: The Free Press.

White, M. (1986). Negative explanation, restraint, and double description: A template for family therapy. *Family Process, 25*(2), 169–184.

White, M. (1988a, Winter). The process of questioning: A therapy of literary merit? *Dulwich Centre Newsletter.*

White, M. (1988b, Spring). Saying hello again: The incorporation of the lost relationship in the resolution of grief. *Dulwich Centre Newsletter,* pp. 21–40.

White, M. (1991). Deconstruction and therapy. *Dulwich Centre Newsletter,* 3, pp. 21–40, Publication NO. SBG l093. Adelaide, Australia: Dulwich Centre Publications.

White, M. (1995). *Re-authoring lives: Interviews and essays*. Adelaide, South Australia: Dulwich Centre Publications.

White, M., & Epston, D. (1990). *Narrative means to therapeutic ends*. New York: Norton.

11/10/05

Solution-Focused Therapy

A Postmodern Approach

Solution-focused therapy originated in the late 1970s. Its founders were Steve de Shazer, Insoo Kim Berg, and their colleagues at the Brief Family Therapy Center of Milwaukee. The model was influenced by Milton Erickson's view that the client, not the therapist, defines the problem (O'Hanlon, 1987). Initially, the model was conceptualized around a *problem* orientation and emphasized the importance of intervening in *problem patterns* as a prerequisite to constructing *solutions*.

From its inception, a unique feature of solution-focused therapy has been its emphasis on looking for *exceptions* to the problem. Examples of these *exception-finding questions* would include, "What's better with your situation? What else are you doing differently that seems to be making a difference?" or "What will you continue doing so this happens more often?"

In its later development, the solution-focused theory stated that it was not necessary to have a *connection* between the problem and the solution. The model shifted from identifying *problems*, then to identifying *exceptions* to problems, and finally, to identifying *solutions to problems*. This movement is illustrated later in this chapter, with the revision of the future-focused miracle question, developed by de Shazer (1988).

Solution-focused therapy, like narrative therapy, is rooted in postmodern or poststructural thinking. This model operates within a conceptual framework that views people living and creating new narratives about their lives that extend beyond their problem-focused ones. Unlike *narrative* therapy, whose name is conceptual and suggests *process*, the term *solution-focused* may lend itself to being misinterpreted as being a set of *techniques* only. This belies the importance in solution-focused therapy of the collaborative process—therapist and client working together to *construct* a solution, not merely giving simple solutions to complex problems.

Since its origin, the miracle question has undergone revisions. For example, the following adaptation illustrates the move from the problem focus of the original miracle question into *goaling talk* (Peller & Walter, 1998, p. 84):

> Suppose tonight while you were sleeping a miracle occurs, and *life is the way you want it to be.* But because the miracle happened while you were sleeping, you didn't know it happened. What would be the sign to you that this miracle had occurred?

Another variation of the miracle question helps the client to consider the *progress* she may be making (Peller & Walter, 1998, p. 85):

> Suppose when you leave here tonight after this appointment life is the way you want, or you are on track to putting your life together in the way that you want, *what signs would you notice that would let you know?*

In addition to the miracle question, *presuppositional* questions can be used to help clients define the "who," "what," "how," and "where" of goal attainment. Examples may include "How will you know that the problem is really solved?" "How will you know when you don't have to come here any more?" or "If you were to gaze into my pretend crystal ball and see your family one month down the road, what will we see happening that is different?"

Exception questions imply that "nothing is always or never" (Becvar & Becvar, 2003, p. 266), and there are circumstances and times when the problem is not being experienced. Focusing on exceptions such as "What is different or better?" helps the client to see that some good things are happening, and the problem may seem less oppressive.

Scaling questions can help to determine a quantitative measurement of the client's problem prior to treatment (on a scale of 1 to 10), where would she like to be at the end of a certain period of time (on a scale of 1 to 10), or how confident the client is that she will be able to resolve the problem (on a scale of 1 to 10). In the following excerpt, the student uses a scaling question to help the client define the progress she has made since coming to therapy. We can see how the student supports the client's ability to make future changes by reinforcing the fact that it is the client herself who has made the changes in her life.

Student: If you had to rate how things have gotten better on a scale of 1 to 10, with one being the lowest and ten the highest, how would you rate yourself when you first came here?

Client: I'd say I was a 4.

Student: And how would you rate yourself now?

Client: I'd say I was a 7 now.

Student: That's a significant amount of change. . . . How have you managed to take such a strong stand for yourself?

Problem-tracking questions are used in work with families (Selekman, 1997). Members are asked to give a detailed description of how each person interacts with each other and with other people. These questions are particularly useful in "interactionalizing" (viewing problems as interactive) rather than locating problems within any one individual. Problem tracking questions can be used with individual clients as well; for example, "When your daughter won't listen to you and refuses to go to bed, what do you do? What does she do in response? What happens next?"

The Editorial Reflection

The solution-focused therapist varies the traditional psychotherapy hour. She may take a break during the session so that the therapist and client each have an opportunity to reflect on what has been transpiring in the session. The consultant may use this time to compose a thoughtful reflection on what has transpired during the session, and also to invite the client to share her reflections. In addition, the consultant uses this time to select appropriate tasks for the client or family members, and considers how she might compliment the client(s) on problem solving or coping strategies that may have been helpful at some point. Some solution-focused consultants work with reflecting teams, who are available to offer different points of view about what transpired in the session. (Reflection teams observe sessions from behind a one-way mirror.) After the break (whether it has been with a reflecting team or alone, in self-reflection) the consultant shares her thoughts with the client. She may, at that time, offer suggestions for how to work on those things she would like to do differently, or suggest keeping a list of times when the problem behavior is not occurring. A specific question, originating in the pioneering days of solution-focused therapy, is the "Formula First Session Task" (FFST): "Between now and next time we meet, I want you to observe, so that you can tell me next time what happens in your life (or marriage, family, or relationship) that you want to continue to have happen" (Molnar & de Shazer, 1987). This is not a homework assignment. The strategy is presented as "clues" suggested by the consultants that may help the client to make desired changes (de Shazer, 1988; Friedman, 1995).

Post-Assessment Session and Self-Reflection

During this phase, the solution-focused therapist reflects on her work with the client or family, considering both the interventions she made and any other interventions she might use in the next meeting. Examples of self-reflective questions, suggested by Selekman (1997, pp. 70–71) in his work with families, include "If I were to conduct this session all over again with the same family, what would I do differently? What family members do I need to spend more time engaging in the next session? Have I been sensitive to cultural issues? Are there power imbalances around gender in this family?"

Solution-Oriented Family Assessment

Selekman (1997, p. 32) designed a "solution-oriented family assessment format" consisting of five components that the therapist and family participate in during their initial meeting.

1. Problem defining and clarification. Although seemingly contrary to solution-focused therapy, Selekman feels it is important to show interest in how the family views its struggles (as problems) and to work with the family to establish a focus for what members are most interested in changing (i.e., finding a solution for). He uses future-oriented questions to help find this focus: "Suppose we were months down the road, long after we successfully completed counseling together, and you each proceeded to tell me the steps you took to get out of counseling. What would you tell me you did?" In addition, the therapist might interject *collaborative problem identification* questions, for example, "Which of these (presenting) problems do you want to change first?" or "If we were to break that problem up into small pieces, what part of the problem do you want to focus on changing first?"

2. Meaning making. Meaning making elicits the family story. Once the family's view of the problem is known, the therapist uses the language of solution-focused therapy to begin to inquire about and understand the important themes in their stories. Selekman (1997, p. 41) reminds us that "there are multiple meanings to the words that family members use to describe their problem situation," and that "their problem stories are stories." He gives particular attention to the reasons why people seek therapy and may engage in conversational questions to seek this information: "If you were to work with the most perfect therapist, what would he/she do that you would find to be most helpful?" If a family has been in prior counseling, the therapist might be interested in exploring their experience further by asking a question such as "Have former therapists tried something with you that you found helpful? We could try doing the same" or "You have seen a therapist(s) before me; what, if anything, has he or she missed with your situation? What, if anything, would you like me to do differently?"

3. Assessing the customer(s) for change in the client system. Here, Selekman draws on de Shazer's (1988) delineation of three possible therapist–family relationship patterns. These are essentially the ways in which the therapist determines how motivated the clients may be and the ways in which she can best respond and engage them in the therapy. The first group is called *visitors*, who are generally those individuals (such as children and adolescents, for example) who may be brought to counseling because someone else in the family thinks they have a problem. Sometimes, entire families can be considered visitors. Visitors require warmth, empathy, and acceptance by the therapist of whatever goal the family (or individual members) may wish to pursue. *Complainants* are those who express their worry or concern and are often hoping that the therapist will correct the problem, as they see it. In order to engage complainants in the treatment process, it is useful to give them some type of observational task that requires their involvement in a positive way (for example, writing down what their child did during the week that was encouraging or writing down ideas about how to be encouraging to the child). Finally, *customers* are those who are most concerned about the identified client's problematic behaviors and most willing to work with the therapist toward new solutions.

4. Goal setting. Solution-focused consultants encourage the client to talk about how she would envision a future without problems. The miracle question(s), presuppositional questions, scaling questions, and problem-tracking questions are used to set goals. Selekman (1997, pp. 64–65) also offers examples of how to use scaling questions within the context of family therapy: "How confident are you today on a scale of 1 to 10 that you will resolve your son's temper tantrums? Let's say we get together in one week's time and you proceed to tell me that you took some steps and got to a 7, what will you tell me that you did?"

5. Collaborative treatment planning. Family sessions are generally structured so that the therapist meets with the family as a whole, with the parents alone, and with the identified child alone. It is important to remember that others outside the immediate family may also be important collaborators in the treatment process (i.e., concerned relatives, schools, family doctors, etc.). The therapist informs the family members that they will be encouraged to do certain tasks and experiments between meetings. The collaborative process extends to empowering families to determine how frequently they feel counseling should occur, when they may need some time away from counseling to practice on their own, and even what *DSM-IV* diagnostic code they feel would be most applicable. When a diagnosis is required for his purposes, the consultant invites the client to discuss the diagnosis that he feels is most appropriate, within a reasonable choice of possibilities.

As with narrative therapy, the therapist works with the family to externalize *DSM-IV* codes that label individual members as identified clients. For example, "How did this problem begin to make trouble for you in school?" may be one way to talk to a child (family) who is brought to counseling for behaviors associated with attention deficit disorder. Other *externalizing the problem* questions Selekman offers are "Have there been any times lately where you stood up to (name the problem; for example, distraction) and didn't allow it to get the best of you?" or "What do you do to achieve victories over (name the problem)?" In all of these ways, solution-focused therapy is committed to client empowerment.

Interdisciplinary Collaboration

Selekman extends a solution-focused approach to interdisciplinary collaboration with other professionals involved in working with a particular family. He cautions that the family consultant needs to be open to other perspectives and opinions (just as she is in working with the family as the client system). This involves a genuine interest in what the other professionals have to say and a willingness, if necessary, to alter one's own views. He raises the important point that professionals from different disciplines speak different languages; therefore, solution-focused consultants must either be versed in these different languages or willing to ask questions nondefensively. In this day of technological advances, it is important to remember that collaboration can be done via instant email, speaker phone, written correspondence, and/or fax (with the family's consent and attention to confidentiality matters).

An interesting twist on interdisciplinary collaboration is the involvement of the child or adolescent client's friend(s) as consultants. This is similar to White and Epston's definitional ceremony (see Chapter 11 on narrative therapy), and Saleebey's (1997) concept of viewing the entire community as a potential resource to be enlisted on behalf of clients. Friends are called upon to offer helpful advice concerning what could be done to make things better for their pal. These friends can also participate in role-plays and offer the support and encouragement of a peer.

Something wraparound does

Solution-Focused Strategies

Introduced by de Shazer (1985, 1988, 1991), these rather creative strategies can be used with children, adolescents, adults, or families. They engage the client(s) in becoming more aware of what works and help them move forward to new solutions to old problems. With the *Prediction Task*, the consultant invites the client to "predict" whether the next day (or other defined period of time) would be a good day, and then to consider and report what made it good. In the *Do Something Different Task*, particularly suited to work with families, the parent(s) or the child(ren) are asked to do something other than what others around them would expect them to do (in response to a particular problematic situation). The idea behind this strategy is that often when one person in the system changes his behavior, others respond differently as well. The client is asked to observe and report on how the other person responds to him or her at that time. The *Pretend the Miracle Happened* strategy suggests to the client that he or she engage in what the other person would consider a miracle behavior. Selekman (1997) suggests that parents use *positive consequences* (rather than negative consequences) as a strategy to employ with children who have pushed the limits. Positive consequences might incorporate skills the child has shown mastery over, such as babysitting for a neighbor or helping to make dinner for several nights. This is in keeping with the solution-focused notion that attention needs to be given to incorporating more of what works (strengths) into making what doesn't work better. These solution-focused strategies bear some resemblance to White's (1991) narrative concept of "erotocizing the domestic," since they are all geared toward making the familiar different. Selekman (1997, pp. 111, 180) offers two other variations on the miracle question with the following question he addresses to parents during the course of family therapy:

> Suppose I had an *imaginary time machine* sitting over here, and I asked each of you to enter it and take it wherever you wished to travel in time. Where would you go? Who would you be with? What would you do there? What difference would that make in your life? Suppose you were to wake up tomorrow and find yourselves in *Parentland,* where parents are totally fulfilled by their important roles, are regarded by society as its most important citizens, and have well-behaved children. What would you observe these parents doing for themselves and their children that makes them feel so fulfilled as parents?

These interventions may be particularly helpful in those challenging family situations where parents (and children) feel stuck, guilty, angry, and helpless. It offers them a sense of empowerment and perhaps a vision (from the imaginary vantage point) of future possibility. It also interjects some lightheartedness in the work—which is often sorely lacking for many of these parents and families.

Case Example: Initial Meeting with the Drew Family

The following example demonstrates an initial family meeting. As consultant, I conduct the assessment according to the solution-focused format suggested by Selekman (1997). This schema appears in **bold** type within the dialog.

Overview

Mrs. Drew initiated the counseling session. In a brief telephone conversation she reported that her 12-year-old son Donald could not be controlled. She identified his problem behaviors as "lying and stealing." She also told me that she and Donald's father had divorced when Donald was 5 years old. She was remarried, and she and Donald's stepfather live with Mr. Drew's 15-year-old daughter. Donald's older brother, age 18, lives with Donald's father and stepmother. Donald sees his father on a very regular basis but the relationship between families is strained.

Before meeting with Mr. and Mrs. Drew and Donald, I obtained Mrs. Drew's permission to call Donald's father to ensure his support and involvement. He gave this readily, and we determined that we would meet together on a separate occasion.

Solution-Focused Family Assessment with Mr. and Mrs. Drew and Donald

In keeping with Selekman's suggested format, I greet each member of the Drew family warmly, introducing myself and taking the time to let them know that I am pleased they have decided to seek some help for whatever is troubling them as a family. I then say, "We'll be meeting for about an hour. We'll spend the first half of our time together talking about your concerns and then we'll turn our attention to some solutions that you might like to see happen."

Mrs. Drew immediately begins to tell her reasons for seeking help at this time. She speaks rapidly and with obvious frustration, "I'm at my wit's end with Donald. His behavior has been getting worse and worse over the past couple of months. My husband and I don't know what else to do. We have tried taking privileges away but he doesn't even care any more. I apologize for not coming sooner but I was hoping that things would get better."

In an attempt to involve Mr. Drew and Donald in this discussion and to get further information about why they decided to seek help at this time, I ask, "Who was the first person who got the idea that you should seek help?" **(meaning making and eliciting the family story)**

Mrs. Drew: What finally prompted me to call was a recent incident when Donald got into trouble again because he signed my name to a test with a failing grade.
Consultant: Who else thought counseling would be helpful now? **(eliciting other meanings)**
Mr. Drew: I did. This was not the first time Donald had lied to us. He seems to be lying more and more to cover up things that aren't going well. Donald also hoards food. He's been doing this since we tried to offer him a healthier diet. His pediatrician suggested that we do this because Donald is gaining weight at a rapid rate. We find empty bowls of cereal and candy wrappers hidden in his room. We suspect that Donald is buying candy with money he periodically steals from his mother's purse.

I note that Mrs. Drew initially presents herself as a *complainant* who has tried all she could to help Donald but now feels that professional help is warranted. I will try to involve her, at a later point in the session, in some type of encouraging, *observational task* concerning her son's behavior—a task she can identify. She clearly wants me to do something to make their situation better. I feel that Mr. Drew is a *customer,* conveying concern about Donald and a willingness to engage in a team effort to make changes.

While Mr. and Mrs. Drew speak, Donald looks down and appears sullen and uncommunicative. Clearly, Donald is a *visitor* at this session, brought because his mom and stepdad feel he has problems that require professional attention. I feel it is time to reach out to him:

Consultant: Donald, what's your theory about why this problem exists? **(problem finding question)**
Donald: (looks somewhat surprised; responds by shrugging his shoulders) I don't know. . . . I think I'm afraid of getting into trouble.
Consultant: Well, that makes a certain amount of sense to me. Now, let me ask you two questions, Donald. How long has this lying about your troubles been taking charge of your life? **(externalizing the problem so that it does not define Donald)** Have there been any times lately where you have stood up to lying and didn't allow it to get the best of you? **(finding exceptions to the problem)**

Case Example **Continued**

Donald (and his parents) smile for the first time and Donald begins to share his story with me. It becomes clear as he speaks that this young boy is having a very difficult time in school—both academically and with his peers.

Donald: The work was hard this year, especially because I started middle school and got confused when I had to change classes. Then the kids started making fun of me because of my weight. They do it when the teachers aren't looking and it makes me sad. They also think I'm dumb because it takes me a long time to do the work, especially math. I don't like school. I'm afraid to bring my work home because my parents will be upset or take away some privilege so I try to hide it from them. And then suddenly I just started lying about everything.

Consultant: Yes, I can see that lying seems to have taken hold of you somehow . . . now . . . can you or you (turning to parents), Mr. and Mrs. Drew, think of any times in the past when Donald was struggling to handle something? What did you do to help him get back on track?

Mr. Drew: Well, we know that the punishment isn't helping because Donald is very sensitive. He just gets upset or shrugs it off and says he doesn't care.

Mrs. Drew: When he was little, I used to bribe him to do things—that would work.

Consultant: You mean using rewards for jobs well done?

Mrs. Drew: Yes.

Consultant: (turning to Donald) Donald, can you think of anything your Mom and Dad could do to help you get this monkey—this lying monkey—off your back?

Mr. Drew: (jumping in) We could try to be more understanding and not be so quick to punish Donald when he gets a bad grade or makes a mistake.

Donald: (smiling) That would help because sometimes I feel like everybody is against me.

Mr. Drew: Perhaps Donald and his mother and father should have a meeting with you. Maybe that would help.

(Here we move from **meaning making** into the process of *goaling*.)

Consultant: These are all good suggestions. I think that by meeting together as we have done today, we can come up with some good solutions to help get family life back on track. Would you like to meet with me again next week? (All agree. I introduce an *observational task*.) Mr. and Mrs. Drew, I would like you to observe Donald over the coming week and write down anything Donald does that is encouraging to the both of you and anything you do that is encouraging to Donald during this difficult time. I also use a *scaling question:* On a scale of one to ten, where would you like to be in a week's time when we meet again?

Mr. Drew: I would be happy with a 4 or a 5.

Mrs. Drew: I agree—that would be nice.

Consultant: (I ask a *presuppositional* question) Let's say all of you are eating dinner tonight and you are talking about how successful today's meeting had been. What will have changed with your situation?

Mrs. Drew: (responding immediately) Donald wouldn't be lying—that's the biggest thing in my mind because I would like to be able to trust him again.

Mr. Drew: I agree.

Donald: I wouldn't be in so much trouble any more.

Consultant: Donald, would you and your family like to participate in an experiment that I think might help Donald kick this lying habit that has taken hold of him?

The family agrees and seems curious. I introduce the ***Do Something Different Task*** hoping to get these three people to begin to act differently as they deal with Donald's problematic behaviors.

Consultant: Donald, I would like you to bring home any school papers no matter whether the grade is good or bad. I'd also like you to leave candy wrappers or empty cereal bowls out in plain view rather than trying to hide them away. And Mr. and Mrs. Drew, I'd like you to let Donald know that you appreciate it when you find the candy wrapper or empty cereal bowl he's left out and to thank him when he shows you a grade that he's not too proud of.

As the session with this family is drawing to an end, I offer Mr. and Mrs. Drew and Donald a framework for making the changes we have discussed. I find the **Formula First Session Task (FFST)** a good way to do this:

Consultant: Between now and next time we meet, if you would like to do so, I want you to observe what happens in your family that you want to continue to have happen. This is very important because sometimes, when people are working hard to make changes, they forget about the positive experiences they have together. Donald, you need to be a detective and really help me out by closely watching, maybe by writing it down and reporting back to me next time, so that I will know what works well in your family. Then, we'll all try to figure out how to make more of those good times happen. You can do this on your own sometimes or you can talk it over with your mom and stepdad. Next time, I'd like to first meet alone with you for a while and we'll have a chance to go over what you have observed. Afterwards, we'll all meet together again and talk about how you each made out with trying the new things we discussed earlier. How does that feel to you?

The Drew family agree to work on this task, and to meet again in one week's time.

Post-Assessment Session and Self-Reflection

Following the sessions, I begin to think about our meeting and develop ideas for our next session. As can clearly be seen from the vignette presented above, Donald is a *visitor* to the counseling session and initially not a happy visitor. Although he did admit to having some problems as the meeting progressed, he was brought to see me because his parents felt he had a problem. In today's session I feel I made some headway by helping Donald to become a ***customer,*** by reaching out to him in an empathic manner. I was very conscious of how small he appeared to be, sitting in between his concerned but quite upset mother and stepfather, and of his rather desperate attempts to let his family know he wasn't feeling all that happy.

Following this first meeting with the Drew family, I consider the interventions I have chosen and whether there might be others that I could have used or would use

(continued)

Case Example **Continued**

in our next meeting. I feel I made a positive connection with each family member, but that more needs to be done to engage Mrs. Drew. I have the sense that if Donald's behavior continues, Mrs. Drew would be unable to ignore it, and she could get really punitive. I decide that next time I will introduce the idea of *positive consequences.* Mrs. Drew has noted that when Donald was little she used to "bribe him" and this got results. **Positive consequences** will enable the Drews to set limits on Donald's behavior in ways that will draw on his strengths and help the family out of this vicious cycle of poor behavior and negative consequences. I consider Mr. Drew's suggestion about having a session with his wife and Donald's father. I feel it is still too early to do this but make a mental note to try and find a way to open up this line of communication in the future. I hope that the Drew family will be able to follow through on the assignments we discussed so that the tension among them can abate. I need to work with Donald alone to give him an opportunity to talk further about his feelings and perhaps help him find more adaptive coping strategies. I think that I might ask Donald how he feels about *inviting one of his friends to the session*—someone who might have some helpful suggestions to offer. I will, of course, have to be sure that Donald feels comfortable with this approach. I make a mental note to get permission to talk to Donald's teachers and to get their perspective on the problems Donald appears to be having in school. I also think it will be important to talk with Donald's pediatrician.

Conclusion

As is illustrated in the Drew family case, solution-focused therapy is a strengths-based model of practice. In this initial assessment, I, as "consultant," reach out to this troubled family with optimism, in order to establish a collaborative working relationship. I respect their right of self-determination, invite the family members to discuss their goals for the consultation, and obtain permission for my interventions. I demonstrate my belief that they are capable of change and growth by engaging them in discussion of ways they have coped with problems in the past. I help them to give new meaning to Donald's "lying and stealing," reframing these behaviors as alien to him as well as to his parents. In the future, I will use interdisciplinary collaboration to further my understanding and marshal additional resources. Together, we will construct a solution that will help this family to replace their anger and frustration with empowerment and hope.

Research Perspectives

Followup reseach done on solution-focused therapy (n = 64, eighteen months after completion at the Milwaukee Brief Family Therapy Center) showed that 84 percent of families experienced long-term improvements. All of these families received fewer than ten sessions of therapy, with an average of three sessions (Wylie, 1990).

Research done in Sweden found that 80 percent of clients completing solution-focused therapy accomplished their stated treatment goals, and the average length of treatment was five sessions (Andreas, "A Follow-Up of Patients in Solution-Focused Brief Therapy," paper presented at the Institution for Applied Psychology, University of Lund, Sweden, cited in Carlson & Kjos, 2002).

Summary

Solution-focused therapy, with its thoughtful and creative use of language, offers a range of new clinical possibilities. Its focus on solutions rather than diagnosis makes it well suited for work with clients of all ages and backgrounds. The reframing of problems to solutions helps clients to overcome the shame and guilt that many feel when seeking therapy for the first time. Solution-focused therapists use a wide range of techniques to engage their clients in collaborative therapeutic relationships. Such relationships are especially helpful when working with children and adolescents who are often in counseling at the request or insistence of others. The solution-focused model also offers concerned families the opportunity to see that their children are doing some positive things. Finally, solution-focused therapy embodies the values of the social work profession as the client's innate strengths and resiliency factors are supported and enhanced in the therapeutic contact.

Learning Assignments

1. Working in small groups, role-play an initial meeting with a family. Practice doing a solution-oriented family assessment. Use collaborative problem identification questions and try to assess whether the family members are customers, complainants, or visitors. Finally, use presuppositional and/or problem-tracking questions to set goals.

2. Working in pairs, role-play an interview between a consultant and a client. Use the miracle question and a scaling question. Switch roles.

3. Working in small groups, role-play several interviews (e.g., with a child, with an adolescent). Practice different solution-focused interventions such as the prediction task, the pretend the miracle happened strategy, or the observational task.

References

Becvar, D., & Becvar, R. (2003). *Family therapy: A systemic integration* (5th ed.). Boston: Allyn and Bacon.

Carlson, J., & Kjos, D. (2002). *Theories and strategies of family therapy*. Boston: Allyn and Bacon.

de Shazer, S. (1985). *Keys to solution in brief therapy*. New York: Norton.

de Shazer, S. (1988). *Clues: Investigating solutions in brief therapy*. New York: Norton.

de Shazer, S. (1991). *Putting difference to work*. New York: Norton.

Friedman, S. (1995). *The reflecting team in action*. New York: Guilford.

Molnar, A., & de Shazer, S. (1987, October). Solution-focused therapy: Toward the identification of therapeutic tasks. *Journal of Marital and Family Therapy, 13*(4), 349–357.

O'Hanlon, W. H. (1987). *Taproots: Underlying principles of Milton Erikson's therapy and hypnosis*. New York: Norton.

Peller, J., & Walter, J. L. (1998). Solution-focused brief therapy. In R. A. Dorfman, *Paradigms of clinical social work* (pp. 71–93). New York: Brunner/Mazel.

Saleebey, D. (Ed.). (1997). *The strengths perspective in social work practice*. New York: Longman.

Selekman, M. D. (1997). *Solution-focused therapy with children*. New York: Guilford.

White, M. (1991). Deconstruction and therapy. In *Postmodernism deconstruction and therapy* (pp. 21–40). Adelaide, Australia: Dulwich Centre Newsletter.

Wylie, M. S. (1990). Brief therapy on the couch. *Family Therapy Networker, 14*, 26–34, 66.

13

Clinical Practice with Children and Adolescents

Clinical treatment of children and adolescents requires a multisystemic, team approach. The team includes the child or adolescent; parents; school personnel; the pediatrician; representatives of environmental influences such as friendship groups, religious and cultural affiliations, child welfare agencies, and the therapist. The social worker—with knowledge of developmental assessment, clinical theory, play therapy, differential diagnosis, and the environmental influences—coordinates the team. In this chapter, we discuss the components of child and adolescent treatment. Case examples—using self-psychological play therapy and behavioral therapy—illustrate two different treatment models that apply to work with this population.

Developmental Assessment

Child and adolescent behavioral and emotional problems occur within a developmental context. Knowledge of child development informs assessment, diagnosis, theoretical conceptualization, and treatment planning (Shirk, 1999). Webb (1996, p. 64) suggests a tripartite assessment that attends to the biological, psychological, and sociocultural factors in the child's support system. Genograms (McGoldrick & Gerson, 1985), ecomaps (Hartman, 1978), and culturagrams (Congress, 1994) are also helpful assessment tools (see Chapter 11 for examples of how these tools can be used). There are various developmental frameworks that provide a context for child psychotherapy. These include Piaget's model of cognitive development (1952a, 1952b), Erikson's psychosocial model (1950, 1959) Freud's model of psychosexual development (1905), Stern's (1977, 1985) model of self development,

Kail's (2001) model of emotional development, and Kohlberg's (1984) model of moral development. Feminist models (see Chapter 8); multicultural developmental models, and those that address gay, lesbian, bisexual, and transgender identity development provide important insights into therapy with children and adolescents whose primary identity is different from that of the dominant culture or who may have a number of ethnic identities (Cramer & Gilson, 1999; D'Augelli, 1994; Eliason, 1996; Gusman, Stewart, Young, et al., 1996; Oetting & Beauvais, 1990; Sue & Sue, 2003). All of the above models provide templates for the cognitive, linguistic, physical, emotional, social, and play development of children within their environmental contexts. It is important to remember that children with the same presenting problems will differ significantly in the cognitive, emotional, and social competencies they bring to therapy as well as in the stresses they face in their everyday lives. Shirk (1999, p. 61) refers to this as a "developmental dialectic between the child's capacities and psychosocial demands."

Childhood Psychopathology

Symptoms of most child and adolescent disorders are manifested during different stages of development, and the clinical challenge is to determine whether the behaviors are maladaptive or within the normal range. Davis (1999) presents a nicely organized chronological summary of normal child development. Infant development takes place from birth to 12 months of age, toddler development (1 to 3 years of age), preschool development (3 to 6 years of age), and middle childhood development (6 to 12 years). Several authors discuss the importance of *equifinality, multifinality,* and *heterotypic continuity* in a developmental understanding of clinical practice. Equifinalty means that a single disorder (e.g., dysthymia) can be produced via different developmental pathways (e.g., as a result of ongoing difficulties with peers or in reaction to family problems and stresses). Multifinality suggests that the same developmental events may lead to different adaptive and/or maladaptive outcomes. The death of a parent, for example, may result in different ways of coping. Heterotypic continuity implies that a given pathological process will be exhibited differently with continued development—bipolar disorder will have different behavioral manifestations in childhood and adolescence. (For further information, see Cicchetti & Rogosch, 2002; Holmbeck, Greenley, & Franks, 2003; Shirk, 1999.) Treatment, therefore, cannot be guided solely by diagnostic manuals such as the *DSM-IV,* because they do not attend to the *developmental* precursors of symptoms and behaviors. The social worker needs to understand the child's cognitive and emotional functioning within a developmental framework and note how this translates into behaviors that can be observed during the clinical interview. These behaviors may include: (1) responsiveness to limit setting, (2) impulsivity, (3) distractibility, (4) level of organization in play, (5) responsiveness to interviewer, (6) mood, (7) use of environment, (8) attention span, (9) recurring themes in play and conversation, and (10) social reasoning (Hughes & Baker, 1990, p. 8). Certain conditions emerge during childhood and adolescence, and a social worker's knowledge of child development helps her to identify these problems and to plan for early intervention. Early identification and intervention help the child or adolescent make a healthier transition to later stages of development.

The Clinical Interview

With the Parent(s)

The clinician needs to obtain information from the child or adolescent as well as the parent. We suggest that the initial interview be conducted with the parent(s) when the child is age 12 or younger. In certain instances, the parent of an older adolescent needs to talk first, and this should be respected. Listening to the parent's concerns, answering questions, and providing education about the interdisciplinary approach fosters the therapeutic partnership. Allow time to take a detailed developmental history and to have the parents sign all necessary releases. Review the mandatory reporting laws and limits of confidentiality, because the client needs to know your role as a mandated reporter of child abuse and neglect.

If the parents are divorced, establish who has custody of the child and discuss how each parent (including the parent who may not be present during the initial interview) will be involved. Contact with both parents, if seen by the child on a regular basis, is always preferable (Wachtel, 1994; Webb, 1996). The initial interview with the parents is also the time to establish what other therapeutic partners might need to be consulted in order to complete the diagnostic picture. Request permission to talk with the child's pediatrician and obtain results of a recent health examination. Consider getting information from the school adjustment counselor or a teacher. A child psychiatrist, clinical psychologist, or speech-language therapist might be part of the treatment team, especially if the parent or the clinician suspects the presence of a learning disability, Attention Deficit Hyperactivity Disorder (ADHD), or other problems that are manifest in childhood.

Finally, advise the parent how to explain the therapy to her child. Use developmentally appropriate language. You might, for example, coach a parent of a 4-year-old child attending preschool and not wanting to leave the parent in the morning to say: "I met a very nice woman who plays with children who don't like to say goodbye to their mommies in the morning." Be prepared to talk with the parent about your plan for assessing the child in the child's first interview and how you will be working as you proceed with treatment. This helps the parent to feel confident that she is in the hands of a competent practitioner.

With the Child or Adolescent

We recommend that the clinician meet with the parents and the child together for the first 10 to 15 minutes of the first session. During this time the child or adolescent (who is still a minor) can hear why the parent has brought her to see the therapist (Wachtel, 1994). This meeting helps establish rapport so that later in the session, when the child or adolescent meets alone with the therapist, he is clear there is a problem. Then, the therapist might say: "I can see your point, but it sounds like your parents see it differently . . . What do you think about their point of view?" Keep toys within view when working with younger children. You may want to sit on the floor and engage in some play as you talk with the parent to find out the reason she is bringing the child to "visit" you. In a developmentally sensitive interview, the communication process may rely more on play than words (Hughes & Baker, 1990).

Adolescent clients are often silent in initial interviews when parents are present. Use the time to establish the boundaries of the relationship with the adolescent and the parents and refrain from pushing the adolescent to talk. Review confidentiality within a developmentally appropriate context. Younger children expect parents to be involved in their lives (Wachtel, 1994), but adolescents may feel differently. We suggest being flexible when discussing the guidelines for disclosure. Use language such as: "I will be meeting alone with ___ but, from time to time, we may want to involve you (to parent) in a session." Be clear and honest with adolescents about the need to inform parents about high-risk behaviors. The following brief examples demonstrate how to engage an adolescent in a discussion of confidentiality:

> *Example 1:* You're telling me some things right now that I have a lot of concern about. I know you won't like hearing this, but I feel strongly that we need to bring your parents on board for this conversation. Tell me how we can work together to tell them.

> *Example 2:* Remember when we first met and I told you there might be things that you might tell me that might make me worry about your safety—and that these were things we would have to share with your parents? Well, today we have to do that. I want us to be able to tell them together in a way that is as okay for you as possible. I know this won't be easy so let's figure out how to best handle it.

Learning Disturbances

Learning problems manifest in a variety of ways. Included are problems of intelligence, specific cognitive disabilities, interrelations of specific cognitive deficits and broader psychological functioning, a specific symptom secondary to other psychological conditions, a reflection of disturbance in object relations, a part of a general character trait, a family-based disinterest in learning, or the result of the effects of poverty and social disadvantages (Elbaum & Vaughn, 2003). Palombo (2001, p. 26) suggests that dyslexia (p. 122–123), ADHD (pp. 144–145), executive function disorders (pp. 164–165), and nonverbal learning disabilities (pp. 192–193) are most often associated with self-esteem problems, because these children are often introspective, self-conscious, and sensitive to others expectations of them. Learning and emotional disorders interface, and mental health clinicians need to team up with practitioners from other disciplines to provide comprehensive services to clients who are at risk of any of these complex disorders. Siegel (1999, p. 21) discusses a model of "interpersonal neurobiology" that integrates scientific findings from a range of disciplines. This model conceptualizes the human mind as developing at the interface of neurophysiological processes and interpersonal relationships. Neuropsychological and educational testing is often warranted in these cases to facilitate an early and accurate diagnoses and intervention plan.

Play Therapy

Play is the child's language of expression. We concur with the definition of play therapy introduced by the Association for Play Therapy (1997) and expanded upon by O'Connor (2000):

> Play therapy consists of a cluster of treatment modalities. It involves the systematic use of a theoretical model to establish an interpersonal process wherein trained play therapists use the therapeutic powers of play to help clients prevent or resolve psychosocial difficulties, achieve optimal growth and development, and re-establish the child's ability to engage in play behaviors as they are classically defined in childhood. (p. 7)

The many theoretical models of play therapy include psychoanalytic, humanistic, cognitive behavioral (Knell, 1997, 1998; Lee, 1997), developmental (Brody, 1997; Jernberg, 1979), and filial play therapy (Guerney, 1997; Van Fleet, 1994). Each model uses play in a different way. In psychoanalytic play therapy, the therapist interprets the child's play metaphorically through the use of objects in the play. Play, in a behavioral approach, is used to reinforce or extinguish behaviors. Cognitive play therapy encourages modeling of adaptive behaviors and thought processes (O'Connor, 2000). Play therapies are further differentiated by styles. In *directive play therapy,* the therapist assumes responsibility for guidance and interpretation of the play (Gil, 1991). *Nondirective play therapy* relies on the child's ability to direct the process and pace of the play. The developmental age of the child further defines the type of play therapy plan (see O'Connor, 2000).

Each of the theories presented in this book (as well as many other theoretical models that exist outside of this volume) may contribute to an understanding of different aspects of a child's development. Behavioral protocols that involve parents are appropriate for young children. Older children with more advanced cognitive abilities may benefit from a cognitive approach that relies on the modification of cognitive structures and processes (Kendall, 2000). Research has shown that cognitive-behavioral treatment for depression with adolescents is quite successful because adolescents are capable of the level of abstract reasoning central to this form of therapy (Kendall, 2000; Marcotte, 1997). Strategies that focus on self control may also be more useful with older adolescents (Holmbeck, Greenley & Franks, 2003). Psychodynamic models of play therapy are useful in work with young children. Play has an abreactive value, can help to establish a relationship, and is useful in gathering information related to intrapsychic conflict. Older children and adolescents with some capacity for verbal expression and insight may benefit from interpretations that make the client's conflicts conscious and allow for behavioral change (O'Connor, 2000). Finally, it is important to appreciate the importance of cultural competence in the application of any of these models to work with children and adolescents.

The following three examples demonstrate the application of two different child and adolescent therapy models—self-psychological play therapy and behavioral modification.

Case Example

Rosa: A Child Suffering from Selective Mutism

Client Information.   Rosa, a 10-year-old Puerto Rican girl, lives with her mother, father, and two older sisters. The family is Pentecostal, Spanish-speaking, with a large extended family living in Puerto Rico. They visit Puerto Rico at least twice a year. Rosa was referred for school-based counseling services by her teacher because she was "not speaking in school." Rosa was diagnosed with selective mutism, "a disorder of childhood characterized by the total lack of speech in at least one specific situation (usually the classroom) despite the ability to speak in other situations" (Dow, 1995, p. 1). Rosa's mother described her as "only speaking in the home" and "not outside the home," even when in the company of her family. She reported that this condition began when Rosa was 4 years old, when she soiled herself in preschool after being denied permission to go to the bathroom. Subsequently, Rosa's family moved back to Puerto Rico for a four-year period before returning again to the United States. Rosa, according to her mother, stopped speaking in school after the event, both here and in Puerto Rico.

Assessment of Rosa.   Meyers (1984, pp. 41–42) describes several characteristics common to families where a child has selective mutism. These apply to Rosa and her family and include (1) an intense attachment to another family member, usually the mother (Rosa is very close to her mother); (2) suspicion of the residents in a low socioeconomic inner city (Rosa and her family live in such a city); (3) fear of strangers (Rosa's family may face discrimination as a minority group new to dominant United States); (4) language difficulties (no one in the family speaks English); (5) marital disharmony (Rosa's parents are both on social security/disability and the family lives in poverty with little support); and (6) mutism modeling (Rosa's family may not be able to respond to stress from outside the home because they do not speak English).

Steinhausen and Juzi (1996) write of a cultural component in selective mutism. They suggest that children who fail at mastering a new, second language can develop selective mutism as a way of coping. They also assert that children of immigrants are more likely not to speak in classrooms, regardless of their understanding of the dominant language.

Rosa was 4 years old and mastering language development—bilingual language development—when the bathroom incident occurred. She may have associated her "accident" with a failed attempt at language mastery and retreated into the world of silence. The clinician, in her choice of treatment, used sensitivity in selecting a bilingual approach.

Self Psychological Play Therapy with Rosa.   The clinician, a white, bilingual (English/Spanish) female, recognized the importance of language and culture in treatment of Rosa. She selected a self-psychological approach and conceptualized her role as that of a selfobject who would provide idealizing, mirroring and alterego selfobject functions (see Chapter 7). Therapy was conducted in Spanish in order to establish an empathic relationship. Landreth (2002), in his book *The Art of the Relationship in Play Therapy*, emphasizes the importance of the therapist's authenticity, warmth, and acceptance, as well as an ability to connect to the child's world. Miller's (1996) application of self psychology to work with children further helps us to understand Rosa. He speaks of (1) the child's need for others, (2) the child's will to do, and (3) the principle of internal harmony. These are necessary for the development of a healthy self-structure, are present in a fragmented form by mutism, and are described in detail.

Need for Others.   Rosa's *need for others* may not have always been optimally met outside of her home. Disruptions in language acquisition, compromised by numerous moves between English- and Spanish-speaking countries, may have contributed to difficulties in Rosa's development of a sense of self at the crucial developmental stage when words are important in interpersonal relationships. Her parents, able to function psychologically as protectors and as providers of emotional support in the home, may not have been able to do so in the larger, English-speaking environment because of their own language constraints. How frightening this must have been for Rosa—precipitously torn from the selfobject merger with her parents because of language. The idealizing relationship with the parents provides a model for the self-organization of the child. It is interesting and not surprising that Rosa speaks in her house, where Spanish is the language of the family.

Will to Do.   Rosa's refusal to speak tells everyone of her power. However, her *will to do* is not free to focus on the normal developmental tasks of her age, such as school performance and social interaction with peers. Rosa remains caught in a bind: She can either succeed at maintaining her sense of cohesion or fail at growing up.

Internal Harmony.   The principle of *internal harmony* is both a motivational force and the main mechanism of experience that becomes part of the self-structure. Rosa is trying her best to integrate the frustration, anger, and loneliness of unmet selfobject needs with the conflicts of her developmental age, and so she stops speaking.

Rosa's need for others, will to do, and internal harmony begin to be met in new ways by the therapist through play therapy conducted in Spanish. The English-speaking therapist can negotiate the English-speaking environment on behalf of her clients and can provide an important anxiety-reducing buffer for Rosa. As a primary selfobject support, the therapist becomes a role model and figure for identification (Miller, 1996). She affirms Rosa as the admired child within the context of play therapy. This admired child has a fuller command of the language (Spanish) that she and the therapist need to use to communicate. This is demonstrated in the following exchange between Rosa and the worker. The play puppets hold Rosa's voice until she is able to speak herself.

(continued)

Case Examples   Continued

Therapist: Tiger? (speaking to tiger puppet) Do you think you can help me with my Spanish today?

Rosa: (no response)

Therapist: My Spanish is pretty bad and tigers know a lot.

Rosa: (no response)

Therapist: Tiger? Are you there?

Rosa: (walks over to the puppet box that I was sitting in and puts Tiger on the window of the box)

Therapist: So, will you help to teach me Spanish, Tiger?

Rosa: (nods the tiger's head yes)

Therapist: Wonderful . . . you know so much Spanish . . . I will be lucky to have your help . . . thank you so much.

This type of exchange, interspersed with moments of sharing—another important part of both mirroring and idealizing relationships—continued throughout the play sessions. Miller (1996, p. 41) describes sharing "as an awareness of the underlying unity of self and object that defines all self object experiences." The therapist and Rosa share the experience of reading books (in Spanish), using play telephones, and writing notes. Therapy culminates with Rosa writing a book about her life, sharing it with the therapist during sessions, and reading it when it is completed.

Source: Case material supplied by Ariel Perry.

Behavioral Therapy

Behavioral therapy is particularly effective with young children, as it can be taught to the parent, who then applies the method at home. The parent learns from the experience and can then take credit for being instrumental in producing change. This success leads to other successes in parenting. One can obtain rapid results with behavior therapy, and the pretreatment and intervention periods can be monitored by using single-subject design methodology (see Chapter 14 on integrating research and practice). This next case illustrates behavioral therapy for a child with temper tantrums.

Case Examples

Jenny: Working with a Parent

Jenny is a 4-year-old African American child whose single mother requested help. Jenny's behavior in school was appropriate, but at home she exhibited temper tantrums whenever she did not get her way. Jenny's mother, Mrs. P., frustrated and angry, tried bribing, screaming, spanking, and punishing to end the tantrums—all to no effect. The worker determined that she would intervene with Mrs. P., and not Jenny, because of Jenny's development stage. She selected a behavioral protocol from Phelan (1995)—a simple counting method combined with a "no talking–no emotion" rule. She instructed Mrs. P. that when unacceptable behavior occurred, Jenny was to be told that the behavior was "unacceptable," followed by the words: "That's ONE." If Jenny did not respond, Mrs. P. was to say: "Jenny, that's TWO." If Jenny did not comply by the third time, Mrs. P. was to say "Jenny, That's THREE, take four minutes" (one minute for each year of her age). Jenny was then immediately sent to a time-out area to serve the allotted four minutes of time. If Jenny had a temper tantrum before the time out, Mrs. P. was instructed to wait until the tantrum was over and then re-quest, calmly, that Jenny serve the time-out. Mrs. P. was also encouraged to reinforce all of Jenny's positive behavior with praise and extra incentives such as delaying bed-time to watch a special TV movie or playing a special game. The worker developed a daily chart with Mrs. P. so that she and Jenny could keep track of Jenny's temper tantrums (see Figure 13.1). Jenny would receive a sticker on the chart every day that she did not get a time-out. Seven stickers would earn her special privileges.

Mrs. P. collected baseline data for seven days before intervention took place. The therapist and client looked at the data and learned that when Mrs. P. asked for com-pliance and Jenny didn't wish to obey, a tantrum followed. The program began in the second week. Jenny had a rapid, positive response. She adjusted quickly, and her tem-per tantrums decreased. Data on baseline and intervention phases of the work is vi-sually demonstrated in Figure 13.1. Graphing data allows both worker and client to see if results have been obtained just by "eyeballing." The downward direction of the trend line informs us immediately that Jenny's temper tantrums have decreased.

Mrs. P. felt gratified that the treatment was so effective and was able to re-establish a loving relationship with her child.

Bruce: A Child Diagnosed with ADHD and ODD

Mrs. J., a 35-year-old white, single mother, sought treatment for her 12-year-old son who was having difficulty progressing in school. Mrs. J. felt that Bruce was immature for his age and oppositional at home. Homework was a major struggle. The social worker used the multisystemic team approach described earlier in this chapter. A psychologist and psychiatrist were consulted and evaluations were completed. Bruce was diagnosed with attention deficit disorder and oppositional defiant disorder and prescribed psychotropic medication. The social worker also met with his teachers and the child study team to help them understand his behaviors within a developmental context, and, as a result, academic adjustments were made to provide educational support services and an individualized educational plan.

Obviously, Mrs. J. needed help in parenting this difficult child. The worker might have intervened with Bruce in behavioral play therapy, but this would not have helped Mrs. J. to feel empowered in her role as parent. Again, as in Jenny's case, the parent became the client. Homework was selected as the target for change and a token economy was employed as the intervention. Token economies work well with children and adolescents (see, for example, Barkley, 2002, 2003), because they

(continued)

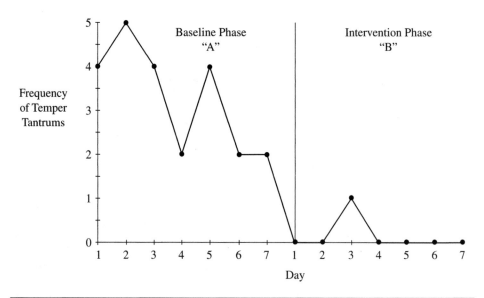

FIGURE 13.1 *Jenny's Temper Tantrums*

Everyday	Weekends	Specials
½ hour of ball playing (10 points)	Eating @ restaurant (50 points)	Extra trip to New York (120 points)
½ hour of video games (15 points)	Renting a video game (50 points)	Having a sleep over (90 points)
1 hour ball playing (15 points)	Play day (50 points)	
1 hour video games (20 points)		
Eating at McDonald's (20 points)		

FIGURE 13.2 *Bruce's Rewards*

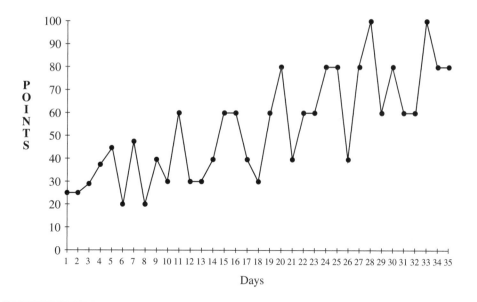

FIGURE 13.3   *Points Earned during Five-Week Intervention*

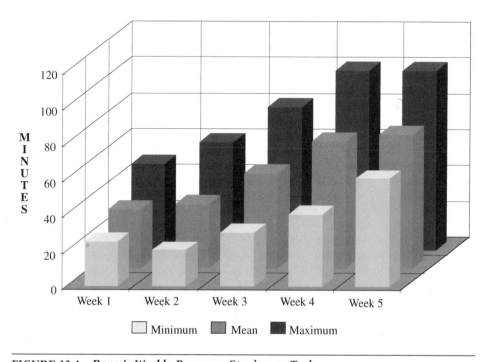

FIGURE 13.4   *Bruce's Weekly Program: Staying on Task*

Case Examples Continued

involve positive reinforcement with tokens that can then be exchanged for privileges or material rewards.

The worker taught Mrs. J. how to develop this system with Bruce, using poker chips as tokens. The poker chips had different colors; together, Mrs. J. and Bruce designated a value to each chip and made a special bank where the chips could be placed. Everyday rewards had lower point values, while weekend and special rewards had higher values. A red poker chip, for example, was worth 5 points, and Bruce could earn one for every 20 minutes of staying on task with homework, without giving up or demonstrating oppositional behavior. (After 20 minutes, Bruce was given a 5-minute break and then instructed to return to the task.) Figure 13.2 (p. 202) illustrates Bruce's reward system.

During the first week (baseline) there was no reinforcement for Bruce's target behavior—staying on task with homework for 20 minutes without quitting or displaying oppositional behaviors. Bruce spent between 25 and 48 minutes on task without his behavior deteriorating during this time period. Reinforcement for appropriate behavior began in week two. Over the next four weeks, Bruce's time spent on task gradually grew longer. Bruce was reinforced with poker chips for appropriate behavior. As the amount of time spent doing homework increased, so did the number of chips that Bruce received. These chips had a point value and were redeemed for rewards (see Figure 13.3 on page 203).

As treatment progressed, Bruce was able to increase the weekly time that he spent on homework without arguing, crying, making demands on his mom, quitting, or otherwise displaying oppositional behaviors. He spent more time per week working on his own. As can be seen in Figure 13.4 (p. 203), Bruce's appropriate homework behavior climbed from a weekly average of 33 minutes to a weekly average of 75 minutes (note the minutes on the vertical axis). The minimum and maximum times spent on task also increased. Mrs. J. felt relieved that Bruce was more compliant, proud of his increasing academic success, and empowered in her role as parent.

Summary

The knowledge base of child and adolescent therapy has depth and breadth. It includes an understanding of child development, the environment, cultural and religious factors, various theoretical models and styles of play therapy, and learning disturbances. Social workers need a multitude of skills. Some, to name a few, are techniques of play therapy, child behavioral management, and coping and self-management strategies. Knowledge of family treatment and group work is also important. Treatment of abused and neglected children requires another set of skills. Additionally, social workers must be comfortable facilitating and often leading a treatment team. They need to know the community resources and the legislation that effects the lives of children and adolescents. An appreciation of the difficulties of parenting in today's complex world and empathy for parents' struggles is also imperative. Beginning workers need to be careful to not overidentify with the child client, because they may risk alienating the parent. The clinician may spend one hour a week in an office with a child or adolescent, but the parent is never off duty. The parents, whenever possible and appropriate, need to be part of the therapeutic process, and their input and hard work must be respected. Finally, children and adolescents are the most vulnerable of clients, and the social worker must have a holistic, person-in-environment perspective—a central tenant of social work practice—to do justice in meeting their needs.

Learning Assignments

1. Attempt a developmental assessment of a child. Select a potential treatment plan based on your understanding of the child's behavior within this developmental schema.

2. Working in pairs, role-play an initial interview with a parent. Switch roles and role-play the initial interview with the child.

3. Select a child or adolescent client from your practice. Using a multisystemic approach, consider who would be included in the treatment team. How would you include these resource persons, what would be your rationale, and how might they be of use?

References

Association for Play Therapy. (1997). A definition of play therapy. *The Association for Play Therapy Newsletter, 16*(1), 7.

Barkley, R. A. (2002). *Defiant children: A clinician's manual for parent training*. New York: Guilford.

Barkley, R. A. (2003). *Defiant adolescents*. New York: Guilford.

Brody, V. (1997). Developmental play therapy. In K. O'Connor & L. Braverman (Eds.), *Play therapy theory and practice: A comparative presentation*. New York: John Wiley & Sons.

Cicchetti, D., & Rogosch, F. A. (2002). A developmental psychopathology perspective on adolescence. *Journal of Consulting and Clinical Psychology, 70*, 6–20.

Congress, E. P. (1994). The use of culturagrams to assess and empower culturally diverse families. *Families in Society, 75*(9), 531–539.

Cramer, E. P., & Gilson, S.F. (1999). Queers and crips: Parallel identity development processes for persons with nonvisible disabilities and lesbian, gay and bisexual persons. *Journal of Gay, Lesbian and Bisexual Identity, 4*, 23–37.

D'Augelli, A. R. (1994). Identity development and sexual orientation: Toward a model of lesbian, gay and bisexual development. In E. J. Trickett, R. J. Watts, & D. Birman (Eds.), *Human diversity: Perspectives on people in context* (pp. 312–333). San Francisco: Jossey-Bass.

Elbaum, B., & Vaughn, S. (2003). Self-concept and students with learning disabilities. In H. L. Swanson, K. R. Harris, & S. Graham (Eds.), *Handbook of learning disabilities* (pp. 229–242). New York: Guilford.

Eliason, M. J. (1996). Identity formation for lesbian, bisexual and gay persons: Beyond a "minoritizing" view. *Journal of Homosexuality, 30*(3), 31–58.

Erikson, E. (1950). *Childhood and society*. New York: Norton.

Erikson, E. (1959). Identity and the life cycle: Selected papers. Psychological Issues Monograph, 1(1). New York: International University Press.

Freud, S. (1905). Three essays on the theory of sexuality. In J. Strachey, Jr. (Ed.) (1953–1974)

Standard edition of the complete psychological works of Sigmund Freud (7: 125–245). London: Hogarth Press.

Gil, E. *(1991).* The healing power of play: Working with abused children. New York: Guilford.

Guerney, L. (1997). Filial therapy. In K. O'Connor & L. Braverman (Eds.), *Play therapy theory and practice: A comparative presentation* (pp. 131–159). New York: Wiley.

Gusman, F. D., Stewart, J., Young, B. H., Riney, S. J., Abueg, F. R., & Blake, D. D. (1996). A multicultural developmental approach for treating trauma. In A. Marsella, M. Friedman, E. Gerrity, & R. Scurfield (Eds.), *Ethnocultural aspects of posttraumatic stress disorder* (pp. 439–457). Washington, DC: American Psychological Association.

Hartman, A. (1978). Diagrammatic assessment of family relationships. *Social Casework, 59,* 465–476.

Holmbeck, G. N., Greenley, R. N., & Franks, E. A. (2003). Developmental issues and considerations in research and practice. In A. Kazdin & J. Weisz (Eds.), *Evidence-based psychotherapies for children and adolescents* (pp. 21–41). New York: Guilford.

Hughes, J. N., & Baker, D. B. (1990). *The clinical child interview.* New York: Guilford.

Jernberg, A. (1979). *Theraplay.* San Francisco, CA: Jossey-Bass.

Kail, R. (2001). *The development of memory in children.* New York: Freeman.

Kendall, P.C. (2000). *Child and adolescent therapy: Cognitive-behavioral procedures.* New York: Guilford.

Knell, S. (1997). Cognitive-behavioral play therapy. In K. O'Connor & L. Braverman (Eds.), *Play therapy theory and practice: A comparative presentation.* New York: Wiley

Knell, S. (1998). Cognitive-behavioral play therapy. *Journal of Clinical Child Psychology, 27*(1), 28–33.

Kohlberg, L. (1984). *Essays on moral development: Vol II. The psychology of moral development.* New York: Harper & Row.

Landreth, G. L. (2002). *The art of the relationship.* New York: Brunner-Routledge.

Lee, A. (1997). Psychoanalytic play therapy. In K. O'Connor & L. Braverman (Eds.), *Play therapy theory and practice: A comparative presentation* (pp. 46–78). New York: Wiley.

Marcotte, D. (1997). Treating depression in adolescence: A review of effectiveness of cognitive-behavior treatments. *Journal of Youth and Adolescence, 26,* 273–283.

McGoldrick, M., & Gerson, R. (l985). *Genograms in family assessment.* New York: W. W. Norton.

Meyers, S. (1984). Elective mutism in children: A family systems approach. *The American Journal of Family Therapy, 12*(4), 39–45.

Miller, J. P. (1996). *Using self psychology in child psychotherapy.* Northvale, NJ: Jason Aronson.

O'Connor, K. (2000). *The play therapy primer.* New York: John Wiley & Sons.

Oetting, G. R., & Beauvais, L. (1990). Orthogonal cultural identification theory: The cultural identification of minority adolescents. *International Journal of the Addictions, 25,* 655–685.

Palombo, J. (2001). *Learning disorders and disorders of the self in children and adolescents.* New York: Norton.

Phelan, T. (1995). *1-2-3-Magic: Effective discipline for children 2–12.* Glen Ellyn, IL: Child Management Press.

Piaget, J. (1952a). *The language and thought of the child.* London: Routledge & Kegan Paul.

Piaget, J. (1952b). *The origins of intelligence in children.* New York: International Universities Press.

Shirk, S. R. (1999). Developmental therapy. In W. K. Silverman & T. H. Ollendick (Eds.), *Developmental issues in the clinical treatment of children* (pp. 63–70). Boston: Allyn and Bacon.

Siegel, D. J. (1999). *The developing mind.* New York: Guilford.

Steinhausen, H., & Juzi, C. (1996). Elective mutism: An analysis of 100 cases. *Journal of the American Academy of Child and Adolescent Psychiatry, 35*(5), 606–615.

Stern, E. N. (1977). *The first relationship: Infant and mother.* Cambridge, MA: Harvard University Press.

Stern, E. N. (1985). *The interpersonal world of the infant.* New York: Basic Books

Sue, D. E., & Sue, D. (2003). *Counseling the culturally diverse.* New York: John Wiley & Sons.

VanFleet, R. (1994). *Filial therapy: Strengthening parent-child relationships through play.* Sarasota, FL: Professional Resource Press.

Wachtel, E. (1994). *Treating troubled children and their families.* New York: Guilford.

Webb, N. B. (1996). *Social work practice with children.* New York: Guilford.

14

Integrating Research and Practice

Quantitative Research Methods for Clinical Practitioners

There are two methods of research that we believe are particularly appropriate for clinical social workers. The quantitative single-system design is a clinical tool that helps us to evaluate the effectiveness of our practice. The qualitative inquiry helps us add to the body of knowledge about our clients lived experiences and the agencies in which we work. In this chapter we will discuss and illustrate both of these designs.

Single-System Design Methodology

Social work practitioners need to be accountable—to show what they have done. The single-system design (SSD) demonstrates outcomes. This is particularly critical in today's managed care environment, where funding sources insist on seeing results. Single-system designs (SSDs) are quasi-experimental designs, with an *n* of 1. Several versions of this design are considered "uncontrolled" because an intervention is not systematically withheld or varied so that one might observe what happens in its absence (Bloom & Fischer, 1982). In effect, the patient acts as his own control by use of the preintervention baseline. The most rudimentary version of this design requires little more than accurate and complete recording of what many practitioners routinely do: conduct an assessment of a case situation, intervene in it, record interventions, and assess progress. This design evolves into a research design when the practitioner wants to learn about the effects of some type of intervention on a case situation and takes an additional step to collect systematic data on intervention targets and methods.

A core function of this design is to enable the practitioner to compare the level of a client's problems before and after an intervention and to make inferences regarding causality. To do so, one systematically obtains baseline data on target problems in a pretreatment phase or preintervention phase and then makes a comparison to data obtained in exactly the same way during subsequent time periods for the same client. This differs from the classical experimental control group design in which the comparison is made between groups.

The single-system design is a time series design. There are many forms, and for a thorough discussion of this single-system design methodology we refer the reader to Bloom, Fischer, and Orme's (1999) excellent text on this subject. The case illustration in this chapter uses the most basic form—the A-B design. This design yields data on change coincident with or after introducing the intervention. Central to the basic time series design is the notion of repeated measurements of a given variable over time. The baseline is the preintervention phase in which planned observations of targeted problems and events take place. This is symbolized by the letter "A." The intervention period is another phase in which some planned effort to change the client/system's problems, together with a planned observation of targeted problems and events, takes place. Intervention can be thought of as a single procedure, or as a combination of techniques packaged together. It is the formal and planned nature of the intervention that distinguishes it from the baseline, or assessment period. Intervention is represented by the letter "B."

A variety of instruments are suitable for single-system designs. For a full discussion of measures, we refer the interested reader to Bloom, Fischer, and Orme (1999). One set of standardized measures that we highlight, the WALMYR Assessment Scales (WAS; Hudson & Faul, 1998), are well suited for social work practice as they can rapidly assess depression, anxiety, alcohol involvement, peer relations, marital satisfaction, partner abuse, parental and child attitudes, and family relations. They are easy to administer and easy to score. The important point in choosing an instrument is that it needs to measure the problem for which intervention is sought. If a client appears sad in an interview, but also claims that she feels bad about herself and that she and her partner argue a lot, look for an instrument that measures the most distressing or potentially self-injurious behavior first. In the abovementioned case, the worker should get data about the client's depression before looking at the other clinical problems.

The virtue of single-system designs is that, after data is collected on the behaviors, feelings, cognitions, and attitudes that are the targets of intervention, this data can be visually demonstrated on a graph. This allows both worker and client to see if results have been obtained just by "eyeballing" the data—looking to see if the trend line moves up or down, or stays the same. If, for example, a client has scored high for depression during baseline—as indicated by her scores on a depression measure—the data points would be moving upward, or would at least be located in the upward region of the graph. A downward trend line in the intervention period would indicate that depression was declining and that the intervention had been effective. A flat trend line would indicate that no change had taken place. Displaying results visually on a graph serves to motivate the client, who can visually see the progress she has made. It is extremely helpful to the practitioner, as it either validates that the intervention was effective, or tells him that he needs to change the course of treatment because the intervention did not work. Another benefit of single-system design methodology is that statistical analysis is not required. While there are personal computer programs that generate graphs and do statistical analysis (see, for example, Bloom et al., 1999; or the Computer Assisted Social Service [CASS] system in Hudson, 1990a, 1990b; Nurius & Hudson, 1993), this level of sophistication is not required for routine practice evaluation.

In our following case example, we illustrate the use of single-system design methodology.

Case Example: Treatment of a Client with Obsessive-Compulsive Disorder

Recall that the client with obsessive-compulsive disorder, discussed in Chapter 10 on behavioral theory, was completely overwhelmed with the tasks of performing fifty-four washing, cleaning, checking, and counting rituals on a daily basis. To monitor the effectiveness of the treatment (modeling, exposure, and response prevention), the worker turned to single-subject design methodology. Because there were several behaviors to examine, a multiple-baseline approach, more useful in demonstrating causality than the basic A-B design, was utilized. This approach calls for replication and is nicely detailed in Bloom et al. (1999). Of the fifty-four rituals that the client regularly performed, three target behaviors were selected for monitoring, although intervention addressed all fifty-four items. The behaviors targeted were (1) how often she opened and closed her makeup cases after application (referred to as "makeup cases"); (2) the length of time spent rinsing in the shower ("rinsing"); and (3) how she counted her belongings while carrying them with her when she moved from place to place ("belongings"). I introduced the client to the notion of self-monitoring by using language from Bloom et al. (1999), who referred to the "psychological thermometer." I told the client the following:

"Just as a doctor needs to have specific information about the problem at hand before he attempts to treat his patient, I need to have very accurate information of a psychological nature in order to help you. A doctor might want to take your temperature for a while, to establish a baseline before he prescribes treatment, and he might take your temperature afterward to see if the treatment has been effective. If your temperature goes down, you are on the right track. Social workers can use a 'psychological thermometer.' You will be asked to make daily entries on three of your rituals, using 3" × 5" cards. This will tell us how frequently these rituals occur. We will take the 'makeup cases' item, the 'rinsing' item, and the 'belongings' item for our recording (one from the low end of your anxiety hierarchy, one in the middle range, and the last from the high end). Make a small vertical line on the card every time you perform the targeted behavior. (I hand her a card and demonstrate how she is to make rows of hatch marks.) I would like you to do this for a week until we meet again. Then we can see just how many times a day you are doing the ritual. To record the number of minutes spent showering, you will need to keep a kitchen timer near the shower. You've estimated that you rinse for 45 minutes to an hour after soaping. Set the timer

(continued)

Case Example   **Continued**

for an hour, and when you are finished, look at the timer and write down the number of minutes you actually spent rinsing."

I then discussed with the client whether she felt there would be any obstacle in the way of her monitoring. Although her thinking was quite obsessive and detailed (e.g., she wanted to know if she should count the rinsing minutes when she shaved her legs and washed her hair and what would happen if her 3" × 5" cards got wet), I patiently addressed her concerns, and she was able to comply with the process. The client recorded diligently. As we reviewed the data, she was actually surprised to learn just how much time she was spending on these sample behaviors. Because of the collaborative nature of behavioral treatment, the client could participate in setting goals, monitoring her progress, and evaluating the outcome.

Data Analysis

By eyeballing the data on the graphs below, the reader can see that the behavioral techniques that were used—modeling, exposure, and response prevention—were effective in reducing the client's ritualizing (see Figures 14.1 through 14.3). Intervention on the nine makeup cases (Figure 14.1) reduced the number of clicks, presses, or twists of her makeup cases to one click per makeup item. Rinsing behavior decreased to a maximum of 9.5 minutes (Figure 14.2). Before intervention on the "belongings" item, 57 percent of the time that the client carried her belongings, she was obsessively counting them. After intervention, this counting behavior completely stopped. Needless to say, she was thrilled to see the graphs of her target behaviors because they offered concrete proof of her accomplishments (see Figures 14.1, 14.2, and 14.3). As

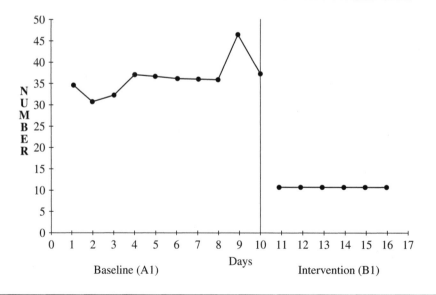

FIGURE 14.1   *Number of Twists, Presses, and Clicks of Makeup Case by Client Each Morning at Baseline (A1) and after Intervention (B1)*

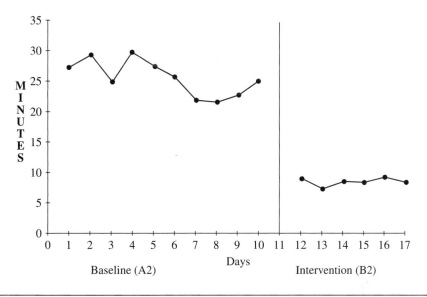

FIGURE 14.2   *Minutes Client Spent Rinsing in Shower at Baseline (A2) and after Intervention (B2)*

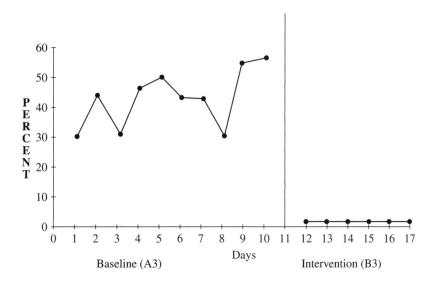

FIGURE 14.3   *Percentage of Times Client Counted Belongings When Carrying Them at Baseline (A3) and after Intervention (B3)*

Case Example   Continued

mentioned in Chapter 10, the client's rapid success is attributed to her high degree of motivation, her ongoing relationship with me (two years of psychodynamic psychotherapy prior to the introduction of behavioral therapy), as well as the demonstrated effectiveness of the treatment protocol as established in the research.

Graphic Illustration of Ineffectual Treatment

Let's suppose that my use of the treatment protocol had not been effective. The next graph (Figure 14.4) shows how it would look if the treatment had not been successful in reducing the client's rituals on the "makeup case" item.

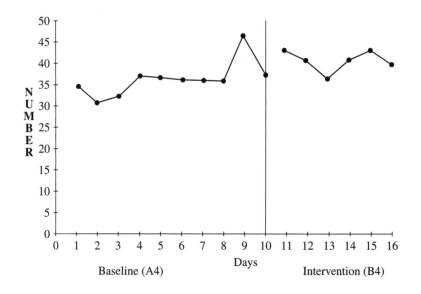

FIGURE 14.4 *Number of Twists, Presses, and Clicks of Makeup Case by Client Each Morning at Baseline (A4) and after Intervention (B4) If Intervention Was Not Successful*

Qualitative Research

The next research design that we will discuss is the qualitative inquiry. We include it in this chapter because of its natural fit with social work practice. Qualitative research uses the interviewing skills, concern, and curiosity of clinicians to obtain knowledge about clients' lives and also provides clinicians with additional insight into the agencies in which they work.

Qualitative research is naturalistic inquiry. It is a human interaction, well suited to social work practice, as the researcher is also a participant who relies on conversations between himself and his respondents to understand the problem that is being studied. In many ways, qualitative research resembles a clinical interview. The researcher uses an interview guide and active listening skills to obtain information on his subject of inquiry. This information then generates new questions and ideas to be further explored in a continual search for meaning and understanding.

Qualitative research methods have their roots in anthropology. The method originated with the nineteenth-century ethnographers, who, like Margaret Mead and Gregory Bateson (the famous explicators of remote and exotic cultures), took copious field notes (known as "thick description") to understand their own unique experiences. There are many types of qualitative designs, and the interested reader is referred to the following sources for a detailed description: Guba and Lincoln (1981), Lincoln and Guba (1985), and Miles and Huberman (1984). For a highly student-friendly book on qualitative research, see Padgett (1998).

How Knowledge Is Constructed

The qualitative researcher and respondent construct knowledge together. Data is gathered from individual interviews, or in focus groups (usually consisting of seven to ten persons, unfamiliar to each other, who come together to discuss some common concern). Qualitative research is highly labor intensive. The researcher takes abundant notes of each interview or makes video or audiotapes that must then be immediately transcribed. Padgett (1998) notes that transcribing an audiotape of a 2-hour interview can take 10 hours and produce thirty pages of transcription data. The data is then searched for themes that must be tested out on the study participants. New data then emerges, requiring further transcription and another return to the respondents to verify the hypotheses generated by these emergent themes. This process of going back and forth from the data to the participants repeats itself until the researcher is convinced that credibility has been achieved. The purpose of qualitative research is to get as many points of view as possible. The process is iterative and interactive—the worker tries not to make prior assumptions, so as to get at the greatest breadth on the subject of inquiry.

The Researcher as Instrument

The qualitative researcher as a person is the method, the research instrument (Kavale, 1995). Although she follows an interview guide, she also uses spontaneous probes (such as "Can you tell me more about it?" [Padgett, 1998]) to further her collection of data. The researcher is flexible as a collector of data. She can adapt to differing contexts and informational needs, which frees her to explore a given context until she is satisfied that the subjects have provided as much information as possible. The immediate transcription of interviews—usually within 24 hours—enables the researcher to change the direction of the inquiry as necessary and to return to the respondents for additional discussion.

Data Collection and Data Analysis

The detailed description of situations; events; people and interactions; observed behaviors; direct quotations from people about their experiences; attitudes; beliefs and thoughts; or excerpts from documents, correspondence, records, and case histories comprise the data sources for qualitative research (Patton, 1980). In qualitative research, data analysis is concurrent with data collection. It is an integrative, cyclical process wherein patterns and themes are generated from the data. For a detailed description of data analysis, see Glaser and Strauss (1967); Patton (1980); and Miles and Huberman (1984).

In qualitative research one comes up with the widest amount of data and then culls it down—reduces it—in order to extract common themes and categories that capture the essence of the data through specific coding procedures, which are described in the literature. Through this process of inductive conceptualization, the researcher develops core categories that capture the essence of the data. Coding ends when we begin to see repetition and redundancy. This state of grace is known as "saturation," a term meaning the "cooking" process is drawing to an end (Padgett, 1998). Saturation occurs when additional analysis no longer contributes anything new about a category.

This analysis of categories is written up in the form of memos—a process called memoing—that link different pieces of data to show their evidence of a general concept. Direct quotes from study participants can be incorporated in the memos to illustrate particular points. Thus, the researcher ensures that the analysis is grounded in the actual data and not in the researcher's interpretation. Qualitative research requires that the data be confirmed once it is obtained. Methods used to accomplish this include cross-validation strategies such as triangulation, member checks (taking the data back to the study participants for verification), and using an auditor to review the consistency of the study by checking the researcher's decision-making process and actions.

Case Example

The following excerpts are from a study undertaken by the authors in collaboration with the Jamaica Association of Social Workers. The study took place in August 2003 in Kingston, Jamaica, West Indies, where poverty, drugs, and migration are significantly associated with crime and violence ("The Caribbean's Tarnished Jewel," 1999; Crawford-Brown, 2001; Dunn, 2001; Ricketts, 2000; Williams, 2001). The authors sought to gather information on the effects of violence on the families and children living in this area in order to develop culturally specific clinical interventions to help them to deal with posttraumatic stress.

Methodology

Our collaborators arranged for focus groups and interviews with key informants in anticipation of our visit. We arrived with topic guides for these interviews (see Figures 14.5 and 14.6) and permission from the human subjects review boards of our universities to interview our informants.

(continued)

1 Structure of Jamaican child welfare system
2 Reporting system for child abuse and neglect
3 Definition of child maltreatment in Jamaica
4 Legal consequences for perpetrators of physical and sexual abuse on children
5 Service providers—identity and academic and professional qualifications
6 Mechanism for a child entering care system
7 Facilities and length of stay for children in care
8 Government resources for children in care
9 Existence of prevention programs
10 Primary access roads to care
11 Migratory patterns of Jamaicans and impact on child welfare
12 Rate of unemployment and governmental support for families in poverty and maintaining children at home

FIGURE 14.5 *Topic Guide for Individual Interviews*

1 Direct experience working with abused and neglected children
2 Jamaican view of child maltreatment, specifically child sexual abuse
3 Perception by children and families of treatment providers
4 Religious and cultural beliefs of children and families that promote or forestall problem
5 Current treatment modalities, resources, and culturally sanctioned interventions
6 Cultural aspects that can be harnessed to promote change
7 Culture's effective use of support networks
8 Effects of care on children and their families
9 Prioritization and actualization of family reunification
10 Post-care support networks for children and families
11 Perception by Jamaican social service system and families of core social work values, i.e., self-determination and confidentiality
12 Unique Jamaican practice approaches that can be incorporated in United States to help culturally diverse clients

FIGURE 14.6 *Topic Guide for Focus Groups*

Case Example   Continued

Focus Groups

We conducted three focus group meetings, lasting approximately an hour and a half each. One group, held at a school, was attended by the female school principal, a male social worker with an MSW degree, a female MSW student and her female supervising social worker, a female guidance counselor, and a female community social worker who is also a nun. Another focus group consisted of the executive board members of the Jamaica Association of Social Workers. Attending the third focus group, held at an agency, were the agency director/supervisor, a colleague from the University of the West Indies, and the current president of the Jamaica Association of Social Workers. Individual interviews were held with a male MSW social worker, the president of the Jamaica Association of Social Workers, and a faculty member from the University of the West Indies who had been a visiting faculty member at a college in the northeastern United States.

All interviews were recorded on cassette tapes and transcribed upon our return. The real work of searching the voluminous amount of data for themes then began. We applied the grounded theory approach to the data analysis, including open, axial, and selective coding to develop coding categories. This procedure involves the constant comparative method and the development of coding paradigms to develop themes. A Word computer program was used to undertake the line-by-line coding. This program enabled two windows to open on the computer. The left window contained original transcriptions with each line numbered. The right window was used for copying, pasting, and organizing of material from the left window, defining emerging themes and categorizing salient data (pieces of quotations) beneath each theme. Trustworthiness of the data was established through triangulation, a cross-validation strategy, in which we compared and contrasted the consistency of what was said by the different participating groups. We used member check to summarize and confirm interpretation of our data.

Presentation of Data

The themes and supporting data of quotations are explicated below. They were culled directly from the transcript of the focus group sessions and individual interviews.

The Themes

1. *Frequent exposure of children to violence with resulting trauma.* The extent and pervasiveness of violence and sexual abuse in Jamaica are for its victims not unlike the experiences and consequences of those living in a war zone. The human damage can lead to a demoralizing cycle of more violence and abuse with very serious harm to affected children, parents, caregivers, and society. Violence begets violence.

   "All kinds of violence, murdered, you know, fires. There are lots of fires."

   "There was one night where we had a lot of shooting."

   "Trauma that they experience every single day because there's guns, they go to bed at night and they hear it. They wake up in the morning so all the students see, actually see the murders right there from their school here."

"Well, the violence really does have a serious impact on the way the children operate in school."

"[Children's] attention span seems to be very short. They become distracted very easily and I don't think that some of them think that there is much more to their existence than, you know, just being here, going through the motions until it is time for whatever is to happen to them should happen because you know, there are not long-term goals, you know. They just go from day to day. Catch as catch can and you know, the seriousness about life I find it's just not there. And so we find that the students don't, many of them, don't want to sit down in class and really put their minds to what is taught in a real serious way. . . . [They will be unable] to . . . move up the social ladder.

"Many of them feel trapped and, and they know that they are victims of circumstance, many of them."

"It was like an innocent child said to me. He just couldn't, he couldn't take the gunshots any more. He would just shake."

"The children . . . they're depressed. . . . A child will . . . say, 'I'm going to kill this person' and you say 'would you go to prison?' And [they] say, 'Miss, but it's not anything' . . . that's your hopelessness and depression, . . . their attention span is very limited . . . their reasoning ability is not there. They're not able to reason out things and, and sometimes . . . they're impulsive."

"Among youngsters now . . . there are suicides a lot . . . high level of it."

"When they play there's so much conflict sometimes I'm watching and there's so much aggression."

2. *Intrafamilial violence.* Abuse is by no means limited to occurrences between strangers but can affect a family and its members at the most basic level. People who under "normal" circumstances would have a very positive relationship with one another are capable of causing grievous injury.

"The problem is . . . quite deep rooted and it's also at home. It appears it comes from home most of the time. The home environment is also what influences these situations.

"There's violence, children against parent, going on."

"The hopelessness and the agitation a child shall experience. Going back home to the environment . . ."

"[At home] she's a tiny little girl but her mother hit her with a cutlass [i.e., type of knife] . . . Her mother . . . couldn't take it any more. . . . The mother tries but that's how she punishes her . . . tries not to cut her. The mother . . . just . . . doesn't know what else to do."

"Her son tends to bring violence on his own sister, bringing home violence."

"Violence in the family . . . in speech, in action, everything."

3. *Cultural desensitization to violence and sexual abuse due to poverty.*
"The necessities of day-to-day living such as affording food and shelter can cause people to make gut-wrenching compromises for the sake of survival. If repeated frequently by enough members of society, harmful acts can lead to

(continued)

Case Example   **Continued**

a numbing desensitization until the line between normal and abnormal becomes blurred."

"I'll say, 'What's the matter?' 'Miss, I'm hungry." "They don't have breakfast and they don't have lunch and they don't have dinner . . . It's a serious problem . . . you are trying to work with them and they're hungry . . . then you have to solve the problem of hunger."

"They're provoked, they are going to retaliate so that is why . . . that's the experience of this year round and people retaliate an eye for an eye and they raise the violence. There's tolerance . . . jungle justice . . . a kind of subculture . . ."

"The class issues in Jamaica are very stark . . . and the educational system is built upon a class system . . ."

"They like to tease each other and they like to make the violence. They don't see a way because they don't have the skills to manage their anger. Because they don't see that out in the community or at home."

"Sometimes what you have is that parents are not so much behind the children to take them to get this help [or medicine] because you identify factors and then you say, all right, and make that appointment for you to go and get some help at this appointment and you come back next week and tell them. . . . But what you find is that they tell you, I have to go to work. I don't have the time. They're not really able to spare the time and make the effort to see that the best results come for the children. And when they finish they don't go for follow[up]. There is no followup. You will take them this far but even to bring the parents in so that you can have sessions with them."

4. *Different stresses on gender.*

"Not surprisingly, boys and girls, woman and men, have dissimilar experiences and are treated differently as well."

"In our school what we have is we have more boys who are . . . leaders and we find that there is more aggression among that set . . ."

"In the reading streams . . . there are more girls than boys . . . you find a great concentration of aggression among boys . . . I think parents pay more attention to the girls' education than boys."

"The boys get the chance to run the streets because they're boys and they will not become pregnant so I have no fear, you know, but recently there is another fear with some persons who fear that they might go out there, they might pick up the guns."

"Incest also happens . . . it's just coming out of the closet now . . . There are laws . . . [against incest but] it's not reported."

"Sexual abuse in Jamaica among children is kept covert for many reasons . . . it is feared that the breadwinner will be lost."

"Sometimes they (the parents) report it, but when it comes to a person charging, the parents will not press charges and that's when the police have to withdraw because they're saying you either live with it or you lose your bread. I have met children who have been told just that. And the parents will tell you, 'Miss, if I send my man out of the house we'll lose our bread.' So they have to live with it. Yes. And so they will not press charges. They report it but when they are told they say, no. Because they can be killed, too."

"It's very hard to get a child in Jamaica to admit that they have been sexually molested. Blood is thicker than water."

"The perpetrator's in the home because we have single-parent homes in Jamaica a lot."

"There is also some amount of child prostitution . . . mother sends her out into places . . . where she performs acts . . . she has sex for money . . . she does [it] to support the mother and the other children in the house."

"Here in Jamaica we have a thing that you call adults, we call them aunties or uncles. It doesn't have to be related in many things . . . with the incest . . . it's almost a cultural thing where a father may say, 'I'm the first to have my daughter before any other male.' That happens. And so because of that it's kept covert and the children are told it's because you are loved . . . it's linked to a kind of kinship system in a way."

"But it is also an objectification of children."

5. *Poor societal resources to deal with violence, abuse, and their impact.* Economic poverty and lack of opportunity leads to a dearth of treatment resources and solutions. Governmental institutions that should offer relief can perpetrate additional harm and actually increase distrust and hopelessness.

"[The system] will intervene . . . if they thought it was serious then . . . the child will be taken to court and you know, the court intervenes and decide whether the child can be taken away from the parent, passed on to another relative, or be placed at the children's home." But often the laws "have no teeth." This is changing with the passage of the Child Care and Protection Act . . . it will make reporting mandatory.

"[Victims and advocates] don't want to be in the courts because the police, because they have poor, real poor, understanding of sexual abuse. They are unsympathetic in many cases . . . that is one of the reasons why training is so important . . ."

"What also happens in the system many times is that the private practitioner's fees are higher than the state is willing to pay so they end up not going to see appropriate practitioner or they end up going to Family Court or to anybody that will take it on. Maybe a counselor or someone who is not necessarily a trained practitioner . . ."

"Family Court of Probation Service . . . handles these matters . . . Those are not clinical practitioners."

"At the Children's Hospital they have trained psychologists who are paid by the state but again the case load is high so you find that many other persons like the children in this are who should be benefiting from services don't get them. So there's a distinction, you see, in Jamaica in terms of the trained

(continued)

Case Example   **Continued**

practitioners versus the person who's doing social work in court and is not trained or equipped to deal with the clinical elements of the person."

"Our practitioners here are ill equipped [to treat incest] and that's why the training is so important."

"[We have a] shortage of trained practitioners here in Jamaica. We have psychologists but again the psychologists' fees are expensive."

"There's a terrible lack of skill here . . . the need is so great now for the clinical aspect of treatment here . . . It is unbelievable . . . We really need that kind of training here because people . . . have such minimal training, like four months training . . . maybe a year."

"Many of the persons who are working in this kind of field do not have exposure to that kind of training so there is really, really a dying need for persons to be trained because they are doing the work and can create more harm."

6. *Hunger for strategies to help break cycle of abuse.* In spite of momentous challenges, affected stakeholders (parents, children, clinicians) continue to look for improvements and solutions. They are eager for additional training from credible sources. Optimism endures.

"There is a great love of young children here in Jamaica."

"There is a strong sense of spiritual and religious belief."

"Parents wanted to know how to cope. . . . How do I cope with what is happening around me?

"There is stigma about mental health care so we'd have to try and break it gently with them. . . . I just want a psychiatrist to come in and do something with [parents] about, you know, self-care. That's what we are calling it. Because if we call it anything else, they're not coming."

"But there are some parents who would [try mental health and medicine] because they are at their wit's end. So, of course we organized a session. And they, the parents themselves have suggested the area that they wanted us to go into."

"Conflict resolution was a major, one of the things that the focus was on."

"They wanted a way to improve themselves in terms of training or to generate an income."

"Children themselves . . . are being educated to realize that . . . [incest] is wrong."

"Then there are children advocates. Not just among social workers . . ."

"[Children surviving incest] will go through a series of counseling sessions where we try and help them. . . . That is a difficult thing so we want to get to that stage where we can work with them. Work through the traumas and refer them to other evaluations that we feel are necessary. Work with the parents. Try to get the perpetrator in and we have had perpetrators come in. I've had them who come in and admit. And we will refer them to the police."

"Counseling programs for the perpetrator . . . [exist]. [Victim] . . . might get some money."

"[Government] introduced a bill about four years ago, something called Victim's Support where . . . persons who have experienced any kind of violence, be it sexual or otherwise, can get help . . . in the form of . . . from my experience, probably relocation sometimes . . . [though] the actual matter of material assistance is very difficult."

"There is a national health fund and I think children are in there now . . . . So they can get the medication but we need to inform people within this community that this exist[s]."

"We also are doing something for the teachers this semester because . . . they have been affected by the violence themselves . . . the children's behavior and their experience in the community."

Conclusion

This qualitative research provides a powerful human voice to the sobering sociological challenges facing Jamaica. It also affirms that clinicians and parents are eager to try solutions. The primary researchers believe that poverty, drugs, and massive migration are three root causes for the situation in Jamaica. Despite the daunting trials faced by the focus group participants and their peers, the island has a long history of loving and nurturing relationships between parents and children, respect for authority, and graciousness that was clearly evident to us during our visit to impoverished communities and schools. The researchers, in collaboration with our colleagues in Jamaica, are working to harness the strengths in the culture and the findings from this qualitative analysis to develop effective therapeutic interventions to be given back to the Jamaican clinicians and human service workers. We are returning to Jamaica to interview parents and children directly about their experiences in hope of ensuring that any training supports their voices on the community level. We are interested in hearing more about the specific reasons for migration, childcare arrangements, and the parents' and children's ideas about what happens when children are left behind in the care of others. This approach will increase treatment effectiveness at the micro level while agencies and government, the authors hope, would perhaps make progress respectively on the mezzo and macro levels. Note that the qualitative research process provides the finely drawn detail necessary to help create and tailor an intervention unique to a particular culture. It captures specificity wholly representative of its participants.

Summary

In this chapter we have presented two forms of research that are particularly applicable to clinical social work practice: single-subject design methodology and qualitative inquiry. It is our belief that social work clinicians should engage in multiple methods of research, including undertaking empirical studies, literature reviews, and evaluating program outcomes. There is a push today for social workers to participate in evidence-based practice. Evidence-based practitioners, according to Gambrill (1999), seek out the best available external evidence from practice-related research findings and share this with their clients. If they cannot find evidence for an intervention that they are recommending, they inform the client of this and describe the theoretical rationale for their treatment decision. We encourage all social workers to always draw on existing knowledge when making decisions for those who are in their care. We also encourage them to develop new theory based on their practice with clients and to develop and analyze policies and services that affect clinical practice. In this capacity, social workers will provide the leadership that advances the profession.

Learning Assignments

1. Select a client from your practice and identify a target problem. Find an instrument that might measure this problem (e.g., a depression or anxiety scale).

2. Use this measurement to collect at least four baseline data points. Then write about (a) what you have learned about your client's problem from using this measurement and (b) how it guides you to select an intervention.

3. Intervene with your client and repeat the measurement at least twice. Has there been any change in the client's target problem?

4. Working in small groups, consider a research question regarding clinical practice that you would like to further explore. Develop an interview guide to be used with prospective research participants.

5. Working in the same small groups, practice using the interview guide, changing roles as researcher and participant. Have members of the group observe the interview and offer feedback. Consider whether additional questions might be incorporated into subsequent interviews.

References

Bloom, M., & Fischer, J. (1982). *Evaluating practice: Guidelines for the accountable professional*. Englewood Cliffs, NJ: Prentice-Hall.

Bloom, M., Fischer, J., & Orme, J. (1999). *Evaluating practice: Guidelines for the accountable professional* (3rd ed.). Boston: Allyn and Bacon.

The Caribbean's Tarnished Jewel. (1999, October 2). *Economist, 353*(8139), 37–38.

Crawford-Brown, C. (2001). The impact of migration on the rights of children and families in the Caribbean. In C. Barrow (Ed.), *Children's rights: Caribbean realities* (pp. 227–223). Kingston, Jamaica, WI: Ian Randle Publishers.

Dunn, L. L. (2001). Jamaica: Situation of children in prostitution: A rapid assessment. Geneva: ILO.

Gambill, E. (1999). *Evidence-based practice: An alternative to authority-based practice*. Washington, DC: National Academy Press.

Glaser, B., & Strauss, A. (1967). *The discovery of grounded theory*. Chicago: Aldine.

Guba, E. G., & Lincoln, Y. S. (1981). *Effective evaluation*. San Francisco: Jossey-Bass.

Hudson, W. W. (1990a). *Computer-assisted social services*. Tempe, AZ: WALMYR.

Hudson, W. W. (1990b). Computer-based clinical practice: Present status and future possibilities. In L. Videka-Sherman & W. H. Reid (Eds.), *Advances in clinical social work research* (pp. 105–117). Silver Spring, MD: National Association of Social Workers Press.

Hudson, W. W., & and Faul, A. C. (1998) *The clinical measurement packager: A field manual* (2nd ed.). Tallahassee, FL: WALMYR.

Kavale, S. (1995). *Interviews: An introduction to qualitative research interviewing.* Thousand Oaks, CA: Sage.

Lincoln, Y. S., & Guba, E. G. (1985). *Naturalistic inquiry.* Beverly Hills, CA: Sage.

Miles, M., & Huberman, M. (1984). *Qualitative data analysis: A sourcebook of new methods.* Beverly Hills, CA: Sage.

Nurius, P., & Hudson, W. W. (1993). *Human services: Practice, evaluation and computers.* Pacific Grove, CA: Brooks/Cole.

Padgett, D. K. (1998). *Qualitative methods in social work research.* Thousand Oaks, CA: Sage.

Patton, M. (1980). *Qualitative evaluation methods.* Newbury Park, CA: Sage.

Ricketts, H. (2000, November). *Parenting in Jamaica: A situation assessment and analysis.* Jamaica's Coalition for Better Parenting: UNICEF.

Williams, S. (2001). "The mighty influence of long custom and practice." Sexual exploitation of children for cash and goods in Jamaica. In C. Barrow (Ed.), *Children's rights: Caribbean realities* (pp. 330–349). Kingston, Jamaica, WI: Ian Randle Publishers.

Index